# *Advance praise for*
# More Healthy Homestyle Cooking

"Tribole has done it again! Now there is no excuse not to eat healthy. Whether you're time-challenged, cooking phobic, health-unconscious, or just ready for a change of taste, this book is for you. Even my kids loved the recipes!"

**—Elizabeth Somer, R.D.,**
author of *Food & Mood*

"Evelyn is innovative, creative, and crystal clear in everything she does. She doesn't follow trends; she sets them!"

**—Graham Kerr,**
author and international
culinary consultant

"You may never have to open another cookbook again! *More Healthy Homestyle Cooking* combines flavor, health, and convenience. Plus, it's filled with usable, down-to-earth tips."

**—Debra Waterhouse, R.D.,**
author of *Outsmarting the Midlife Fat Cell*

"If there's a way to make a recipe more healthy, Evelyn knows how to do it."

**—Jennifer Lowe,**
deputy food editor, *Los Angeles Times*

"Once again, Evelyn has created quick, great-tasting, healthy food that the whole family will enjoy. Plus, she reveals her secrets in every recipe!"

**—Mindy Hermann, R.D.,**
children's nutrition columnist
and coauthor of *The American
Medical Association Family Health Cookbook*

**Other Books by Evelyn Tribole**

*Stealth Health*

*Healthy Homestyle Desserts*

*Intuitive Eating* (coauthor)

*Healthy Homestyle Cooking*

*Eating on the Run*

200 All-New Recipe Makeovers

# MoreHealthy Homestyle Cooking

## Evelyn Tribole, M.S., R.D.

author of the million-copy bestseller
*Healthy Homestyle Cooking*

RODALE

First published 2000
First published in paperback 2002

Illustrations © 2000 by Kris Wiltse
All photographs © 2000 by Rodale Inc., except pages 133 and 191 © 2000 by Thom DeSanto

Front cover recipes: Quick Praline Rolls (page 42), Spicy Cashew-Chicken Stir-fry (page 207), Broiled Breaded Scallops (page 141) and Orzo Salad (page 277), Lemon Heaven Meringue Squares (page 346)

The recipe for Hot Spinach-Artichoke Dip on page 94 is from Evelyn Tribole's "Recipe Makeovers" column, © June 2000 *Shape* magazine. Reprinted with permission.

"Top Five Reduced-Fat Products" chart on page 20 is from the Calorie Control Council National Consumer Survey.

Cover Designer: Tara A. Long
Interior Designer: Christina Gaugler
Photographers: Mitch Mandel/Rodale Images, Thom DeSanto
Illustrator: Kris Wiltse
Food Stylist: Diane Simone Vezza
Prop Stylist: Debra Donahue

**Library of Congress Cataloging-in-Publication Data**

Tribole, Evelyn, 1959–
    More healthy homestyle cooking : family favorites you'll make again and again : 200
all-new recipe makeovers / Evelyn Tribole.
        p.      cm.
    Includes index.
    ISBN 1–57954–117–8 hardcover
    ISBN 1–57954–663–3 paperback

    1. Cookery.   2. Low-fat diet—Recipes.  I. Title.
TX714 .T763  2000
641.5'638—dc21                                     00–039060

**Distributed to the book trade by St. Martin's Press**

      4  6  8  10  9  7  5       hardcover
2  4  6  8  10  9  7  5  3  1   paperback

RODALE

WE INSPIRE AND ENABLE PEOPLE TO IMPROVE
THEIR LIVES AND THE WORLD AROUND THEM

FOR MORE OF OUR PRODUCTS
WWW.RODALESTORE.COM
(800) 848-4735

*To my parents*

# Contents

# Acknowledgments

I sincerely appreciate and am thankful for guidance and help from:

The Rodale Test Kitchen and Rodale editing team, including David Joachim, Anne Egan, and Mary Goodbody.

David Smith, my literary agent, champion, and sounding board.

My team of taste testers—families and friends, including the Burt family, Gagnon family, Jakowatz family, Pavlish family, Peck family, and my sister, Elaine Roberts. I would turn up at all hours on their doorsteps awaiting their opinions on the newest recipe creation.

And publicists past and present, who are the unsung heroes of book promotion. Thanks especially to Mary Lengle and Alisa Wyatt.

I offer special thanks and love to my family—Jeff, Connor, and Krystin—for patiently putting up with me. Especially to Connor, who awaits his own book. During the middle of this project, he was diagnosed with celiac disease and was unable to participate in tasting but kept saying, "The next book is for me, Mom." And so it will be.

# Nutrition Update

Margarine versus butter. Calories versus fat. Protein versus carbohydrates. Over the years, there have been numerous nutritional debates like these. New studies come out showing that one food or nutrient is better or worse than another, the media spreads the news, and the debates begin.

I'm sure you've seen headlines that one day proclaim a certain food to be healthful, while the next day another headline says that the same food is, in fact, dangerous. No wonder people are confused. Some of my nutrition clients say that they just want to wait until the researchers make up their scholarly minds before they make any changes in their personal eating habits. I can't blame them, but I urge them—and you—to be patient because, believe it or not, none of this is an exact science.

Research studies are evolutionary by nature. A single study will not make or break an idea or dietary change. While nutrition research has evolved, the long-standing pillars of healthful eating have not changed. Only the fine-tuning has. For example, we've known for eons that it is important to eat plant-based foods such as vegetables. But researchers are just now finding out exactly why. They've discovered numerous healthful substances in plant foods such as lycopene, a natural red pigment in tomatoes and watermelon, that may play an important role in fighting cancer, especially for men; and phenolic flavonoids, found in grape juice and red wine, which help lower cholesterol.

This doesn't mean that we should run out and purchase these promising compounds in a bottle. In fact, that approach may backfire. Once a singular compound is isolated from food and packaged as a supplement, it may lose its purported health properties and may even become damaging. For instance, when beta-carotene was first isolated and taken as a supplement, it was found in two major studies to increase the risk for developing cancer among smokers rather than offering lung protection as the researchers had originally hoped.

What we continue to learn from research is that there is no shortcut or magic bullet to healthful eating. It's still a good idea to eat those vegetables and whole grains—and even some fat—regardless of whether you are taking supplements or not.

If there's one thing that nutrition research has made clear, it's this: A healthy diet can make a vital difference in your overall well-being and quality of life. Decades of studies have shown that diet-related conditions such as a stroke, heart disease, and osteoporosis are preventable. Even if the possibility of these conditions seems years away, remember that most of these diseases result from years of eating and lifestyle habits. Fortunately, it doesn't take quite as long to reap the rewards of eating healthfully. One important study showed that high blood pressure can be lowered within just 2 weeks with changes to diet alone.

In this chapter, I review some long-standing nutrition basics and clear up the confusion surrounding carbohydrates, sodium, trans fatty acids, and even phyto-chemicals—that exciting new category of healing substances.

## Pillars of Healthful Eating

I'll never forget a client of mine, a financial planner, who said, "If you don't have a target, how will you know if you reached the mark?" When he asked me this question, I handed him the USDA Food Guide Pyramid.

The pyramid is a target for healthful eating. It illustrates the major food groups and shows how much emphasis to place on each one. Surveys indicate that most people are aware of the pyramid's recommendations (such as "get your five-a-day of fruits and vegetables"). Yet it's an entirely different story when it comes to trans-lating awareness into action on our plates. One USDA report found that we're still eating too many of the things that contribute to poor health (fat, cholesterol, and calories) and falling short with critical nutrients like folate and calcium. Most Americans are not even meeting the minimum recommendations for the pyramid's major food groups.

Let's take a closer look at these food groups and see just where we're missing the mark.

Get Your Grains

Recommended amount:
6–11 servings

*What counts as a serving:* 1 slice bread; ½ cup cooked ce-real, pasta, or rice; 1 ounce cold cereal
*How we're doing:* Grains form the base of the pyramid. We should eat breads, pasta, rice, and cereal more than any other food. For the most part, we do. Yet when it comes to eating *whole* grains, the average American is below the sug-gested level, averaging only one serving per day. The minimum recommendation is

# The Whole Truth

Whole grains are one of our best sources of fiber. To boost your intake, work some of the following foods into your meals.

| Whole Grain | Fiber (g) |
|---|---|
| ½ cup cooked bulgur (cracked wheat) | 4 |
| ¼ cup wheat germ | 4 |
| ½ cup cooked pearl barley | 3 |
| ½ cup cooked brown rice | 2 |
| ½ cup cooked whole oats | 2 |
| 1 slice whole wheat bread | 2 |

six servings of grains a day, and at least three of those should be from whole grains. Why go for whole grains? Simply put, they are nature's entire grain package, including the nutritious germ, bran, and endosperm. These are what give whole grains their hearty texture and nutty taste. They also supply you with a healthy amount of soluble fiber, which helps lower blood cholesterol levels. Studies show that whole grains have other benefits, too.

Researchers at the University of Minnesota in Minneapolis studied 34,000 postmenopausal women and found that those who ate whole grain foods every day had a 15 to 25 percent reduction in their risk of dying from all causes, including heart disease and cancer.

The Nurses' Health Study at Harvard Medical School gathered data from nearly 69,000 nurses over a 10-year period and found that eating whole grains significantly lowered the risk of having a fatal heart attack. Women in the study who consumed an average of 23 grams of fiber a day had a 23 percent lower risk of heart attack than women who averaged only 12 grams a day. (The recommended amount is at least 20 to 35 grams of fiber a day.) Interestingly, only fiber from grains was linked to cardiac protection.

To get more whole grains in your diet, eat breads that contain oat flour or whole wheat flour. Use oats and barley in your cooking. Try whole wheat pasta. And use brown rice instead of white rice when you can. Don't forget, corn is a whole grain, too.

Recommended amount:
3–5 servings

***What counts as a serving:*** 1 cup fresh leafy vegetables, ½ cup other cooked or fresh vegetables, ¾ cup vegetable juice
***How we're doing:*** The USDA findings on vegetables are a little tricky. On the surface, we seem to be doing better at meeting the minimum goal of eating three servings of vegetables a day—that is, until you take a closer look at the statistics. Those who do eat the recommended amount of vegetables may not be eating enough of the right ones. Potatoes alone account for nearly one-third of our vegetable consumption, and most of these are fried. Ideally, we should eat a much wider variety of vegetables.

Study after study has demonstrated the health benefits of eating vegetables, from lowering the incidence of heart disease to preventing breast cancer. Three servings a day is considered the absolute minimum. And that's pretty easy to do. Simply having 1½ cups cooked vegetables with dinner will meet your quota for the day. Or you could eat smaller amounts throughout the day. Add tomatoes and lettuce to your sandwich at lunchtime. Eat a crunchy salad. Snack on carrots and sliced red bell peppers when you're hungry. Or drink a glass of vegetable juice. It's easy to meet the minimums when you get in the habit. And you can't eat too many vegetables, so feast away. To get the most flavor and nutrients, go for a full spectrum of brightly colored vegetables. I like to think of this as eating the rainbow.

Recommended amount:
2–4 servings

***What counts as a serving:*** 1 medium piece of fruit; ½ cup chopped, cooked, or canned fruit; ¾ cup fruit juice
***How we're doing:*** Most people know that eating fruit is healthful, but on any given day, many of us eat absolutely no fruit at all. In the United States, we are not meeting the minimum target of two servings a day. Fresh whole fruit, frozen cut-up fruit, or canned fruit (packed in water, not syrup) are the best choices. Fruit juice counts, too, but it doesn't have the valuable fiber of whole fruits.

Again, meeting the daily requirement is pretty simple, especially because fruit is so sweet and delicious. Slice bananas or strawberries on your morning cereal. Eat an apple or tangerine with your lunch. Spoon sliced peaches over ice cream or sorbet for dessert. Or whip up a yogurt-fruit smoothie for a quick snack.

In addition to the heart-smart fiber and health-boosting vitamins in fruits, the

# Poor Eating Is Expensive

What's the economic cost of poor eating? All told, experts estimate that it adds up to $70.9 billion in medical costs. This number accounts for only the top four diet-related diseases—heart disease, cancer, stroke, and diabetes. The economic toll climbs even higher when you factor in other diet-related problems such as osteoporosis.

latest findings show that fruits and veggies may help protect our bones. Researchers examined 907 members of the Framingham Heart Study in Framingham, Massachusetts, and found that those with the highest intakes of fruits and vegetables had the strongest bones. This may be because of the rich potassium and magnesium content of these foods. Fruits and vegetables account for one-half of the potassium intake in the American diet.

*Proteins from Land and Sea*

Recommended amount:
2–3 servings

*What counts as a serving:* 2 to 3 ounces cooked lean meat, poultry, or fish (1 egg or 2 tablespoons peanut butter count as 1 ounce of lean meat); ½ cup cooked beans

*How we're doing:* The Food Guide Pyramid recommends getting 4 to 6 ounces of lean protein a day. Most folks actually get more protein than that, mostly in the form of red meat. Chicken and turkey consumption has increased by nearly 60 percent since 1980, but red meat continues to be a primary source of protein for many Americans. Beef, veal, pork, and lamb accounted for more than half of our total meat consumption in 1996, nearly double that of poultry.

To keep fat to a minimum when meat is on your menu, look for lean cuts (see page 26 for the best choices). These make all the difference between a meat meal that's healthy and one that's not.

There are plenty of other lean protein sources besides red meat. Poultry, fish, and eggs are excellent choices. So are beans, peas, lentils, and other dried legumes. These plant proteins have less fat than animal proteins, and they are good for us in other ways, too. Beans are a great source of folate, the important B vitamin that can help prevent birth defects. Folate also helps protect your heart because it keeps a substance called homocysteine at normal levels (if homocysteine goes too high, it increases risk of heart disease).

Don't forget about nuts. Peanuts, walnuts, almonds, pecans, and other nuts are included in the protein group. Fortunately, nuts are packed with flavor, so a little goes a long way. In baking, I like to scatter chopped nuts over the top of batters (for breads, muffins, brownies, and cakes) rather then stirring them in. That way, the nuts get "toasted" by the dry heat of the oven, which intensifies their flavor. And they're the first thing you taste.

Kudos to soy protein! One of the most beneficial plant proteins is soy protein, which helps lower blood cholesterol levels. Researchers looked at 38 clinical studies of soy protein consumption and found that in 84 percent of the studies, LDL cholesterol (the "bad" cholesterol) was lowered by 13 percent. Soy protein may also help reduce the risk of other chronic diseases, including osteoporosis and many forms of cancer.

Recommended amount:
2–3 servings

**What counts as a serving:** 1 cup milk or yogurt, 1½ ounces natural cheese, 2 ounces processed cheese

**How we're doing:** Dairy products are our richest source of calcium, and they're readily available. But very few Americans get enough. The target for this food group is three calcium-rich foods a day. Three servings of low-fat dairy foods provides about 900 milligrams of calcium. Yet on average, Americans get only about 680 milligrams of calcium a day. At minimum, all Americans over 8 years of age need at least 1,000 milligrams of calcium a day. Teenagers and pregnant women need 1,200 to 1,500 milligrams. Menopausal women not on estrogens need at least 1,500 milligrams.

Men are not off the hook when it comes to calcium. Men account for one out of five osteoporosis patients (which means that 2 million men have this bone-robbing disease). Each year, men experience one-third of all the hip fractures, and sadly, a third of these men do not live for more than a year after injury. Eating foods high in calcium is part of the solution to this preventable disease.

Pour fat-free milk over your cereal. Dollop plain yogurt on a baked potato or mix it with herbs for a salad dressing or dip. Add reduced-fat shredded cheeses to casseroles and sliced cheeses to sandwiches. Even a cup of hot milk or cocoa counts as a serving. Keep in mind that eating a calcium-rich diet does more than protect your bones. Calcium plays a key role in maintaining healthy blood pressure levels and may also help prevent colon cancer.

Recommended amount:
Use sparingly

***What counts as sparing use:*** Limit sugars to no more than 10 percent and fats to no more than 30 percent of your average daily calories.

***How we're doing:*** The Food Guide Pyramid illustrates sugars and fats as the smallest part of a healthy diet, but we seem to be making a meal of them. We eat about 53 teaspoons of sugar per person per day. In a year, that's 154 pounds of sugar per person (including refined cane and beet sugar, corn sweeteners, and edible syrups, many of which come in the form of soft drinks). Needless to say, we are overdoing it, downing more than five times the amount of the recommended upper limit. The USDA recommends limiting sugars to no more than 10 percent of your average daily calories. That translates into about 10 teaspoons of sugar a day for the average 2,000-calorie diet for adults. Some may argue that sugar is harmless because it contains no fat. While this is true, the fact is that sugar adds loads of calories with no nutritional benefits. And too often, foods that contain sugar also contain fat. Here, we're talking about cookies, cakes, and other sweets. Fortunately, it's easy to check the sugar content of most foods because it's listed in the Nutrition Facts label as "grams of sugars." Note that 4 grams equals 1 teaspoon of sugar.

I'm not suggesting that you banish sweets altogether. One of the worst things you can do is to say, "I will never eat chocolate (or ice cream, cheesecake, doughnuts, chocolate chip cookies, and so on) again!"

Fat is the other food group at the very small tip of the pyramid. Given the proliferation of low-fat and fat-free foods, you would think that Americans have begun to eat less fat. Actually, the reverse is true: We have increased our fat intake. On average, men ages 19 to 50 eat 101 grams of fat per day. Women in the same age range eat about 65 fat grams a day. These figures are better than they were in the 1970s, but since the mid-1990s, our fat intake has gradually crept back up. I discuss the reasons why below.

Keep in mind that fat is necessary for good health. Our bodies need fat to absorb vitamins A, D, E, and K. More important, fat transfers flavors in food (if you have compared fat-free salad dressing with full-fat salad dressing, you know what I mean). But we need only a little fat every day, and it's not hard to come by. To see exactly how much fat we should be eating, see "Total Fat" on page 11.

# The Daily 6-5-4-3 Countdown

To simplify the Food Guide Pyramid's recommendations, I like to use a mnemonic device called the Daily 6-5-4-3 Countdown. These numbers represent the minimum servings from the pyramid's four key food groups: six servings of grains, five servings of fruits and vegetables (combined), 4 ounces—not servings—of lean protein (including plant proteins like beans), and three servings of calcium-rich foods. The 6-5-4-3 Countdown makes it easy to remember what to eat each day. Simply count down the numbers to see if you're getting the recommended amounts. If not, increase your intake of whatever food is coming up short.

# The Plate Model

Some of my clients prefer a meal-by-meal approach rather than a day-by-day approach. I give them a diagram that illustrates what the food proportions should look like on their plates at each meal (see opposite page). This plate model makes meal planning much easier. I also like the fact that the plate resembles the peace symbol, which seems to say that food is our ally, not our enemy. If you're planning to make a casserole, stew, or other dish where many food groups are mixed together, apply the plate model so that the proportions match those in the illustration.

Whichever method you prefer, day-by-day or meal-by-meal, these devices help you make sure that you're hitting the targets for an overall healthy diet.

# Eat Healthy Fats

With all the negative things we hear about fat, it's easy to forget that fats also play a vital role in health. Here's the skinny on which fats to eat and which ones to keep to a minimum.

*Essential fatty acids.* Our bodies require two types of dietary fats that act as vitamins: the omega-6 linoleic fatty acid and the omega-3 alpha-linolenic fatty acids. These are essential to our diets because our bodies cannot manufacture them. They must be harvested from food.

Omega-6's are important because they help reduce blood cholesterol levels. This type of fat is found in nuts, seeds, and the oils made from them.

Omega-3's are found primarily in fish such as salmon and tuna and in some plant foods such as flaxseed and walnuts. Research shows that these fats not only may

help protect your heart but may also be beneficial for rheumatoid arthritis, psoriasis, and hypertension (high blood pressure).

Years ago, before the abundance of processed fat-free foods, it would have been nearly impossible to be deficient in these essential fatty acids. But researchers are beginning to discover that some groups are falling short of recommended amounts.

Research from the large-scale Nurses' Health Study raised concern that widespread use of fat-free salad dressings has eliminated an important source of beneficial fat from women's diets. The oil in salad dressing supplies omega-3 alpha-linolenic acid. The data, based on more than 76,000 women over a 10-year period, show that women who had a higher intake of alpha-linolenic acid had a much lower risk of fatal heart disease. This type of fatty acid is believed to be protective because of its antiarrhythmic effect on the heart. Yet half of all Americans are not getting enough of it.

# Go Nuts for Health Benefits

Nuts and seeds are among the best sources of alpha-linolenic acid, a type of omega-3 fatty acid that can help reduce risk of heart attacks and may help treat rheumatoid arthritis, psoriasis, and hypertension (high blood pressure). Look to the following foods to help supply this essential acid in your diet. Studies show that 50 percent of Americans don't get enough of this type of fat in their diets.

| Food | Percentage of Alpha-Linolenic Acid (by weight) |
| --- | --- |
| Flaxseeds | 55 |
| Flaxseed oil | 51 |
| Walnut oil | 11 |
| Canola oil | 9 |
| Wheat germ | 8 |
| English walnuts | 7 |
| Soybean oil | 7 |
| Soybeans, cooked | 7 |
| Wheat germ oil | 7 |
| Almonds, dry roasted | 0.4 |

Another study has identified essential fatty acid insufficiency as one of the most prevalent nutritional problems. Researchers from the Framingham Offspring Study in Massachusetts expressed concern that a low-fat diet may worsen this problem because these diets are often lacking in whole foods, which supply the small amounts of essential fatty acids that our bodies require.

To make sure that you're getting enough essential fatty acids, keep fish, nuts, and oils in your diet. For particularly good sources of alpha-linolenic acid, see "Go Nuts for Health Benefits."

*Monounsaturated fats.* These fats are found in most kitchens in the form of olive oil and canola oil. Their health advantage is that they lower "bad" LDL cholesterol while helping to maintain "good" HDL cholesterol. Translation: These fats help keep your blood cholesterol at healthy levels, thereby reducing heart disease risk. The easiest way to get these health benefits is to use olive or canola oil in place of saturated fats like butter and bacon drippings. You'll notice that many of my recipes do use light butter or bacon drippings for flavor (and texture, in the case of light butter). I don't swear off these ingredients entirely, but the majority of the fats that I use are monounsaturated in the form of canola oil, olive oil, sesame oil, and peanut oil.

*Saturated fats.* Surprisingly, there is no biological requirement for saturated fats. Perhaps that is why, more than any other component of our diets, saturated fats have the most profound effect on raising blood cholesterol levels and increasing heart disease risk. We simply don't need these fats. Fortunately, saturated fat is listed on food labels, so it's easy to identify and keep to a minimum. Saturated fat is found primarily in animal fats such as butter, full-fat dairy products, meats, and chicken skin and also in tropical oils such as coconut oil.

*Trans fatty acids.* These fats have made headlines because studies show that they behave similarly to artery-clogging saturated fats. They tend to raise blood cholesterol levels and increase heart disease risk. Unfortunately, trans fatty acids are not listed on food labels, so identifying them requires a little know-how.

Trans fatty acids are created during the process of hydrogenation. This process involves adding hydrogen to liquid oils to transform them into solid fats. These hydrogenated oils are used to make margarine (especially stick margarine), most crackers, and some baked goods. They're also used for frying foods in fast-food restaurants.

What's a consumer to do? If you use margarine, buy it in a tub instead of a stick. Liquid oil is the key ingredient in tub margarine, while hydrogenated oil is the key ingredient in stick margarine. This means that tub margarine contains less than half the amount of trans fatty acids as stick margarine. And some tub margarines have no trans fatty acids.

Tub margarine is also a more healthful choice than butter. But if you love the taste of butter, as I do, try light butter instead of regular butter. Light butter has half the saturated fat and half the calories of regular butter. I use light butter in many of the recipes in this book, mostly in baked goods and casseroles.

*Total Fat.* With so many types of fats available, my clients often ask me, "How do I balance my intake of beneficial fats with harmful fats?" Here's the answer: Most health authorities, including the American Heart Association and the National Institutes of Health, agree that no more than 30 percent of our daily calories should come from fat (some nutrition experts recommend even less). Of this amount, no more than 10 percent should be saturated fat. This means that if you are consuming 2,000 calories a day (the average amount for adults), you should limit yourself to about 65 grams of fat a day, and of these, no more than 20 grams should be saturated fat. While the daily figures make it easier to keep track, bear in mind that these guidelines apply to a balanced diet over a period of several days, such as a week. They do not apply to a single food or single meal. The key terms are *balance* and *moderation*.

# Carbohydrates: The Nutrition Nemesis?

Let's get this straight right up front: Carbohydrates do not make you fat.

I believe that because so many of us have become disenchanted with fat-free foods, we sought out a nutritional villain to replace fat. Carbohydrates were the obvious choice. This, combined with the latest round of diet books that bash carbohydrates as the cause of obesity and other ills, has resurrected the old diet myth that carbohydrates are fattening. And consumers have jumped on the bandwagon like never before. According to a 1995 survey by the Wheat Food Council and American Bakers Association, 40 percent of consumers think that bread is fattening, and 35 percent believe that starches should be avoided.

Nothing could be further from the truth. Breads and starches are included in the foundation of any healthy eating plan. As with any food, overeating carbohydrates can cause you to gain weight, but you could also gain weight by eating too many protein bars or too many cartons of fat-free frozen yogurt. There's nothing magical about carbohydrates. It's the calories that come with them that can cause you to gain weight.

Here's some proof. Researchers at the University of Colorado Health Sciences Center in Denver fed men extra calories so that they ate 150 percent of their normal energy requirements every day. Some men consumed all their extra calories as carbohydrates, while others ate them as fat. After 2 weeks, the results showed that eating excess fat led to greater fat storage than did eating excess carbohydrates. This study confirmed that overeating *any* type of calories can result in fat storage, whether the calories are from carbohydrates or from fat itself.

# The Shakedown on Salt

Like sugar and fat, salt is one of those ingredients that can be used sparingly with great results. For instance, just a tiny amount of salt on a potato makes all the difference in flavor. Likewise, in baked goods, just ¼ teaspoon or ½ teaspoon usually does the trick.

Because it is so concentrated, eating high amounts of salt or, more specifically, sodium, is related to many health problems, most of which take years to manifest. Hypertension (high blood pressure) is the condition that is most readily associated with too much sodium. Half of all people with high blood pressure are salt-sensitive, which means that salt is one of the factors contributing to their condition. Studies show that one out of five people can prevent themselves from getting high blood pressure by keeping salt in check.

Eating too much salt also causes the body to eliminate the mineral calcium. This calcium loss can contribute to thinning bones (osteoporosis), especially in women, who often don't get enough calcium in their diets.

Even some cancers, such as stomach and colorectal cancer, are related to over-consumption of sodium.

Because of these health concerns, most health organizations recommend keeping sodium intake under 2,400 milligrams per day. That equals 1 teaspoon of salt a day. Even if you don't use the saltshaker at the table, watch your sodium intake from other sources. Seventy-five percent of the sodium in American diets comes from processed foods that don't even taste salty.

# The DASH Diet

Some of the best news in nutrition research has come from a study called DASH, an acronym for Dietary Approaches to Stop Hypertension. Tested at four major medical centers around the country, the DASH diet has far-reaching results that may affect more than just hypertension. The most significant features of the diet include:

• Boosting fruit and vegetable intake to nearly 10 servings each day (double the current Food Guide Pyramid recommendations)
  • Eating only low-fat dairy products
  • Eating four to five servings of legumes (and nuts) a week
  • Keeping sodium levels at 3,000 milligrams a day

The study found that subjects who followed the DASH diet had significant drops in blood pressure whether or not they had high blood pressure to begin with. Those with high blood pressure had a reduction in blood pressure comparable to using

# DASH Details

Is it possible to lower blood pressure by diet alone? The DASH eating plan (Dietary Approaches to Stop Hypertension) showed that it is. According to DASH, here's what to eat and how much if you'd like to lower your blood pressure fast.

| Food Group | Servings | Serving Size: |
|---|---|---|
| Grains | 7 to 8 daily | 1 slice bread or ½ cup cooked rice, pasta, or cereal |
| Vegetables | 4 to 5 daily | 1 cup raw leafy greens, ½ cup cooked vegetables, or ¾ cup vegetable juice |
| Fruits | 4 to 5 daily | 1 medium piece; ¼ cup dried; ½ cup fresh, frozen, or canned; or ¾ cup fruit juice |
| Dairy (low-fat or fat-free) | 2 to 3 daily | 1 cup milk, 1 cup yogurt, or 1½ oz cheese |
| Meats, poultry, and fish | 2 or less daily | 3 oz cooked |
| Nuts, seeds, and dry beans | 4 to 5 per week | ⅓ cup nuts, 2 Tbsp seeds, or ½ cup cooked dry beans |
| Fats and oils | 2 to 3 daily | 1 tsp tub margarine, 1 Tbsp low-fat mayonnaise, 1 tsp vegetable oil, or 2 Tbsp light salad dressing |
| Sweets | 5 per week | 1 Tbsp sugar or jam, ½ oz jelly beans, or 1 cup lemonade |

antihypertensive drug therapy. Amazingly, the effect of the diet was evident within just 1 week of implementation. Maximum benefits were seen after just 2 weeks. With these extraordinary results, researchers estimate that if Americans adopted the DASH eating plan, we could see a 27 percent reduction of strokes and a 15 percent reduction of heart disease in this country.

Although the DASH diet has slightly more sodium than the current recommended level of 2,400 milligrams a day, another phase of the study (called DASH2) is examining the relationship between blood pressure, eating patterns, and a reduced sodium intake. Meanwhile, it's comforting to know that it doesn't take an ultra low sodium diet to lower blood pressure.

# Phytochemicals

Here's more good news coming out of nutrition research. Science has finally pin-pointed why vegetables and fruits are so good for us. There are dozens of naturally occurring compounds in plants called phytochemicals. These plant compounds have huge health benefits and have been shown to do all of the following:

## The Good Things in Food

Here's just a sampling of the beneficial phytochemicals found in whole foods.

Eat more of the foods in the column at right to get the health benefits of these substances.

| Phytochemical | Health Benefits | Sources |
|---|---|---|
| Anthocyanins | • Inhibit the cholesterol-making process<br>• Act as antioxidants | Strawberries, cherries, cranberries, raspberries, blueberries, grapes, black currants |
| Flavonoids | • Act as antioxidants<br>• Prevent blood from clumping<br>• Have anti-inflammatory properties<br>• Extend vitamin C activity<br>• Protect cholesterol levels | Fruits, vegetables, nuts, whole grains |
| Gingerols and diarylhaptanoids | • Have antioxidant activity greater than vitamin E | Ginger |
| Isothiocyanates | • Cancer inhibitor | Broccoli and other cruciferous vegetables |
| Limonoids | • Cancer inhibitor | Citrus fruits |
| Lycopene | • Cancer inhibitor | Tomatoes, guava, watermelon |
| Phthalides | • Cancer inhibitor | Celery seeds |
| Phytosterols | • Cancer inhibitor<br>• Lowers cholesterol | Nuts, seeds, whole wheat, corn, soybeans |
| Quercetin | • Anti-cancer activity<br>• Protects cholesterol from being converted to a more harmful compound | Red and yellow onions, kale, broccoli, red grapes, cherries, French beans, apples, whole grain cereals |

*Fight cancer:* Sulphoraphane, a natural compound in broccoli, is a potent inducer of enzymes that prevent cancer.

*Protect your heart:* Terpenoids, which are found in citrus fruits, can reduce blood cholesterol levels. And phenolic flavonoids, found in grape juice and red wine, lower cholesterol levels and prevent blood cells from clumping (which can jam up arteries).

*Enhance immunity:* Allylic sulfides, compounds found in onions and garlic, improve immunity and help ward off colds.

This is only the tip of the iceberg. Citrus fruits alone have more than 60 different flavonoids, which offer a wide range of benefits from inhibiting blood clots to fighting tumors. While research is ongoing in this area, it is clear that it pays to eat foods rich in phytochemicals. Again, look to whole foods instead of supplements for these nutrients. Studies suggest that individual phytochemicals exert their spectacular health benefits only when eaten as whole foods since they may work synergistically with other naturally occurring compounds in the food.

As you can tell, I get very enthused about nutrition. After all, it's a big part of my profession. But my true passion is food. Knowing about the nutritional benefits of food is important, but good taste is even more crucial. Who cares how good a meal is nutritionally if it doesn't taste good? Plus, the only way to continue eating a healthy diet is to consistently enjoy the food. I probably would have stopped eating healthfully long ago if I didn't enjoy my food. In the next chapter, I tell all my secrets about how to make healthy food that tastes fabulous.

# Recipe Makeover Secrets: New and Tried-and-True

Taste, taste, taste!" This is my recipe-makeover mantra. I say it over and over to myself when creating new recipes. It's the most critical factor when transforming any dish into a more healthful one. I've found that regardless of how healthful a recipe is, if it doesn't taste good, it's not likely to be featured again on anyone's dinner table.

Of course, my tastebuds are different from yours, so I subjected the recipes in this book to a minimum of two outside tests. Once I was satisfied with the results, I shared the recipe with my family and friends—test number one. If and only if a recipe passed their taste tests did it go on for another round of testing at the Rodale Test Kitchen. At that stage, many recipes were tested several times to ensure that they tasted absolutely delicious.

During the process of creating and testing recipes, you learn a lot. It can be rather humbling but also enlightening and exciting. In this chapter, I offer both new and tried-and-true techniques that work to cut fat and calories while boosting the overall nutrition profile. I also discuss the best uses for the many reduced-fat, fat-free, and healthy convenience products in today's supermarkets.

## Straight Substitutions Don't Always Work

You would think that with more than 5,600 reduced-fat and fat-free foods available to us, most of which did not exist a few years ago, it would be a snap to transform your favorite recipes into lower-fat versions of their former selves. But so often this is not the case. Simply swapping a fat-free ingredient for a full-fat food can be disastrous. For example, toss fat-free cream cheese into a recipe that was developed for full-fat cream cheese, and you may end up with a lumpy mess of curds. Or, try using light butter—which tastes great on the tongue—in baking recipes calling for regular butter, and the results are likely to be disappointing in terms of texture.

I have learned the hard way that you can't take a favorite family recipe and automatically substitute these fat-free and reduced-fat ingredients. Taste and texture

## Every Recipe Is a Cooking Class

If you prefer to learn by doing, turn to a recipe right now. Every recipe in this book explains the techniques I used to reduce calories, fat, cholesterol, and sodium or to boost fiber and other important nutrients. These techniques appear in a bulleted list at the top of the recipe. Every recipe also comes with a "Nutrition Scorecard" (see example at right). The scorecard shows exactly how much the calories and fat were reduced in the recipe. The "before" figures are based on a traditional, less-healthy version of the recipe. The "after" figures are for the healthier recipe shown in the book. A complete nutritional analysis also appears at the bottom of every recipe.

### Nutrition Scorecard
(per serving)

|  | before | after |
| --- | --- | --- |
| Calories | 580 | 386 |
| Fat (g) | 28 | 8 |

often suffer. One thing I have learned, however, is that you can use these products. The trick is making a few other minor adjustments to the recipes.

## Step-by-Step Guide to Recipe Makeovers

The very first step in any recipe makeover is to ask a few simple questions about the role of the ingredients that you'd like to change. The answer will guide you to the best substitution or technique for each ingredient.

1. *Does the ingredient contribute significantly to flavor?* If the role is flavor, you can't simply take out the ingredient. You'll know that something like dark sesame oil, which has an intense nutty flavor, would be sorely missed. When using such a flavorful ingredient, the best method is to reduce the amount rather than omit or replace it.

2. *Does the ingredient contribute significantly to texture?* If the role is texture, ask if the ingredient can be satisfactorily substituted. For example, nuts in a fudge recipe add crunchy texture. Simply eliminating the nuts would leave you with a feeling of something missing. But since texture is the role of the nuts, you can achieve a similar texture by substituting another ingredient, such as crispy rice cereal.

3. *How does the ingredient affect visual appeal?* After all, we eat with our eyes. For example, fat-free (skim) milk is certainly the milk of choice for healthy cooking be-

cause it has zero fat. However, its bluish color can be off-putting to some people, depending on how it is used in a recipe. When the milk will be visible, as in a soup, I recommend using 1% milk instead of fat-free milk. One percent milk has only 2 grams of fat and has the familiar white color of whole milk. Another example: When you decide to reduce the amount of nuts in a batter, it's more appealing to scatter them on top of muffins or brownies rather than mixing them inside, where they will distribute too widely. Plus, you will taste the nuts more readily if they're on top.

4. *What's the best substitute?* Once you spot a fatty ingredient to change, there are several options. You can reduce the amount, substitute it with a lower-fat but comparable ingredient, or omit it altogether. For instance, many recipes call for onions to be sautéed in tablespoons of oil. In this case, the best substitute is simply to use less oil. Usually, 1 to 2 teaspoons of oil is plenty for sautéing. Just be sure to heat the oil before adding the food so that the hot oil cooks the surface of the food rather than getting absorbed by it.

5. *Does a change really need to be made here?* Some ingredients may be too vital to a recipe and should not be changed at all. That's okay. Making even one change is progress. You don't have to challenge every fatty ingredient, especially if it makes an unacceptable compromise in taste. For example, mascarpone cheese, a very fatty type of Italian cream cheese, is critical to the classic Italian dessert tiramisu. It offers such unique sweet flavor and texture that if it were omitted, a recipe for tiramisu would just not be tiramisu. Yet there are other ingredients in the recipe that can be changed quite successfully, as illustrated in the recipe for Tiramisu (page 335).

## The Most Important Makeover Tip

Never reveal your secret ingredients until after everyone has tasted the dish. This strategy heads off the tastebud bias that runs rampant in this country. There continues to be a notion that healthful foods are less flavorful than other foods—or worse, that they don't taste good at all. Sometimes, I don't even tell people that what they're eating is lower in fat than a traditional version of the dish. As long as I know that it's healthy and they know that it tastes good, everyone is happy.

I have to admit that I get a kick out of watching the expressions on people's faces when I do tell them. When they find out that what they've been gobbling up is low in fat or includes a novel ingredient, such as baby food prunes, they are often stunned because it tastes so good. (Of course, if someone has a food allergy or intolerance, you may need to reveal the ingredients before that person takes a single bite.)

# Top Five Reduced-Fat Products

Supermarkets carry thousands of fat-free and reduced-fat products. Here are the five that rise to the top of our shopping lists. Notice that at least half of all Americans purchase the top three foods.

**Percent of adult Americans who consume . . .**

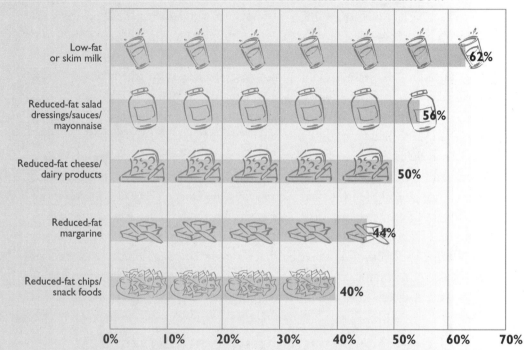

| | |
|---|---|
| Low-fat or skim milk | 62% |
| Reduced-fat salad dressings/sauces/ mayonnaise | 56% |
| Reduced-fat cheese/ dairy products | 50% |
| Reduced-fat margarine | 44% |
| Reduced-fat chips/ snack foods | 40% |

0%   10%   20%   30%   40%   50%   60%   70%

# The Secrets of Using Reduced-Fat Foods

Fat-free and reduced-fat foods have grown enormously in popularity (see "Top Five Reduced-Fat Products" to see just how much). Yet how to use these products baffles many home cooks. I've found that a little tweaking often makes these products perform much better. Here's how to get the most out of common reduced-fat products, including their advantages and limitations.

*Light butter.* This product has half the fat and calories of regular butter. It tastes terrific spread on hot muffins or melted and drizzled over steamed vegetables. The fat is lowered primarily by the addition of water, which means that you just can't toss it into any baking recipe. The solution is to reduce the amount of liquid in the recipe. In cookie dough, for instance, I usually offset the problem by omitting an egg white or two. For muffins or pancake batter, reduce the amount of milk or juice. In frostings, nut toppings, and streusel toppings, light butter works wonderfully without any adjustments to the liquid.

Light butter also works well in pastry dough. The trick here is to prevent overworking the dough so that the crust won't be tough. To solve this problem, I chill the light butter, then shred it. Chilled and grated light butter mixes quickly and evenly into dry ingredients.

*Fat-free cream cheese.* Most recipes call for cream cheese to be beaten with other ingredients. When beating fat-free cream cheese, it starts out just fine, looking smooth and satiny. But the moment you add liquid such as milk, the fat-free cream cheese develops lumps and starts to resemble small-curd cottage cheese. I find that using a combination of fat-free cream cheese and light cream cheese (or light butter) prevents this clumping. Blend the combination of cream cheeses (or cream cheese and butter) first. Then the other ingredients, including liquids, can be added without a problem.

Another tip for fat-free cream cheese: It has very little flavor and no richness on its own. I don't recommend it for bagels. Fat-free cream cheese works and tastes best when combined with other ingredients. It works especially well when mixed with other strong flavors, as in the Blue Cheese–Stuffed Mushrooms (page 88). It also works when combined with light cream cheese, as in Strawberry Cheesecake (page 340).

*Fat-free sour cream.* This product has improved greatly over the years. When it was first introduced, most brands tasted chalky. But today's fat-free sour creams work remarkably well. For the best texture, look for those brands that have little or no gelatin. I find that the gelatin interferes with the texture of baked goods.

*Fat-free ricotta cheese.* Unlike its full-fat counterpart, this ricotta gets too runny when baked. The solution is to add about a tablespoon of unbleached or all-purpose flour for each 15-ounce container of fat-free ricotta. The flour does not alter the taste but stabilizes the cheese. I use this combination for layered and filled pasta dishes such as lasagna and manicotti.

*Powdered egg whites.* I use a lot of fresh egg whites in cooking and baking, and sometimes I run out. I've found that powdered egg whites are a surprisingly good alternative. They offer two advantages: They have a longer storage life, and they are pasteurized. Just follow the package directions on how to use them (usually, you simply add water). You won't find any recipes here that call for powdered egg whites, but you can substitute them in any recipe that uses egg whites.

*Fat-free ice cream.* This is great blended with other ingredients to make smoothies and milkshakes. I don't recommend just scooping fat-free ice cream into a dish for dessert, however. It doesn't have the mouthfeel of regular or even reduced-fat ice cream. Use fat-free ice cream only when mixed with other ingredients.

*Frozen light whipped topping.* I freely substitute this product any time I would normally use regular whipped topping. It tastes good and mixes well with other ingredients to make pie fillings and toppings. Steer clear of the fat-free version, though. It simply does not work.

*Reduced-fat graham cracker crust.* What a convenient solution for healthy pie crust! Most stores carry this product, and there are no glitches in using it with creamy fillings. Another quick solution is to make your own crumb crust by crumbling graham crackers and sprinkling them on the bottom of a baking dish, pie plate, or springform pan. I mix the crumbs with a little sugar and, depending on the recipe, sometimes a little melted light butter before spooning the creamy filling over the top (see Lemon Heaven Meringue Squares on page 346). I also use a similar method with chocolate wafer cookies—and no one has complained yet!

*Fat-free sweetened condensed milk.* No traps or problems here. This is my number one choice as a substitute for regular sweetened condensed milk in dessert recipes. It looks and tastes the same.

*Fat-free evaporated milk.* I use this instead of heavy cream or whole milk to make creamy soups. It works very well and, of course, has no fat.

*Reduced-fat cream soups.* Whether the flavor you want is cream of mushroom or cream of chicken, the reduced-fat versions of these soups are winners. They perform wonderfully in casseroles and can be turned into quick sauces for chicken. You can also make an easy low-fat cheese sauce by stirring low-fat cheese into the heated soup and drizzling it over vegetables, pasta, or rice.

*Reduced-fat lunchmeats.* These have come a long way in the flavor department. I especially like the reduced-fat ham slices flavored with maple or hickory smoke. These work well in sandwiches, savory pies and tortes, roll-ups, wrap-style sandwiches, and chicken rolls.

# Makeover Methods That Work

Over more than a decade of creating healthy recipes, I have tried dozens and dozens of healthy-cooking techniques. Some work and some don't. Below are the tried-and-true methods that I use again and again. To get an idea of the fat and calories that you'll save by using these techniques, refer to "Recipe Makeover Substitutions" on page 28.

## *Using and Replacing Oil and Other Fats*

*Baking.* Fruit purees such as applesauce or baby food prunes work very well in place of some or all of the oil in recipes for muffins, brownies, and boxed cake mixes. I've found that pureed fruits work especially well if buttermilk is the liquid in the recipe instead of plain milk or water.

*Sautéing and stir-frying.* If the oil is used to coat the pan for cooking or browning, nonstick sprays work great as a replacement. If the oil is a flavoring agent, I usually coat the pan lightly with nonstick spray to prevent sticking, then use a smaller amount of oil for flavoring.

*Frying.* To create a crispy texture, try coating foods such as chicken or onion rings with flour, followed by egg whites and then cornflake crumbs. Generously spritz the coated food with nonstick spray and bake it (instead of frying it) in a hot oven—at least 400°F. You'll get wonderfully crispy results without all the fat of deep-frying.

*Butter.* Dabs of butter or margarine used to dot casseroles and fruit desserts can be omitted. Instead, I often mix a small amount of chilled and shredded light butter right into the topping ingredients. Light butter also works well when you simply want the taste of butter—on cooked vegetables, for instance. But when using light butter instead of regular butter in baking, be sure to reduce the liquid in the recipe as detailed on page 20.

*Salad dressings.* Many salad dressing recipes simply yield too much. Two table-spoons of dressing per serving is usually plenty. If your dressing makes more, try scaling back all the ingredients by one-quarter to one-half. There is nothing wrong with using a little less to dress the greens. Just be sure to leave in the key flavorful oils such as extra-virgin olive oil, dark sesame oil, or walnut oil. If the yield is just right on a recipe, try replacing up to two-thirds of the oil with a combination of chicken broth and a neutral-tasting juice such as pineapple juice or white grape

# Six Flavor-Boosting Tricks

It's no secret that fats and fatty ingredients can add wonderful flavors to a recipe. But there are other ways to add flavor without adding fat.

**1. Change the cooking method.** Roasting and grilling give foods a rich, smoky flavor that you can't get from sautéing or browning. These methods work especially well for boosting the flavor of vegetables and meats.

**2. Get herbal.** Herbs, both fresh and dried, add incomparable aromas to foods. Sometimes all a recipe needs is a sprinkling of fresh parsley or basil for the final touch of flavor. When using dried herbs, add them early in the recipe and crush them first between your fingers to release their sleeping aromas.

**3. Spice it up.** Sweet spices such as cinnamon, nutmeg, and ginger enhance the flavor of muffins, breads, and other baked goods. Cinnamon also works well with chocolate in desserts and with lemon zest for chicken dishes.

**4. Give it citrus.** Fresh lemon juice brightens the flavor of almost anything. I use lemon juice in salad dressings, marinades, sauces, and baked goods. For Mexican dishes, try the dynamic duo of lime juice and cilantro. And don't forget the zest. Grated lemon or orange peel works great in baked goods and pasta dishes and on vegetables.

**5. Try the dried stuff.** Dried foods are like little bursts of flavor in a recipe. I use sun-dried tomatoes to flavor up sauces, pizzas, dips, spreads, and salads. For richer soups and sauces, try dried mushrooms. Most supermarkets sell mixed dried wild mushrooms in ready-to-go packets. Even dried fruit is a great flavor booster. I use dried apricots, cherries, and cranberries (craisins) for breads, muffins, and cookies—and even Sacher Torte (page 336). Soften dried fruits and vegetables in hot water before using in recipes. Then add the soaking liquid for even more flavor.

**6. Condiments, anyone?** Here's the easiest way make food taste better: Splash the flavor right onto it. Keep a variety of condiments in your kitchen for last-minute flavor. Some of my favorite condiments include salsa, Worcestershire sauce, prepared horseradish, mustard, and hot-pepper sauce.

---

juice. You can also increase the amount of vinegar or lemon juice and decrease the oil. When using this method, try neutralizing the acidity of the vinegar or juice by adding a small amount of freshly brewed black tea.

*Thickening agents.* I use cornstarch as a thickening agent rather than flour or a combination of flour and butter. Flour-based sauces usually include the butter (or margarine) to prevent clumping. You can avoid clumping by dissolving cornstarch in a little bit of cold liquid before adding it to the recipe. Replace every 2 tablespoons of flour with 1 tablespoon of cornstarch and eliminate any butter or margarine. I also find that cornmeal makes a great thickener for stews or chili recipes. Just stir it right in.

## *Using and Replacing Dairy Products*

*Heavy cream.* Fat-free evaporated milk does a great job in place of cream, especially in casseroles, soups, and quiches. For an even thicker texture, stir in about a tablespoon of cornstarch for every cup of liquid.

*Whipped cream.* Without apology, I find that frozen light whipped topping works very well. Plus, it's mighty convenient.

*Cream cheese.* Often, the best combination for spreads, dips, and cheesecakes is a combination of equal amounts of fat-free cream cheese and light cream cheese (Neufchâtel cheese). But one question that I'm sometimes asked is: Which is better, a block of cream cheese or a tub? The truth is that tub-style cream cheese is a little bit lower in fat than block-style. But I use both styles, depending on the recipe. In this book, use the tub-style cream cheese when it is called for, as in the recipe for Best-Ever Light Cream Cheese Frosting (page 334). All the other recipes can handle either block-style or tub-style cream cheese.

*Hard cheeses.* As a general rule of thumb, reduced-fat cheeses work fine, but fat-free cheeses can be troublesome in terms of flavor and texture. A finely grated fat-free cheese may work in a cheese sauce or other recipe that includes liquid ingredients, but it won't melt well as a gooey topping or in a grilled cheese sandwich. For this reason, I usually stick with reduced-fat hard cheeses. For sandwiches, I like to use slices of light provolone, light Muenster, and light Swiss. When it comes to Parmesan cheese, I heartily recommend using the real thing. Nothing comes close to its flavor. Just use less. Luckily, the delicious, salty flavor of real Parmesan cheese is so potent that a little goes a long way.

*Milk and buttermilk.* Whole milk can be replaced with fat-free, 1 percent, or 2 percent milk in nearly any recipe calling for milk. When the opaque whiteness of the milk is important, go for 1 percent milk instead of skim, which looks thin, blue, and watery and lacks body. If you're curious about fat content, 1 percent milk has 1 gram of fat in every 3 ounces; 2 percent milk has 2 grams of fat in every 3 ounces; and whole milk has a little over 3 grams of fat in every 3 ounces.

Buttermilk, which used to be the liquid left over from the process of making butter, is now a cultured product made by adding a bacterial culture to fat-free or low-fat milk.

This means that it's a great product for low-fat cooking. Buttermilk adds richness and a creamy texture to recipes, and its slight acidity makes it perfect for baked goods.

## Using and Replacing Sweets

*Chocolate chips.* Use mini chocolate chips rather than the regular size. They distribute more widely in doughs and batters so you can use less.

*Baking chocolate.* I often substitute cocoa powder for baking chocolate because it's so much lower in fat. I've found that it can't be used across the board, though. For fudgy brownies (rather than cakelike brownies), it helps to keep at least half of the baking chocolate squares; replace the rest with cocoa powder. Three tablespoons of cocoa powder equals 1 ounce of baking chocolate.

*Sugar.* All sugars, whether granulated white, confectioners', brown sugar, honey, or molasses, are naturally fat-free. But they pack quite a wallop of calories. One cup of sugar has 774 calories. You can simply reduce the amount of sugar in most recipes. To enhance the perception of sweetness, I like to add sweet spices such as cinnamon and nutmeg.

*Pastry.* Phyllo dough is a great substitute for puff pastry and strudel dough. It's fat-free, and most grocery stores carry it in the freezer section. Use nonstick spray in place of melted butter to moisten the sheets when layering them. It's much faster and much lower in fat.

## Using and Replacing Protein Foods (Meats, Eggs, and Nuts)

*Beef.* The leanest choices in beef are the round cuts, such as round steak and top round roasts. Again, cutting fat in the meat department can be as simple as using less than the recipe calls for. To make a 3-ounce portion of meat look more attractive, slice it and fan the slices. Or combine beef with other ingredients, such as vegetables and rice, to make casseroles and stir-fries.

Ground chuck is the hamburger of choice in most households. It's inexpensive, and its natural fat content makes juicy burgers. To reduce the fat, I generally recommend using extra-lean ground beef instead and mixing it with ground turkey breast. If you are a beef purist, try mixing ground chuck with equal amounts of lean ground sirloin.

*Pork.* The leanest cut is pork tenderloin. Three ounces of cooked pork tenderloin has only 4 grams of fat. It is by far the best choice among all cuts of pork.

*Chicken.* It's no secret that skinless chicken breast is the leanest meat; the dark meat is a little higher in fat. To keep skinless chicken moist, marinate it before cooking. Or, simmer it in a flavored liquid so that it doesn't dry out. When cooking whole birds, as in roast chicken, leave the skin on during cooking to keep the meat moist. Remove the skin just before serving to slash fat and calories instantly. This is as important for the dark meat (drumsticks and wings) as it is for the breast meat. To see the difference in fat that a little skin can make, turn to page 213.

*Turkey.* Thanks to the variety of readily available cuts, there are so many good possibilities for cooking with turkey today. Turkey breast tidbits or tenders are great in stir-fries and stews. Ground turkey breast can be used to make burgers, chili, meat loaf, or casseroles. And it's the leanest ground meat available. When using ground turkey, I like to add moisture by mixing the meat with a little grated apple and bread crumbs. I also use turkey sausages. But remember that while turkey sausages are lower in fat than traditional pork sausages, they are still a fairly high fat food. When possible, try to reduce the amounts used.

*Eggs.* Two egg whites can be used in place of each whole egg. This swap works well in most baking recipes. In some other recipes, I find that it's necessary to leave in one or two whole eggs for body and richness, as in Crustless Garden Quiche (page 240). While I recommend egg whites, I generally do not use commercial egg substitutes. I prefer egg whites because their texture is more pleasing, and they perform better in most recipes. If you do use egg substitutes, I suggest limiting them to casseroles or other recipes in which the eggs are used to bind ingredients together. Egg substitutes do not have the ability to be whipped and hold air, which makes them less suitable for baked recipes that require volume such as cakes, or in recipes that require a foam such as meringue.

*Nuts.* The flavor and texture of nuts can't be beat. To cut the fat, simply scale back on the amount of nuts in a recipe. To boost the flavor, toast the nuts before using them. Place them in a dry skillet and toast for a few minutes, or until lightly browned and fragrant. It also helps to place the nuts where you can taste them—scattered on top of a recipe rather than buried inside.

# Other Tips for Healthy Cooking

There's a lot more to healthful cooking than simply cutting fat and calories. Adding nutrients is equally important. I've boosted the nutritional profiles of the recipes

*(continued on page 32)*

# Recipe Makeover Substitutions

A simple switch may be all it takes to lower the fat and calories in your favorite dish. Here are my most reliable fat-saving swaps. They're used in the recipes throughout this book.

| Instead of . . . | Use . . . | Calories Saved | Fat Saved (g) |
| --- | --- | --- | --- |
| **Dairy** | | | |
| 1 cup whole milk | 1 cup fat-free milk | 64 | 8 |
| | 1 cup buttermilk (for baking) | 51 | 6 |
| | 1 cup 1% milk | 48 | 6 |
| | 1 cup 2% milk | 29 | 4 |
| 1 can sweetened condensed milk (14 ounces) | 1 can fat-free sweetened condensed milk (14 ounces) | 155 | 35 |
| 1 can evaporated milk (12 ounces) | 1 can fat-free evaporated milk (12 ounces) | 191 | 25 |
| 1 cup heavy cream | 1 cup 1% milk + 1 tablespoon cornstarch | 688 | 86 |
| | 1 cup fat-free evaporated milk | 622 | 88 |
| 1 cup whipped cream | 1 cup frozen light whipped topping, thawed | 250 | 36 |
| | 1 cup frozen whipped topping, thawed | 171 | 25 |
| 1 cup sour cream | 1 cup fat-free plain yogurt | 355 | 48 |
| | 1 cup fat-free sour cream | 244 | 48 |
| 1 cup shredded Cheddar cheese (4 ounces) | 1 cup shredded fat-free Cheddar cheese | 279 | 37 |
| | 1 cup shredded reduced-fat Cheddar cheese (2% milk) | 185 | 16 |
| 4 ounces blue cheese | 2 ounces blue cheese + 2 ounces fat-free cream cheese | 149 | 16 |
| 4 ounces feta cheese | 2 ounces feta cheese + 2 ounces fat-free cream cheese | 110 | 12 |

| Instead of . . . | Use . . . | Calories Saved | Fat Saved (g) |
|---|---|---|---|
| 4 ounces goat cheese | 2 ounces goat cheese + 2 ounces fat-free cream cheese | 153 | 17 |
| 8 ounces cream cheese | 8 ounces fat-free ricotta cheese | 630 | 79 |
| | 8 ounces fat-free cream cheese (any style) | 586 | 79 |
| | 4 ounces fat-free cream cheese + 4 ounces light cream cheese | 394 | 62 |
| | 8 ounces light cream cheese (tub-style) | 296 | 44 |
| | 8 ounces light cream cheese (block-style) | 200 | 25 |
| 8 ounces mascarpone cheese | 4 ounces mascarpone cheese + 4 ounces fat-free cream cheese | 502 | 52 |

## Fat

| Instead of . . . | Use . . . | Calories Saved | Fat Saved (g) |
|---|---|---|---|
| ½ cup oil | ½ cup fat-free chicken broth (for salad dressings and marinades) | 952 | 109 |
| | ¼ cup unsweetened applesauce + ¼ cup buttermilk (for baking) | 913 | 108 |
| | ½ cup unsweetened applesauce (for baking) | 911 | 109 |
| | ½ cup baby food prunes (for baking) | 799 | 109 |
| | ⅓ cup vinegar + ¼ cup fat-free chicken broth + ¼ cup pineapple juice + 2 Tbsp strong-flavored oil (for salad dressings and marinades) | 681 | 82 |

*(continued)*

# Recipe Makeover Substitutions (cont.)

| Instead of . . . | Use . . . | Calories Saved | Fat Saved (g) |
|---|---|---|---|
| **Fat** (cont.) | | | |
| ½ cup margarine or butter (1 stick) | ½ cup unsweetened applesauce (for baking) | 788 | 92 |
| | ¼ cup unsweetened applesauce + ¼ cup buttermilk (for baking) | 763 | 91 |
| | ½ cup baby food prunes (for baking) | 699 | 92 |
| | ½ cup marshmallow creme (for frostings and fillings) | 436 | 92 |
| | ½ cup light butter | 414 | 48 |
| 2 Tbsp oil | 2 Tbsp fat-free broth (for sautéing) | 238 | 27 |
| | 2 Tbsp wine (for sautéing) | 221 | 27 |
| 1 cup chopped walnuts | ½ cup chopped walnuts, toasted | 385 | 35 |
| 1 cup chopped pecans | ½ cup chopped pecans, toasted | 397 | 40 |
| 1 cup slivered almonds | ½ cup sliced almonds, toasted | 518 | 46 |
| | ½ cup slivered almonds, toasted | 398 | 35 |
| **Protein** | | | |
| 6 ounces pork sirloin, cooked | 6 ounces pork tenderloin, roasted | 167 | 19 |
| 6 ounces flank steak, cooked | 6 ounces round steak, roasted | 46 | 9 |
| 6 ounces chicken thigh, no skin, cooked | 6 ounces chicken breast, no skin, roasted | 76 | 12 |
| 6 ounces dark turkey meat, no skin, cooked | 6 ounces turkey breast, roasted | 16 | 2 |
| 1 whole egg | 2 egg whites | 41 | 5 |
| 6 ounces tuna in oil, drained | 6 ounces tuna in water, drained | 140 | 13 |
| 1 lb ground beef | 1 lb ground turkey breast | 839 | 83 |
| | 1 lb chopped pork tenderloin | 581 | 67 |

| Instead of . . . | Use . . . | Calories Saved | Fat Saved (g) |
|---|---|---|---|
| 1 lb ground beef (cont.) | 1 lb chopped chicken breast | 576 | 67 |
| | 1 lb ground turkey | 257 | 29 |
| | 1 lb extra-lean ground beef (15% fat) | 123 | 17 |
| 6 ounces pork sausage, cooked | 6 ounces turkey sausage, cooked | 258 | 29 |

## Miscellaneous

| Instead of . . . | Use . . . | Calories Saved | Fat Saved (g) |
|---|---|---|---|
| 1 cup frozen whipped topping | 1 cup frozen light whipped topping | 79 | 11 |
| 1 cup chocolate chips | ½ cup mini chocolate chips | 405 | 25 |
| | ½ cup chocolate chips | 300 | 29 |
| | ⅔ cup chocolate chips | 276 | 17 |
| | ¾ cup chocolate chips | 203 | 13 |
| 1 cup flaked coconut | 1 teaspoon coconut extract | 337 | 24 |
| | ½ cup flaked coconut | 176 | 12 |
| 1 cup sliced olives | ½ cup sliced olives | 78 | 7 |
| 1 ounce baking chocolate | 3 tablespoons unsweetened cocoa powder | 111 | 14 |
| Single pie crust | 3 sheets phyllo dough (6 half-sheets) | 779 | 59 |
| 1 can condensed cream of mushroom soup (10.7 ounces) | 1 can condensed reduced-fat cream of mushroom soup (10.7 ounces) | 141 | 16 |
| 1 cup sugar | ¾ cup sugar | 194 | 0 |
| 1 small package flavored gelatin mix (4 servings) | 1 small package sugar-free gelatin mix (4 servings) | 292 | 0 |
| 1 cup basic white sauce (1 cup whole milk, 2 Tbsp flour, and 2 Tbsp butter) | 1 cup basic white sauce (1 cup 1% milk and 1 Tbsp cornstarch) | 111 | 15 |

throughout this book using some simple techniques. Experiment with these methods in your own recipes.

**Try a little whole grain.** Incorporate whole wheat flour whenever possible in cooking and baking. In most recipes, you can easily use half whole wheat flour and half unbleached or all-purpose flour. While this doesn't alter calories or fat grams, it does add a nutrition bonus in the form of extra fiber, vitamins, and minerals. For a similar nutrition boost, I like to add a small amount of wheat germ to baked goods. Another simple switch is to use whole wheat pasta instead of regular. I often use brown rice, too, which is more healthful than polished white rice. In short, any time you can incorporate whole grains into your diet, it's a nutritional plus.

**Buy quality oils.** I almost always use canola and olive oil because they are low in saturated fat and high in healthy monounsaturated fat. For rich, fruity flavor, buy a good-quality extra-virgin olive oil and use it in small amounts. The same goes for specialty oils such as walnut and dark sesame oil. Buy the best and use them judiciously.

**Go nonstick.** Nonstick pans make a world of difference in healthy cooking. When using a nonstick pan, a spritzing of nonstick cooking spray may be all you need to sauté or brown foods. If you do need oil, 1 or 2 teaspoons should be enough to sear the outside of the food and keep it from sticking to the pan.

**Take a second look at salt.** I reduced the salt in most of the recipes in this book. In many recipes (except baking), you can cut the salt by one-fourth to one-half without a problem. When a recipe says "season to taste with salt," I suggest following the advice literally. Taste the dish first, then add salt only if it needs it, sprinkling in a little at a time. To lift flavor without salt, add fresh ground pepper, fresh lemon juice, or fresh herbs. For more ideas, see "Six Flavor-Boosting Tricks" on page 24.

**Stock healthy convenience products.** These can make a big difference when you need to save time *and* cook a healthy meal. On hectic nights, these products can spell the difference between a healthy home-cooked meal and high-fat takeout. Reduced-fat cream soups and instant brown rice are staples in my pantry, as is low-sodium chicken broth. Note that many recipes in this book call for these products by the can or the package. This way of listing ingredients makes shopping easier. I also specify the can size; for example, 1 can reduced-fat cream of mushroom soup (10¾ ounces). When you shop, don't worry if the can size in your market isn't exactly the same as the one listed in the recipe. In most cases, we're talking about less than an ounce difference. Rule of thumb: Use the can size closest to the one specified in the recipe.

# Homestyle Bakery

I love to fill the house with the warm, welcoming aromas of baked goods. On weekend mornings, nothing beats the taste of fresh muffins, biscuits, scones, or breads from the oven.

I have used some classic fat-cutting techniques in these recipes, such as replacing oil and butter with applesauce, and whole eggs with egg whites. I rely on reduced-fat cheeses, milk, sour cream, and buttermilk. But I have been careful not to take out too much fat. Fats play an important role in tenderizing baked goods and carrying key flavors.

You'll find some surprise ingredients here, too. In the Triple-Light Angel Biscuits, I replace the shortening with fat-free cottage cheese that is pressed through a sieve, then combined with shredded light butter. When chilled, light butter shreds as easily as cheese, and the shredding helps create a more tender texture in the final product. These biscuits are so light and tender, I use them as the basis for Quick Praline Rolls.

Of course, there is more to healthful eating than cutting the fat. Upping the fiber and reducing cholesterol are important, too. I have incorporated whole wheat flour into some recipes, and a few recipes include healthful ingredients like bran and wheat germ. For a boost in flavor and nutrition, I add fruits and nuts in several recipes such as Chocolate Chip Pecan Loaf and, a personal favorite, Cranberry Bread.

I've also streamlined these recipes whenever possible. All of my muffins come together in less than 30 minutes. Even yeast breads like Easy Cheesy No-Knead Batter Bread are simple. No kneading, and two risings allow you to do other things while the dough gets light and airy. I especially like this savory bread with tomato soup. If my kids had their way, we would eat it at every meal.

# Pineapple Upside-Down Muffins

These are such pretty muffins. I reduced calories and fat by:

❖ *Using light butter in place of regular butter*
❖ *Replacing the oil with applesauce*
❖ *Using low-fat buttermilk instead of whole milk*
❖ *Using egg whites instead of whole eggs*

*Nutrition Scorecard*
(per muffin)

|            | before | after |
|------------|--------|-------|
| Calories   | 207    | 152   |
| Fat (g)    | 8      | 1     |

*Photo on page 57*

¼ cup packed brown sugar
2 tablespoons light butter, melted
6 maraschino cherries, halved
1 can crushed juice-packed pineapple (8 ounces), drained
1 cup unbleached or all-purpose flour
¾ cup whole wheat flour
⅔ cup granulated sugar
2 teaspoons baking powder
¼ teaspoon salt
¼ teaspoon ground ginger
⅔ cup 2% buttermilk
⅓ cup unsweetened applesauce
2 egg whites
1 teaspoon vanilla extract

Preheat the oven to 400°F. Lightly coat a 12-cup muffin pan with nonstick spray.

In a small bowl, stir together the brown sugar and butter. Divide evenly among the prepared muffin cups. Place a cherry half, cut side up, in the center of each muffin cup. Divide the pineapple evenly among the cups. Set aside.

In a medium bowl, stir together the unbleached or all-purpose flour, whole wheat flour, granulated sugar, baking powder, salt, and ginger. Make a well in the center of the flour mixture.

In another bowl, combine the buttermilk, applesauce, egg whites, and vanilla extract. Scrape into the well in the flour mixture. Stir just until the batter is moistened.

Divide the batter evenly among the muffin cups. Bake for 18 to 20 minutes, or until a wooden pick inserted in the center of a muffin comes out clean. Cool in the pan on a rack for 10 minutes. Invert onto the rack and serve warm or at room temperature. (If topping sticks to the pan, scoop it up and spread it back onto the muffins with a knife.)

### Makes 12 muffins

*Per muffin: 152 calories, 3 g protein, 33 g carbohydrates, 1 g fat, 0.5 g saturated fat, 3 mg cholesterol, 164 mg sodium, 1 g fiber*

# Raspberry-Lemon Muffins

Raspberries are one of those fruits that say "summertime" to me. But these muffins can be made year-round with frozen raspberries, too. The calories, fat, and cholesterol were reduced and fiber was boosted by:

*Nutrition Scorecard*
(per muffin)

|  | before | after |
|---|---|---|
| Calories | 266 | 162 |
| Fat (g) | 13 | 0.5 |

❖ *Using low-fat buttermilk in place of half-and-half*
❖ *Replacing the oil with applesauce*
❖ *Using egg whites instead of whole eggs*
❖ *Incorporating whole wheat flour*

1½    cups unbleached or all-purpose flour
1    cup sugar
½    cup whole wheat flour
1    tablespoon baking powder
½    teaspoon finely shredded lemon peel
¼    teaspoon salt
1    cup 2% buttermilk
½    cup unsweetened applesauce
3    egg whites
1    teaspoon lemon extract
1    cup fresh or frozen raspberries (without syrup and unthawed, if frozen)

Preheat the oven to 400°F. Lightly coat a 12-cup muffin pan with nonstick spray. Set aside.

In a large bowl, mix together the unbleached or all-purpose flour, sugar, whole wheat flour, baking powder, lemon peel, and salt. Make a well in the center of the flour mixture.

In a small bowl, whisk together the buttermilk, applesauce, egg whites, and lemon extract. Scrape into the well in the flour mixture. Stir just until the batter is moistened. Fold in the raspberries.

Divide the batter among the prepared muffin cups. Bake for 15 to 20 minutes, or until a wooden pick inserted in the center of a muffin comes out clean. Cool in the pan on a rack for 5 minutes. Invert onto the rack and serve warm or at room temperature.

## Makes 12 muffins

*Per muffin: 162 calories, 4 g protein, 36 g carbohydrates, 0.5 g fat, 0.5 g saturated fat, 1 mg cholesterol, 247 mg sodium, 4 g fiber*

# Spiced Apple Muffins

The aroma of cinnamon warms a room like nothing else can. This recipe keeps friends and neighbors coming back for more. I reduced the calories, fat, and cholesterol and boosted fiber by:

❖ *Replacing the oil with applesauce*
❖ *Using low-fat buttermilk*
❖ *Reducing the amount of walnuts*
❖ *Using egg whites instead of whole eggs*
❖ *Incorporating whole wheat flour*

*Nutrition Scorecard*

| (per muffin) | | |
|---|---|---|
| | before | after |
| Calories | 215 | 156 |
| Fat (g) | 9 | 2 |

## MUFFINS

1½ cups unbleached or all-purpose flour

¾ cup packed brown sugar

½ cup whole wheat flour

2 teaspoons baking powder

1 teaspoon baking soda

¼ teaspoon salt

¼ teaspoon ground nutmeg

1 cup 2% buttermilk

¼ cup unsweetened applesauce

2 egg whites

2 teaspoons vanilla extract

2 apples, peeled, cored, and finely chopped (about 2 cups)

¼ cup chopped walnuts

## TOPPING

1 tablespoon sugar

1 teaspoon ground cinnamon

TO MAKE THE MUFFINS: Preheat the oven to 400°F. Lightly coat a 12-cup muffin pan with nonstick spray.

In a large bowl, mix together the unbleached or all-purpose flour, brown sugar, whole wheat flour, baking powder, baking soda, salt, and nutmeg. Make a well in the center of the flour mixture.

In a small bowl, whisk together the buttermilk, applesauce, egg whites, and vanilla extract. Scrape into the well in the flour mixture. Stir just until the batter is moistened. Fold in the apples and walnuts.

Divide the batter evenly among the prepared muffin cups.

TO MAKE THE TOPPING: In a small cup, stir together the sugar and cinnamon. Sprinkle evenly over the muffins. Bake for 20 to 22 minutes, or until a wooden pick inserted in the center of a muffin comes out clean. Cool in the pan on a rack for 5 minutes. Invert onto the rack and serve warm or at room temperature.

**Makes 12 muffins**

*Per muffin: 156 calories, 4 g protein, 31 g carbohydrates, 2 g fat, 0.5 g saturated fat, 1 mg cholesterol, 266 mg sodium, 2 g fiber*

*Homestyle Hints:* I like to use a crisp, juicy apple such as Cortland, Gala, or Granny Smith for these muffins.

I sometimes mix the walnuts into the sugar and cinnamon to make a nut topping.

## An Apple a Day . . .

*Apples are one of the best sources of boron in the American diet. Boron is a mineral that is essential for our brains and for calcium metabolism. Hungry for a snack? Have a sweet, crisp apple.*

# Orange-Date Bran Muffins

Orange peel and chopped dates lend delightful flavors to these wholesome muffins. The calories, fat, and cholesterol were reduced by:

❖ *Replacing the whole milk with orange juice*
❖ *Replacing the oil with applesauce*
❖ *Using egg whites instead of whole eggs*

| | |
|---|---|
| 1 | cup unprocessed bran |
| 1¼ | cups orange juice |
| ¼ | cup honey |
| ¼ | cup molasses |
| ¾ | cup unbleached or all-purpose flour |
| ¾ | cup whole wheat flour |
| 2 | teaspoons baking powder |
| ½ | teaspoon baking soda |
| ½ | teaspoon salt |
| ½ | cup unsweetened applesauce |
| 2 | egg whites |
| 4 | teaspoons grated orange peel |
| ½ | cup chopped dates |

Preheat the oven to 400°F. Lightly coat a 12-cup muffin pan with nonstick spray.

In a large bowl, stir together the bran, orange juice, honey, and molasses. Set aside for about 5 minutes.

In a medium bowl, stir together the unbleached or all-purpose flour, whole wheat flour, baking powder, baking soda, and salt.

Stir the applesauce, egg whites, and orange peel into the bran mixture. Add the flour mixture and stir just until combined. Fold in the dates.

Divide the batter evenly among the prepared muffin cups. Bake for 18 to 20 minutes, or until a wooden pick inserted in the center of a muffin comes out clean. Cool in the pan on a rack for 5 minutes. Invert onto the rack and serve warm or at room temperature.

### Makes 12 muffins

*Per muffin: 145 calories, 4 g protein, 35 g carbohydrates, 0.5 g fat, 0 g saturated fat, 0 mg cholesterol, 147 mg sodium, 4 g fiber*

*Homestyle Hint:* You'll need about 2 oranges to get 4 teaspoons grated orange peel.

# Pumpkin-Nut Muffins

These cakelike muffins are one of my favorites. To dress them up, place a walnut half on top of each muffin before baking. I reduced the calories and fat and gave fiber a boost by:

- ❖ *Reducing the amount of walnuts*
- ❖ *Using egg whites instead of whole eggs*
- ❖ *Replacing the oil with applesauce*
- ❖ *Incorporating whole wheat flour*

| | |
|---|---|
| 1 | cup unbleached or all-purpose flour |
| 1 | cup sugar |
| ⅔ | cup whole wheat flour |
| 2 | teaspoons pumpkin pie spice |
| ⅛ | teaspoon ground cloves |
| 1 | teaspoon baking soda |
| ¼ | teaspoon salt |
| 1 | cup canned plain pumpkin puree |
| ⅔ | cup 2% buttermilk |
| ⅓ | cup unsweetened applesauce |
| 3 | egg whites |
| ½ | cup chopped walnuts |

Preheat the oven to 400°F. Lightly coat a 12-cup muffin pan with nonstick spray.

In a large bowl, mix together the unbleached or all-purpose flour, sugar, whole wheat flour, pumpkin pie spice, cloves, baking soda, and salt. Make a well in the center of the flour mixture.

In a small bowl, whisk together the pumpkin puree, buttermilk, applesauce, and egg whites. Scrape into the well in the flour mixture. Stir just until the batter is moistened. Fold in the walnuts.

Divide the batter among the prepared muffin cups. Bake for 17 to 20 minutes, or until a wooden pick inserted in the center of a muffin comes out clean. Cool in the pan on a rack for 5 minutes. Invert onto the rack and serve warm or at room temperature.

### Makes 12 muffins

*Per muffin: 167 calories, 5 g protein, 33 g carbohydrates, 2 g fat, 0.5 g saturated fat, 0 mg cholesterol, 224 mg sodium, 2 g fiber*

*Homestyle Hint:* Take care to buy plain pumpkin puree, not spiced puree that may be labeled "pie filling."

# Tuxedo Brownie Muffins

Crowned with a luscious cream-cheese topping, these fancy-looking muffins are surefire crowd pleasers. I reduced the calories, fat, and cholesterol by:

❖ *Using fat-free cream cheese in place of regular cream cheese*
❖ *Replacing regular chocolate chips with mini chips and using a smaller amount*
❖ *Replacing the oil with baby food prunes*
❖ *Reducing the amount of walnuts*
❖ *Using low-fat buttermilk in place of whole milk*
❖ *Using egg whites instead of whole eggs*

*Nutrition Scorecard*
(per muffin)

|  | before | after |
|---|---|---|
| Calories | 240 | 151 |
| Fat (g) | 15 | 3 |

*Photo on page 57*

## TOPPING

8 ounces fat-free cream cheese, at room temperature

¼ cup sugar

2 teaspoons unbleached or all-purpose flour

2 egg whites

½ cup mini chocolate chips

## MUFFINS

1 cup unbleached or all-purpose flour

1 cup sugar

½ cup whole wheat flour

⅓ cup unsweetened natural cocoa powder

2 teaspoons baking powder

⅛ teaspoon salt

¾ cup 2% buttermilk

1 jar baby food prunes (2½ ounces)

2 egg whites

¼ cup chopped walnuts

TO MAKE THE TOPPING: Place the cream cheese, sugar, and flour in a bowl. Using an electric mixer set on medium speed, beat until mixed. Add the egg whites and beat just until blended. Fold in the chocolate chips. Set aside.

TO MAKE THE MUFFINS: Preheat the oven to 350°F. Lightly coat 18 muffin cups with nonstick spray (if using two 12-cup muffin pans, fill the empty cups with water).

In a large bowl, combine the unbleached or all-purpose flour, sugar, whole wheat flour, cocoa, baking powder, and salt. Make a well in the center of the flour mixture.

In a small bowl, whisk together the buttermilk, prunes, and egg whites. Scrape into the well in the flour mixture. Stir just until moistened. Fold in the walnuts.

Divide the batter evenly among the prepared muffin cups. Top each muffin with about 1 tablespoon of the cream-cheese mixture. Bake for 20 to 22 minutes, or until the cream cheese begins to turn golden and a wooden pick inserted in the center of a muffin comes out clean. Cool in the pans on a rack for 5 minutes. Invert onto the rack and serve warm or at room temperature.

**Makes 18 muffins**

*Per muffin: 151 calories, 5 g protein, 28 g carbohydrates, 3 g fat, 1 g saturated fat, 1 mg cholesterol, 100 mg sodium, 2 g fiber*

*Homestyle Hint:* Natural cocoa powder is also called nonalkalized cocoa powder. Hershey's Cocoa is natural cocoa powder.

## Carbohydrates Boost Memory in the Morning

*To study the effects of eating carbohydrates in the morning, researchers gave people between the ages of 58 and 77 lemonade early in the morning on two separate occasions. Those who drank the lemonade sweetened with glucose—a carbohydrate—performed better on memory tests than those who drank lemonade sweetened with an artificial sweetener.*

# Quick Praline Rolls

The first time I made these sweet rolls, my family begged me to make them again for a week! The recipe gets a head start by using a quick biscuit dough. I reduced calories and fat by:

❖ *Using reduced-fat biscuit dough*
❖ *Using light butter*
❖ *Using wheat germ instead of pecans in the filling*

*Photo on page 59*

### DOUGH

1    recipe Triple-Light Angel Biscuit dough (page 50)

### FILLING

2    teaspoons light butter, melted

½    cup packed brown sugar

2    tablespoons wheat germ

1¾   teaspoons ground cinnamon

### TOPPING

¼    cup chopped pecans

¼    cup packed brown sugar

2    teaspoons light butter

Preheat the oven to 400°F. Lightly coat a baking sheet with nonstick spray.

TO MAKE THE DOUGH: Prepare the dough according to the recipe directions. Knead the dough on a floured work surface and roll into a 15" × 10" rectangle.

TO MAKE THE FILLING: Brush the butter evenly over the rectangle of dough. In a small bowl, mix together the brown sugar, wheat germ, and cinnamon. Sprinkle evenly over the butter.

Starting with one of the longer sides, roll the dough into a tight cylinder, pinching the edges to seal. Gently cut the cylinder into 12 slices. Set 1 roll in the center of the baking sheet, then arrange the remaining rolls around it so that their edges touch each other.

TO MAKE THE TOPPING: Sprinkle the pecans evenly over the rolls. In a small microwaveable cup, combine the brown sugar and butter. Microwave on high power for 15 to 30 seconds, or until melted. Stir well and drizzle over the rolls. Bake for 15 to 20 minutes, or until light golden brown. Serve warm.

**Makes 12 rolls**

*Per roll: 182 calories, 4 g protein, 32 g carbohydrates, 5 g fat, 0.5 g saturated fat, 8 mg cholesterol, 382 mg sodium, 2 g fiber*

# Chocolate Chip Pecan Loaf

Speckled with mini chocolate chips and pecans, this lightly sweetened bread makes a perfect accompaniment to coffee or tea. The calories, fat, and cholesterol were reduced and fiber got a boost by:

*Photo on page 58*

- ❖ *Using rum extract in place of bourbon*
- ❖ *Reducing the amounts of chocolate chips and pecans*
- ❖ *Using egg whites instead of whole eggs*
- ❖ *Incorporating whole wheat flour*
- ❖ *Using applesauce in place of butter*

| | |
|---|---|
| 1½ | cups unbleached or all-purpose flour |
| ½ | cup whole wheat flour |
| ⅓ | cup packed brown sugar |
| 1 | teaspoon baking powder |
| ¾ | teaspoon baking soda |
| ½ | teaspoon salt |
| ½ | cup 2% buttermilk |
| ½ | cup pure maple syrup |
| ½ | cup unsweetened applesauce |
| 4 | egg whites |
| 2 | teaspoons rum extract |
| ½ | cup chopped pecans |
| ⅓ | cup mini chocolate chips |

Preheat the oven to 350°F. Coat a 9" × 5" loaf pan with nonstick spray.

In a large bowl, stir together the unbleached or all-purpose flour, whole wheat flour, brown sugar, baking powder, baking soda, and salt. Make a well in the center of the flour mixture.

In a medium bowl, whisk together the buttermilk, maple syrup, applesauce, egg whites, and rum extract. Scrape into the well in the flour mixture and stir just until moistened. Fold in the pecans and chocolate chips.

Scrape the batter into the prepared pan. Bake for 45 to 50 minutes, or until the bread begins to pull away from the sides of the pan. Allow the bread to cool in the pan for 10 minutes. Remove from the pan and cool completely on a rack.

### Makes 1 loaf; 12 slices

*Per slice: 195 calories, 4 g protein, 34 g carbohydrates, 5 g fat, 1 g saturated fat, 1 mg cholesterol, 241 mg sodium, 2 g fiber*

# Cranberry Bread

When fresh cranberries are available, I buy extra bags and freeze them. That way, I can enjoy this bread all year. I reduced calories, fat, and cholesterol and boosted fiber by:

❖ *Using dried cranberries in place of nuts*
❖ *Replacing the oil with applesauce*
❖ *Using egg whites instead of whole eggs*
❖ *Incorporating whole wheat flour*

*Photo on page 56*

1½   cups unbleached or all-purpose flour
½   cup whole wheat flour
½   cup wheat germ
½   cup packed brown sugar
½   cup granulated sugar
2   teaspoons finely grated orange peel
2   teaspoons baking powder
1   teaspoon baking soda
¾   cup orange juice
⅓   cup unsweetened applesauce
2   egg whites
1   teaspoon vanilla extract
1   cup coarsely chopped fresh or frozen cranberries
½   cup dried cranberries

Preheat the oven to 350°F. Coat a 9" × 5" loaf pan with nonstick spray.

In a large bowl, stir together the unbleached or all-purpose flour, whole wheat flour, wheat germ, brown sugar, granulated sugar, orange peel, baking powder, and baking soda. Make a well in the center of the flour mixture.

In a medium bowl, whisk together the orange juice, applesauce, egg whites, and vanilla extract until thoroughly blended. Scrape into the well in the flour mixture and stir just until moistened. Fold in the chopped and dried cranberries.

Scrape the mixture into the prepared pan. Bake for 50 to 55 minutes, or until the bread begins to pull away from the sides of the pan. Allow the bread to cool in the pan for 10 minutes. Remove from the pan and cool completely on a rack.

### Makes 1 loaf; 12 slices

*Per slice: 171 calories, 4 g protein, 37 g carbohydrates, 1 g fat, 0.5 g saturated fat, 0 mg cholesterol, 199 mg sodium, 2 g fiber*

# Apricot Tea Bread

If you love dried apricots, you'll love this bread. I reduced the calories, fat, and cholesterol and boosted fiber by:

❖ *Reducing the amount of nuts*
❖ *Replacing the margarine with applesauce*
❖ *Using fat-free sour cream*
❖ *Using egg whites instead of whole eggs*
❖ *Incorporating whole wheat flour*

| | |
|---|---|
| 1½ | cups unbleached or all-purpose flour |
| 1 | cup sugar |
| ½ | cup whole wheat flour |
| 1½ | teaspoons baking powder |
| 1 | teaspoon baking soda |
| 6 | ounces dried apricot halves (about 1 cup) |
| 1 | cup fat-free sour cream (without gelatin), 8 ounces |
| ½ | cup unsweetened applesauce |
| 4 | egg whites |
| 2 | teaspoons vanilla extract |
| ⅓ | cup chopped pecans |

Preheat the oven to 350°F. Coat a 9" × 5" loaf pan with nonstick spray.

In a large bowl, stir together the unbleached or all-purpose flour, sugar, whole wheat flour, baking powder, and baking soda. Using kitchen shears or a sharp knife, snip the apricots into small pieces and drop them into the flour mixture. Toss to combine. Make a well in the center of the flour mixture.

In a medium bowl, whisk the sour cream, applesauce, egg whites, and vanilla extract. Scrape into the well in the flour mixture and stir just until moistened. Fold in the pecans.

Scrape the batter into the prepared pan. Bake for 50 to 55 minutes, or until the bread begins to pull away from the sides of the pan. Allow the bread to cool in the pan for 10 minutes. Remove from the pan and cool completely on a rack.

**Makes 1 loaf; 12 slices**

*Per slice: 229 calories, 5 g protein, 47 g carbohydrates, 3 g fat, 0.5 g saturated fat, 0 mg cholesterol, 201 mg sodium, 2 g fiber*

*Homestyle Hint:* To prevent the dried apricots from sticking during cutting, dip the shears or knife into the flour mixture frequently.

# Savory Parmesan Popovers

While I'm all for cutting fat, when it comes to flavor, I find that there's no substitute for fresh, traditionally made Parmesan cheese. The taste is worth every gram of fat. Adding basil enhances the flavor of these popovers, too. I reduced the calories, fat, and cholesterol and boosted fiber by:

❖ *Slightly reducing the amount of Parmesan cheese*
❖ *Using fat-free milk instead of whole milk*
❖ *Replacing some of the whole eggs with egg whites*
❖ *Replacing butter with olive oil, and using less of it*
❖ *Incorporating whole wheat flour*

| | |
|---|---|
| 1 | cup fat-free milk |
| ⅔ | cup unbleached or all-purpose flour |
| ⅓ | cup whole wheat flour |
| 1 | teaspoon olive oil |
| ¾ | teaspoon dried basil |
| ¼ | teaspoon salt |
| 1 | egg |
| 2 | egg whites |
| 3 | tablespoons freshly grated Parmesan cheese |

Place the oven rack on the next-to-lowest shelf of the oven. Preheat the oven to 450°F. Coat 6 popover cups, deep muffin cups, or custard cups with nonstick spray.

In a medium bowl, stir together the milk, unbleached or all-purpose flour, whole wheat flour, oil, basil, and salt. Vigorously whisk in the egg and egg whites.

Spoon the batter into the prepared cups. Sprinkle the Parmesan evenly over the batter in the cups. Bake for 15 minutes. Reduce the oven temperature to 350°F. Do not open the oven door. Bake for 15 to 20 minutes longer, or until deep golden brown and puffed up. Remove the popovers from the oven and cool in the cups on a rack for 5 minutes. Carefully remove from the cups and serve.

## Makes 6 popovers

*Per popover: 127 calories, 7 g protein, 18 g carbohydrates, 3 g fat, 1 g saturated fat, 39 mg cholesterol, 205 mg sodium, 1 g fiber*

*Homestyle Hint:* If you open the oven door during baking, the popovers might deflate. They do not keep well and should be made shortly before serving.

# Easy Cheesy No-Knead Batter Bread

This is one of the simplest yeast breads I know. I reduced calories, fat, and cholesterol and boosted fiber by:

❖ *Replacing margarine and whole milk with buttermilk*
❖ *Using egg whites instead of whole eggs*
❖ *Using reduced-fat cheese*
❖ *Incorporating whole wheat flour*

*Photo on page 129*

|   |   |
|---|---|
| 1 | package active dry yeast (¼ ounce) |
| ¼ | cup warm water (110° to 115°F) |
| 2 | cups unbleached or all-purpose flour |
| ½ | cup whole wheat flour |
| 2 | teaspoons sugar |
| 1½ | teaspoons salt |
| 1 | cup shredded reduced-fat sharp Cheddar cheese (4 ounces) |
| 1 | cup 2% buttermilk, at room temperature |
| 6 | egg whites |

In a small bowl, combine the yeast and water and stir gently to dissolve.

In a large bowl, stir together 1 cup of the unbleached or all-purpose flour, the whole wheat flour, sugar, and salt. Stir in the cheese. Add the yeast mixture and, using an electric mixer set on low speed, beat until the mixture resembles coarse crumbs. Add the buttermilk and beat just until moistened. Add the egg whites and beat on high speed for 3 minutes. Reduce the speed to low and beat in the remaining 1 cup unbleached or all-purpose flour (the batter will be slightly runny). Cover the bowl loosely with plastic wrap. Let rise in a warm place (80° to 85°F) for 1 hour, or until light and doubled in volume.

Lightly coat a 1½- to 2-quart shallow baking dish with nonstick spray. Gently push down the dough and transfer it into the dish. Cover loosely with plastic wrap and let rise in a warm place for 20 minutes, or until light and nearly doubled in volume.

Preheat the oven to 350°F. Uncover the dough and bake for 35 to 40 minutes, or until a deep golden brown. Immediately remove the bread from the dish and cool on a rack.

### Makes 1 loaf; 16 slices

*Per slice: 107 calories, 7 g protein, 16 g carbohydrates, 2 g fat, 1 g saturated fat, 6 mg cholesterol, 297 mg sodium, 1 g fiber*

# Glazed Orange Bread

This moist, flavorful bread is bursting with the fresh flavor of oranges, so it's hard to believe that it's practically fat-free. The calories, fat, and cholesterol were reduced and fiber was boosted by:

❖ *Replacing the butter with applesauce*
❖ *Using egg whites instead of whole eggs*
❖ *Using fat-free sour cream*
❖ *Using less orange juice and confectioners' sugar in the glaze*
❖ *Incorporating whole wheat flour*

*Nutrition Scorecard*

(per slice)

|  | before | after |
|---|---|---|
| Calories | 297 | 192 |
| Fat (g) | 13 | 0.5 |

*Photo on page 56*

## BREAD

| | |
|---|---|
| 1½ | cups unbleached or all-purpose flour |
| 1 | cup sugar |
| ½ | cup whole wheat flour |
| 4 | teaspoons finely grated orange peel |
| 1 | teaspoon baking powder |
| 1 | teaspoon baking soda |
| 1 | cup fat-free sour cream (without gelatin), 8 ounces |
| ½ | cup unsweetened applesauce |
| ¼ | cup orange juice |
| 3 | egg whites |

## GLAZE

| | |
|---|---|
| 2 | tablespoons orange juice |
| ¾ | cup confectioners' sugar |

TO MAKE THE BREAD: Preheat the oven to 350°F. Coat a 9" × 5" loaf pan with nonstick spray.

In a large bowl, stir together the unbleached or all-purpose flour, sugar, whole wheat flour, orange peel, baking powder, and baking soda. Make a well in the center of the flour mixture.

In a medium bowl, whisk together the sour cream, applesauce, orange juice, and egg whites. Scrape into the well in the flour mixture and stir just until moistened.

Scrape the batter into the prepared pan. Bake for 55 to 60 minutes, or until the bread begins to pull away from the sides of the pan. Allow the bread to cool in the pan for 10 minutes. Remove from the pan and set on a rack.

TO MAKE THE GLAZE: In a small bowl, stir together the orange juice and confectioners' sugar until smooth. Drizzle a thin layer of the glaze on the bread while it is still warm. When the glaze is dry, add another layer. Repeat until all the glaze is used. Let the bread cool completely before serving.

**Makes 1 loaf; 12 slices**

*Per slice: 192 calories, 5 g protein, 43 g carbohydrates, 0.5 g fat, 0 g saturated fat, 0 mg cholesterol, 135 mg sodium, 2 g fiber*

*Homestyle Hint:* Fresh orange juice is best for this recipe, but good-quality frozen or refrigerated juice works well, too.

# Oranges—More Than Vitamin C

*Both citrus pulp and the white parts of oranges are rich in glucarates, which are phytochemicals. These may play a role in preventing breast cancer and lowering the risk of symptoms of premenstrual syndrome. Whenever possible, eat whole oranges. Of course, drinking orange juice is never a bad idea—it remains a top-notch source of vitamin C.*

# Triple-Light Angel Biscuits

I knew these biscuits were a hit when a professional baker I know proclaimed them to be "amazingly delicious!" The dough has three leavening agents—yeast, baking powder, and baking soda—which make the biscuits especially light in texture. The calories, fat, and cholesterol were reduced and fiber was boosted by:

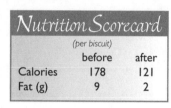

*Photo on page 128*

| Nutrition Scorecard | | |
|---|---|---|
| *(per biscuit)* | | |
| | before | after |
| Calories | 178 | 121 |
| Fat (g) | 9 | 2 |

- ❖ *Replacing the shortening with a combination of light butter and fat-free cottage cheese*
- ❖ *Shredding the butter for a flakier texture*
- ❖ *Incorporating whole wheat flour*

|  |  |
|---|---|
| 1½ | teaspoons active dry yeast |
| 2 | tablespoons warm water (110° to 115°F) |
| 2 | cups unbleached or all-purpose flour |
| ½ | cup whole wheat flour |
| 2 | tablespoons sugar |
| 1 | tablespoon baking powder |
| ¾ | teaspoon salt |
| ½ | teaspoon baking soda |
| ¼ | cup fat-free cottage cheese (2 ounces) |
| ¼ | cup chilled light butter |
| 1 | cup 2% buttermilk |

Preheat the oven to 400°F. Lightly coat a baking sheet with nonstick spray.

In small bowl, combine the yeast and water and stir gently to dissolve. Set aside.

In a large bowl, stir together the unbleached or all-purpose flour, whole wheat flour, sugar, baking powder, salt, and baking soda.

Place the cottage cheese in fine-mesh sieve over a bowl. Using the back of a spoon, push all of the cottage cheese through the sieve. Add to the bowl with the flour mixture, but do not mix.

Using a cheese grater, shred the butter into the flour mixture. Using a pastry cutter or a fork, cut the butter and the cottage cheese into the flour mixture until the mixture resembles coarse crumbs. Add the buttermilk and the yeast mixture and toss briskly with a fork just until the dough holds together.

Turn the dough out onto a floured work surface. Knead lightly for 1 minute. Roll to an even thickness of ⅝". Using a 2½" biscuit cutter or glass, stamp out biscuits. Dip the cutter into flour between cuts to prevent sticking.

Transfer the biscuits to the prepared baking sheet, leaving about 1" space between. Bake for 13 to 15 minutes, or until the biscuits are puffed and lightly browned. Serve immediately.

**Makes 12 biscuits**

*Per biscuit: 121 calories, 4 g protein, 21 g carbohydrates, 2 g fat, 0.5 g saturated fat, 6 mg cholesterol, 370 mg sodium, 1 g fiber*

*Homestyle Hint:* Light butter is readily available in supermarkets. The butter must be very cold to shred well. Work rapidly once the butter is shredded, as it softens quickly.

## How Much Fiber Do Kids Need?

It's a simple formula called Age + 5. Take your child's age and add 5 to determine the number of grams of fiber that your child should eat each day. For example, a 7-year old needs 12 grams of fiber (7 + 5 = 12). How to make sure your kids get it? Offer them whole grain muffins, cold cereals that are high in fiber, sandwiches on whole grain bread, and plenty of dishes with brown rice and green leafy vegetables.

# Jalapeño Cornbread

Olé! This festive cornbread is sure to tingle your tastebuds. Serve it with soups, stews, and chili. The calories, fat, and cholesterol were reduced and fiber was boosted by:

❖ *Replacing the oil with a combination of pureed corn and applesauce*

❖ *Using reduced-fat cheese, and less of it*

❖ *Using egg whites instead of whole eggs*

❖ *Using fat-free sour cream*

❖ *Incorporating whole wheat flour*

| | |
|---|---|
| 1 | small onion, finely chopped |
| 1¼ | cups cornmeal |
| ½ | cup unbleached or all-purpose flour |
| ¼ | cup whole wheat flour |
| 2 | tablespoons sugar |
| 4 | teaspoons baking powder |
| ¾ | teaspoon salt |
| 1½ | cups corn kernels |
| 1 | cup fat-free sour cream (without gelatin), 8 ounces |
| 4 | egg whites |
| 2 | tablespoons unsweetened applesauce |
| ¾ | cup shredded reduced-fat sharp Cheddar cheese (3 ounces) |
| 1 | can diced jalapeño or green chile peppers (4 ounces), drained |

Preheat the oven to 400°F. Lightly coat a 9" × 9" baking dish with nonstick spray.

Lightly coat a small skillet with nonstick spray and warm over medium-high heat. Add the onion and cook, stirring occasionally, for 5 minutes, or until soft. Set aside.

In large bowl, stir together the cornmeal, unbleached or all-purpose flour, whole wheat flour, sugar, baking powder, and salt.

In a food processor, pulse the corn until almost creamy but still lumpy (this will not work in a blender). Transfer to a bowl and whisk with the sour cream, egg whites, and applesauce. Pour into the flour mixture and stir just until moistened. Fold in the onion, cheese, and chile peppers.

Scrape the batter into the prepared baking dish. Bake for 30 minutes, or until the corn-bread is golden brown. Cool for 5 minutes in the pan. Cut into 9 squares.

**Makes 9 squares**

*Per square: 212 calories, 10 g protein, 38 g carbohydrates, 2 g fat, 1 g saturated fat, 7 mg cholesterol, 613 mg sodium, 3 g fiber*

*Homestyle Hint:* Frozen corn kernels do not need to be thawed before they are pulsed in the food processor.

# Yolks, Whites, and Cholesterol

*Eggs are the number one source of cholesterol in the American diet. They account for almost one-third of the cholesterol consumed by adults. This doesn't mean that you should give up eggs—just try eating them less often to lower your cholesterol intake. And when you can, use egg whites in place of whole eggs because all of the cholesterol is in the yolk.*

# Rosemary-Cheddar Scones

I like to pair these savory scones with hearty soups like Roasted Garlic–Potato Soup (page 156) and Sweet-and-Sour Stew (page 162). Calories, fat, and cholesterol were reduced and fiber got a boost by:

❖ *Using light butter in place of regular butter*
❖ *Using reduced-fat cheese, and less of it*
❖ *Using low-fat buttermilk*
❖ *Incorporating whole wheat flour*

| *Nutrition Scorecard* | | |
|---|---|---|
| *(per scone)* | | |
| | before | after |
| Calories | 324 | 233 |
| Fat (g) | 16 | 7 |

*Photo on page 125*

1¾ cups cake flour (not self-rising)

1 cup whole wheat flour

2 teaspoons finely chopped fresh rosemary or 1 teaspoon dried

1½ teaspoons baking powder

1½ teaspoons sugar

¾ teaspoon salt

¼ cup chilled light butter

1¼ cups 2% buttermilk

1½ cups shredded reduced-fat sharp Cheddar cheese (6 ounces)

Preheat the oven to 350°F. Lightly coat a baking sheet with nonstick spray.

In a large bowl, stir together the cake flour, whole wheat flour, rosemary, baking powder, sugar, and salt.

Using a cheese grater, shred the butter into the flour mixture. Using a pastry cutter or fork, cut the butter into the flour mixture until it resembles coarse crumbs. Stir in the buttermilk to form a moist dough. Mix in the cheese.

Turn the dough out onto a floured work surface. Knead lightly and form into a disk with a thickness of ¾". Cut into 8 wedges.

Transfer the wedges to the prepared baking sheet. Bake for 30 to 35 minutes, or until puffed and lightly browned. Serve warm.

### Makes 8 scones

*Per scone: 233 calories, 12 g protein, 30 g carbohydrates, 7 g fat, 3 g saturated fat, 24 mg cholesterol, 537 mg sodium, 2 g fiber*

*Homestyle Hint:* If you don't have 1¾ cups cake flour, you can replace it with 1½ cups unbleached or all-purpose flour mixed with 3 tablespoons cornstarch.

**Savory Parmesan Popovers** *(page 46)*

Glazed Orange Bread *(page 48)* and Cranberry Bread *(page 44)*

Pineapple Upside-Down Muffins *(page 34)* and Tuxedo Brownie Muffins *(page 40)*

**Chocolate Chip Pecan Loaf** *(page 43)*

**Quick Praline Rolls** *(page 42)*

59

**Stuffed French Toast** *(page 72)*

Sour Cream–Streusel Coffee Cake *(page 84)*

61

**Artichoke Frittata** *(page 79)*

**Gingerbread Pancakes** *(page 74)*
63

Southwest Soufflé Roll-Up *(page 76)*

**Mini Spring Rolls with Plum Sauce** *(page 106)*

65

**Mini Pizza Turnovers** *(page 105)* **and Corn Dog Bites** *(page 99)*

Hot Spinach-Artichoke Dip *(page 94)*

**Festive Cheese Log** *(page 92)*
68

**Blue Cheese–Stuffed Mushrooms** *(page 88)*
69

**Thai-Style Chicken Pizza** *(page 115)*

70

# Brunch Specials

During the week, breakfast at our house is usually rushed or grabbed on the go. But on the weekends, especially on Sundays, I like to make a more satisfying morning meal for my family. Traditional breakfast and brunch dishes can be high in fat. Here's what I do to lower the fat and calories while keeping the rich flavors.

🕯 When it comes to egg dishes, I replace at least half of the whole eggs with egg whites (use 2 whites in place of each whole egg). I prefer egg whites to egg substitute because, while substitutes are nutritionally similar to real eggs, they don't perform nearly as well in cooking. For example, you can't whip egg substitute into the stiff foam required for recipes like Southwest Soufflé Roll-Up or Sour Cream–Streusel Coffee Cake. I prefer to stick with real eggs, using a mixture of whole eggs and egg whites (which are fat-free, cholesterol-free, and very low in calories).

🕯 Turkey sausage has come a long way in terms of taste and texture. It works remarkably well in place of pork sausage. But while turkey sausage is much leaner than pork sausage, it is still high in fat overall. Take care not to use too much. One to 2 ounces per person is about right.

🕯 Always check the use of oil, butter, and other fats in a breakfast or brunch recipe. Often, the oil is splashed in the pan to cook eggs or potatoes even when it's not necessary or when you could use less. This is especially true if you use nonstick pans and coat them with nonstick spray. If you need the flavor of butter, light butter does a fabulous job. It has half the fat and half the calories of regular butter. When chilled, light butter can be shredded and cut into the dry ingredients for baked goods just like regular butter.

# Stuffed French Toast

This is one of my all-time favorite breakfasts. The cream cheese filling has just enough fruit preserves and walnuts mixed in to give it a heavenly flavor. Do not substitute fat-free cream cheese for light cream cheese. Calories, fat, and cholesterol were reduced by:

Photo on page 60

* *Using a mixture of light cream cheese and fat-free cream cheese in place of regular*
* *Reducing the amount of nuts*
* *Replacing heavy cream with 1% milk*
* *Replacing half of the whole eggs with egg whites*

## FILLING

4   ounces light cream cheese

4   ounces fat-free cream cheese

2   tablespoons confectioners' sugar

2   tablespoons apricot or strawberry preserves

⅓   cup finely chopped walnuts

## FRENCH TOAST

1   loaf French bread, about 16" long (16 ounces)

4   egg whites

2   eggs

1   cup 1% milk

1   teaspoon vanilla extract

½   teaspoon ground cinnamon

½   teaspoon ground nutmeg

TO MAKE THE FILLING: In a small bowl, using an electric mixer, beat together the light cream cheese and fat-free cream cheese. Mix in the confectioners' sugar and preserves. Stir in the walnuts.

TO MAKE THE FRENCH TOAST: Trim ½" off each end of the bread loaf and discard. Cut the loaf into ten 1½"-thick slices. Cut a pocket in the top of each slice without cutting all the way through. Fill each pocket with about 1½ tablespoons of the filling.

Coat a nonstick griddle or large skillet with nonstick spray and warm over medium heat.

In a shallow bowl, beat together the egg whites, eggs, milk, vanilla extract, cinnamon, and nutmeg. Using tongs, dip the bread in the egg mixture to coat completely (take care not to squeeze out the filling).

Cook the bread in batches over medium heat for 2 minutes on each side, or until golden brown. (Using tongs, hold the crusts against the griddle for a few seconds to cook all sides.)

**Makes 10 slices**

Per slice: 241 calories, 12 g protein, 31 g carbohydrates, 8 g fat, 3 g saturated fat, 54 mg cholesterol, 370 mg sodium, 2 g fiber

*Homestyle Hint:* Light cream cheese may be labeled "Neufchâtel cheese."

# Fiber Up at Breakfast

*To boost your fiber intake in the morning, look for breads and cereals that have a whole grain as the first ingredient. Whole grains include whole oats, whole wheat, and brown rice.*

# Gingerbread Pancakes

My kids like their pancakes in different shapes. Gingerbread man–shaped pancakes are always a hit with this batter. Of course, it makes great round griddle cakes, too. I reduced the calories, fat, and cholesterol and boosted fiber by:

Nutrition Scorecard
(per pancake)

|  | before | after |
|---|---|---|
| Calories | 117 | 96 |
| Fat (g) | 4 | 1 |

Photo on page 63

❖ *Replacing the butter with molasses*
❖ *Using low-fat buttermilk instead of whole milk*
❖ *Using egg whites instead of whole eggs*
❖ *Incorporating whole wheat flour*

1¼ cups unbleached or all-purpose flour
1 cup whole wheat flour
2 tablespoons brown sugar
1½ teaspoons baking powder
1½ teaspoons baking soda
1 teaspoon ground cinnamon
1 teaspoon ground nutmeg
1 teaspoon ground ginger
½ teaspoon ground cloves
½ teaspoon salt
2 cups 2% buttermilk
¼ cup molasses
2 egg whites

In a wide-mouth pitcher or large mixing bowl, combine the unbleached or all-purpose flour, whole wheat flour, brown sugar, baking powder, baking soda, cinnamon, nutmeg, ginger, cloves, and salt.

In small bowl, whisk together the buttermilk, molasses, and egg whites. Stir into the flour mixture just until moistened.

Coat a nonstick griddle or large skillet with nonstick spray and heat over medium heat. For each pancake, pour or ladle about ¼ cup batter onto the hot griddle. Cook for 1 to 2 minutes, or until the pancakes are bubbly and slightly dry around the edges. Turn over and cook briefly until golden. Serve immediately.

## Makes 16 pancakes

Per pancake: 96 calories, 4 g protein, 20 g carbohydrates, 1 g fat, 0 g saturated fat, 1 mg cholesterol, 27 mg sodium, 1 g fiber

*Homestyle Hint:* I like these pancakes topped with a fruit sauce, like apple or pear.

# Overnight Brunch Bake

This hassle-free dish is ideal for entertaining or a relaxing breakfast. All the effort occurs the night before. The old-fashioned breakfast bread pudding soaks up the liquid while you're sleeping, and come morning, you just have to put the casserole in the oven. Calories, fat, and cholesterol were reduced by:

*Nutrition Scorecard*

(per serving)

|  | before | after |
|---|---|---|
| Calories | 604 | 300 |
| Fat (g) | 45 | 11 |

❖ *Using turkey sausage, and less of it*
❖ *Using reduced-fat cheese*
❖ *Replacing the heavy cream with a mixture of fat-free evaporated milk and 1% milk*

| | |
|---|---|
| 6 | ounces bulk turkey sausage or 2 links (3 ounces each), casings removed |
| 6 | slices potato bread, crusts removed |
| 1½ | cups shredded reduced-fat sharp Cheddar cheese, preferably sharp (6 ounces) |
| 6 | egg whites |
| 1 | can fat-free evaporated milk (12 ounces) |
| ½ | cup 1% milk |
| 1 | teaspoon mustard powder |
| ¼ | teaspoon salt |

Coat an 11" × 7" baking dish with nonstick spray.

Coat a small nonstick skillet with nonstick spray and warm over medium heat. Add the sausage and cook, stirring to break it up, until crumbly and no longer pink. Remove from the heat and set aside.

Cut the bread into ½" cubes. Place half of the bread cubes in the prepared baking dish. Top with ¾ cup of the cheese. Top with the remaining bread cubes and the sausage. Sprinkle the remaining ¾ cup cheese evenly over the top.

In a medium bowl, beat together the egg whites, evaporated milk, 1% milk, mustard powder, and salt. Pour over the bread, cover, and refrigerate overnight.

Preheat the oven to 350°F. Uncover and bake for 45 minutes, or until golden and puffy. Serve immediately.

**Makes 6 servings**

*Per serving: 300 calories, 27 g protein, 23 g carbohydrates, 11 g fat, 6 g saturated fat, 47 mg cholesterol, 784 mg sodium, 1 g fiber*

# Southwest Soufflé Roll-Up

This dish may sound complicated at first, but don't let it fool you. It's easy to make, yet elegant to serve. If you can roll up a cake jelly-roll style or form the dough for cinnamon rolls, you can make this. In this recipe, you roll a cooked egg mixture instead of a cake or dough. The filling is made from cooked, savory vegetables. Calories, fat, and cholesterol were reduced by:

*Photo on page 64*

❖ *Replacing most of the whole eggs with egg whites*
❖ *Eliminating the butter for cooking the vegetables*
❖ *Using reduced-fat cheese*
❖ *Using 1% milk instead of whole milk*

## SOUFFLÉ

5 egg yolks
2 tablespoons unbleached or all-purpose flour
¼ teaspoon salt
¾ cup 1% milk
10 egg whites
1 teaspoon cream of tartar

## FILLING

2 potatoes, peeled and cut into ¼" cubes
1 red bell pepper, chopped
1 green bell pepper, chopped
1 onion, chopped
½ teaspoon dried oregano
½ teaspoon salt
2 ounces bulk turkey ham (not slices), chopped
½ cup shredded reduced-fat Cheddar cheese (2 ounces)
1½ cups salsa

TO MAKE THE SOUFFLÉ: Preheat the oven to 400°F. Coat a 15" × 10" baking dish with nonstick spray. Line with waxed paper, then coat the waxed paper with nonstick spray.

In a medium bowl, using an electric mixer set on high speed, beat the egg yolks for 5 minutes, or until thickened and lemon colored. Reduce the speed to medium and beat in the flour and salt. When incorporated, beat in the milk.

In a large, clean bowl, beat the egg whites on high speed with clean, dry beaters until foamy. Add the cream of tartar and beat until stiff peaks form when the beaters are lifted. Fold into the yolk mixture. Spread into the prepared baking dish. Bake for 20 minutes, or until golden. Cool on a rack for 5 minutes.

TO MAKE THE FILLING: Meanwhile, coat a large skillet with nonstick spray and warm over medium-high heat. Add the potatoes, peppers, onion, oregano, and salt and cook, stirring occasionally, for 10 to 15 minutes, or until tender. Stir in the turkey ham and remove from the heat.

Carefully invert the warm soufflé onto a clean kitchen towel. Peel off the waxed paper. Top evenly with the filling. Sprinkle with the cheese. Beginning at a short end, roll up, jelly-roll style. Place, seam side down, on a serving plate. Serve warm or at room temperature. Cut into 8 slices and serve with the salsa.

**Makes 8 servings**

*Per serving: 155 calories, 12 g protein, 15 g carbohydrates, 5 g fat, 2 g saturated fat, 143 mg cholesterol, 853 mg sodium, 3 g fiber*

## The Calcium Connection

*Diets high in protein cause the body to kick out calcium in the urine. For every 50 grams of protein eaten, the body loses 60 milligrams of calcium. To avoid unnecessary calcium loss, avoid eating more protein than you need each day. A whole roasted skinless chicken breast (two halves) has about 53 grams of protein—enough to meet a woman's needs for the entire day.*

# Sausage and Hash Brown Casserole

It's hard to believe that this savory breakfast dish has half the calories and a third of the fat of the original recipe. Yet it's as filling and delicious as ever. I reduced the calories, fat, and cholesterol by:

❖ *Using turkey sausage, and less of it*
❖ *Adding red bell pepper to compensate for less sausage*
❖ *Replacing whole milk with 1% milk*
❖ *Using reduced-fat cheese*

|  |  |
|---|---|
| 12 | ounces bulk turkey sausage (not slices) |
| 1 | red bell pepper, chopped |
| 1½ | cups 1% milk |
| 3½ | teaspoons cornstarch |
| 1 | pound frozen shredded potatoes or 2 cups shredded potatoes |
| ½ | cup chopped fresh chives |
| ¾ | cup reduced-fat shredded Cheddar cheese (3 ounces) |

Preheat the oven to 350°F. Coat an 8" × 8" square baking dish with nonstick spray.

Coat a large nonstick skillet with nonstick spray and warm over medium-high heat. Add the sausage and cook, stirring to break it up, until crumbly and no longer pink. Stir in the pepper and cook for 2 minutes. Add all but 2 tablespoons of the milk.

In a cup, dissolve the cornstarch in the remaining 2 tablespoons milk. Add to the sausage mixture and cook, stirring, for 2 minutes, or until bubbly.

Arrange the potatoes in a single layer in the prepared baking dish. Top with ¼ cup of the chives and ½ cup of the cheese. Spread the sausage mixture over the potatoes and top with the remaining ¼ cup cheese. Bake for 45 minutes, or until the potatoes are tender. Sprinkle with the remaining ¼ cup chives and serve.

**Makes 6 servings**

*Per serving: 252 calories, 20 g protein, 16 g carbohydrates, 13 g fat, 5 g saturated fat, 59 mg cholesterol, 533 mg sodium, 1 g fiber*

# Artichoke Frittata

A frittata is a cross between an omelet and a quiche. Artichoke hearts and roasted red peppers give this one a Mediterranean flavor. Calories, fat, and cholesterol were reduced by:

❖ *Replacing most of the whole eggs with egg whites*
❖ *Eliminating the butter for cooking the vegetables*
❖ *Using reduced-fat mozzarella cheese*

*Nutrition Scorecard*
(per serving)

|  | before | after |
|---|---|---|
| Calories | 255 | 169 |
| Fat (g) | 18 | 6 |

*Photo on page 62*

|   |   |
|---|---|
| 1 | large onion, chopped |
| 4 | ounces mushrooms, sliced |
| 1 | can water-packed artichoke hearts (14 ounces), drained and coarsely chopped |
| 1 | jar roasted red peppers (7 ounces), drained and chopped |
| 1 | teaspoon dried oregano |
| ¾ | teaspoon ground black pepper |
| ½ | teaspoon salt |
| 10 | egg whites |
| 2 | eggs |
| 1 | cup reduced-fat shredded mozzarella cheese (4 ounces) |
| 3 | tablespoons freshly grated Parmesan cheese |

Coat a large nonstick ovenproof skillet with nonstick spray and warm over medium heat. Add the onion and mushrooms and cook, stirring, for 5 minutes, or until tender. Add the artichokes, roasted peppers, oregano, ¼ teaspoon of the black pepper, and ¼ teaspoon of the salt. Cook, stirring, for 4 minutes, or until heated through.

In medium bowl, combine the egg whites, eggs, the remaining ½ teaspoon black pepper and the remaining ¼ teaspoon salt. Stir in the mozzarella. Pour over the vegetables and cook for 5 minutes. As the eggs begin to set, run a spatula around the edges, allowing any uncooked egg to run under the cooked portions. Do not stir. When the eggs are almost set, cover, reduce the heat to low, and cook for 8 to 10 minutes, or until the eggs are set.

Meanwhile, preheat the broiler. Sprinkle the Parmesan on top of the eggs. Broil for 4 minutes, or until the cheese browns. Cut into wedges and serve.

## Makes 6 servings

*Per serving: 169 calories, 17 g protein, 12 g carbohydrates, 6 g fat, 3 g saturated fat, 84 mg cholesterol, 711 mg sodium, 5 g fiber*

# Tex-Mex Frittata

The toppings really enhance this Southwest-inspired dish. Don't be scared off by the fat-free sour cream; it works very well. But quality differs remarkably from brand to brand. The key is to use a brand that you like and trust. Calories, fat, and cholesterol were reduced by:

| *Nutrition Scorecard* | | |
|---|---|---|
| (per serving) | | |
| | before | after |
| Calories | 255 | 209 |
| Fat (g) | 16 | 7 |

* *Reducing the amount of oil*
* *Replacing most of the whole eggs with egg whites*
* *Using fat-free sour cream instead of regular sour cream*

|   |   |
|---|---|
| 1 | teaspoon canola oil |
| 3 | corn tortillas (6" diameter), cut into thin strips |
| 1 | small onion, chopped |
| 12 | egg whites |
| 4 | egg yolks |
| 1 | cup salsa |
| ¼ | cup fat-free sour cream (without gelatin), 2 ounces |
| 2 | tablespoons chopped fresh chives |

Warm the oil in a large nonstick skillet over medium-high heat. Add the tortillas and onion. Cook, stirring, for 5 minutes, or until the onions are tender.

In a medium bowl, beat together the egg whites and egg yolks. Pour over the tortilla mixture and reduce the heat to medium. As the eggs begin to set around the edges, run a spatula around the edges, lifting the eggs slightly to allow any uncooked egg to run under the cooked portions. Do not stir. When the eggs are almost set, cover, reduce the heat to low, and cook for 8 to 10 minutes, or until the eggs set. Divide into servings and top each with salsa, sour cream, and chives.

## Makes 4 servings

*Per serving: 209 calories, 16 g protein, 19 g carbohydrates, 7 g fat, 2 g saturated fat, 213 mg cholesterol, 860 mg sodium, 3 g fiber*

# Baked Cheddar Grits

This is one of my son's favorite breakfast meals. If you've never tried grits, try these. The sharp Cheddar cheese adds great flavor and a creamy texture. I reduced the calories, fat, cholesterol, and sodium by:

❖ *Eliminating margarine*
❖ *Replacing whole milk with 1% milk*
❖ *Replacing most of the whole eggs with egg whites*
❖ *Using reduced-fat cheese*
❖ *Reducing the amount of salt*

3½ cups 1% milk

2 cups water

¾ teaspoon salt

1¼ cups quick-cooking grits

2 cups shredded reduced-fat sharp Cheddar cheese (8 ounces)

4 egg whites

2 eggs

1 teaspoon hot-pepper sauce

¼ teaspoon ground black pepper

Preheat the oven to 350°F. Coat a shallow 2½-quart casserole with nonstick spray.

In a large saucepan, combine 1½ cups of the milk, the water, and salt. Bring to a boil over medium-high heat. Gradually add the grits, stirring constantly to prevent lumps. Reduce the heat to low, cover, and cook, stirring occasionally, for 5 minutes, or until the grits are stiff. Remove from the heat. Stir in 1¾ cups of the cheese.

In a large bowl, combine the egg whites, eggs, and the remaining 2 cups milk. Gradually stir in the grits. Transfer to the prepared casserole and sprinkle with the remaining ¼ cup cheese. Bake for 45 minutes, or until golden and a wooden pick inserted in the center comes out clean. Serve immediately, seasoned with hot-pepper sauce and black pepper.

## Makes 6 servings

*Per serving: 326 calories, 25 g protein, 33 g carbohydrates, 10 g fat, 6 g saturated fat, 104 mg cholesterol, 711 mg sodium, 1 g fiber*

# Home-Fried Potatoes

A little bit of oil goes a long way in this classic breakfast potato dish. Calories, fat, cholesterol, and sodium were reduced by:

* *Replacing the butter with canola oil, and using much less of it*
* *Reducing the amount of salt*

*Nutrition Scorecard*
(per serving)

|  | before | after |
|---|---|---|
| Calories | 194 | 113 |
| Fat (g) | 12 | 2 |

2  teaspoons canola oil

4  potatoes, peeled and finely chopped

1  onion, chopped

¾  teaspoon salt

¼  teaspoon ground black pepper

Warm the oil in a large nonstick skillet over medium-high heat. Add the potatoes and onion and cook, stirring, for 5 minutes, or until the onions are soft. Season with the salt and pepper. Reduce the heat to medium, cover, and cook for 10 minutes, or until the potatoes are browned on one side. Uncover and cook, turning occasionally, for 10 minutes longer, or until the potatoes are tender. Serve immediately.

**Makes 4 servings**

*Per serving: 113 calories, 3 g protein, 21 g carbohydrates, 2 g fat, 0.5 g saturated fat, 0 mg cholesterol, 274 mg sodium, 2 g fiber*

## *Breakfast Adds Up*

Children who eat breakfast do better with math, attendance, and behavior at school. Plus, they have less hyperactivity. In fact, research shows that children who regularly ate the school-provided breakfast averaged almost a whole letter-grade higher than kids who rarely ate breakfast. Youngsters don't have to eat breakfast at school to reap these rewards. Before they leave the house, give them a bowl of cereal, a piece of toast spread with peanut butter, or yogurt mixed with fruit.

# Shortcut Sticky Rolls

This is a very quick recipe that always gets praise. Its humble beginnings include store-bought refrigerator breadstick dough, which is quickly transformed into glorious sweet rolls worthy of any breakfast or brunch table. I reduced the calories, fat, and cholesterol by:

**Nutrition Scorecard**

*(per roll)*

|          | before | after |
|----------|--------|-------|
| Calories | 267    | 228   |
| Fat (g)  | 8      | 4     |

- *Replacing heavy cream with a mixture of fat-free evaporated milk and light butter*
- *Using raisins instead of pecans*

| | |
|---|---|
| ½ | cup packed brown sugar |
| 1 | tablespoon fat-free evaporated milk |
| 1 | tablespoon light butter |
| ⅓ | cup raisins |
| 1 | package refrigerator breadstick dough (11 ounces) |
| ⅓ | cup unsweetened applesauce |
| ½ | teaspoon ground cinnamon |

Preheat the oven to 350°F.

In a small microwaveable bowl, combine the brown sugar, milk, and butter. Microwave on high power for 30 seconds, or until the butter melts. Stir until smooth. Pour into an 8" round pan. Sprinkle the raisins over the brown sugar sauce.

Place a sheet of waxed paper, about 15" long, on a work surface. Coat with nonstick spray. Unroll the breadstick dough on the waxed paper, but do not separate into breadsticks. Spread the applesauce over the dough and sprinkle evenly with the cinnamon. Roll up from a short end, jelly-roll style, using the waxed paper as a guide. Using a serrated knife, separate the dough at the 6 horizontal perforations to make 6 coiled dough rolls. Arrange in the pan on top of the brown sugar sauce.

Bake for 30 to 35 minutes, or until golden brown. Cool for 1 minute. Invert the pan onto a heatproof platter. Let stand for 1 minute so that the sauce drizzles over the rolls. Remove the pan and serve warm.

**Makes 6 rolls**

*Per roll: 228 calories, 6 g protein, 44 g carbohydrates, 4 g fat, 0 g saturated fat, 3 mg cholesterol, 375 mg sodium, 2 g fiber*

# Sour Cream–Streusel Coffee Cake

This beautiful coffee cake has two cinnamony ribbons of streusel running throughout. It is soooo good! I reduced the calories, fat, cholesterol, and sodium and boosted fiber by:

- ❖ *Reducing the amount of walnuts for the streusel and replacing them in part with wheat germ*
- ❖ *Using egg whites in place of whole eggs*
- ❖ *Replacing butter with applesauce*
- ❖ *Using low-fat sour cream instead of regular sour cream*
- ❖ *Reducing the amount of salt*
- ❖ *Incorporating whole wheat flour*

## STREUSEL

1¼ cups packed brown sugar

⅓ cup wheat germ

4½ teaspoons ground cinnamon

4½ teaspoons unsweetened cocoa powder

⅔ cup chopped walnuts

⅓ cup currants or chopped raisins

## COFFEE CAKE

2 cups cake flour (not self-rising)

1 cup whole wheat flour

1½ cups sugar

1½ teaspoons baking powder

1½ teaspoons baking soda

½ teaspoon salt

⅛ teaspoon ground nutmeg

6 egg whites

2 cups low-fat sour cream (without gelatin), 16 ounces

¾ cup unsweetened applesauce

## GLAZE

½ cup confectioners' sugar

2 teaspoons 1% milk

TO MAKE THE STREUSEL: In a medium bowl, combine the brown sugar, wheat germ, cinnamon, and cocoa. Mix in the walnuts and currants or raisins.

TO MAKE THE COFFEE CAKE: Preheat the oven to 350°F. Coat a 12-cup Bundt pan with nonstick spray.

In a large bowl, combine the cake flour, whole wheat flour, sugar, baking powder, baking soda, salt, and nutmeg.

In another large bowl, using an electric mixer set on high speed, beat the egg whites for 1 minute, or until frothy. Mix in the sour cream and applesauce. Add half of the flour mixture and beat until moist. Add the remaining flour mixture and beat for 1 minute, or until well-blended.

Pour one-third of the batter into the prepared pan. Sprinkle half of the streusel mixture evenly over the batter. Spread another third of the batter over the streusel and top with the remaining streusel. Spoon the rest of the batter over the streusel. Bake for 50 to 60 minutes, or until a wooden pick or cake tester inserted near the center comes out clean. Cool in the pan on a rack for 10 minutes. Using a dull kitchen knife, loosen the cake around the edges and invert onto a platter to cool until warm, about 1 hour.

TO MAKE THE GLAZE: In a small bowl, combine the confectioners' sugar and milk and whisk until smooth. Drizzle over the cake. Serve slightly warm.

**Makes 12 servings**

*Per serving: 386 calories, 10 g protein, 72 g carbohydrates, 8 g fat, 3 g saturated fat, 12 mg cholesterol, 412 mg sodium, 3 g fiber*

*Homestyle Hint:* If you don't have cake flour, mix together 1¾ cups unbleached or all-purpose flour and ¼ cup cornstarch.

## Get a Little Nutty

*Nuts may help lower blood pressure. In a special diet study called DASH (Dietary Approaches to Stop Hypertension), participants ate nuts and beans four or five times per week and had a dramatic drop in blood pressure, even if it was not high in the beginning. Nuts were found to be a key component of the diet. (For more details on the DASH diet, see page 13).*

# Hearty Hot Cereal

My daughter is a big fan of this grainy cereal, so I cook a big batch on the weekends and store it in individual microwaveable containers. Calories, fat, and cholesterol were reduced by:

* ❖ *Eliminating the butter*
* ❖ *Reducing the amount of sugar*

| *Nutrition Scorecard* | | |
|---|---|---|
| *(per serving)* | | |
| | before | after |
| Calories | 334 | 272 |
| Fat (g) | 7 | 2 |

| | |
|---|---|
| 7 | cups water |
| ½ | cup pearl barley |
| ½ | cup short-grain brown rice |
| ½ | cup Irish oats or old-fashioned rolled oats |
| ½ | cup chopped dates |
| ½ | cup raisins |
| ¼ | cup packed brown sugar |
| ½ | teaspoon salt |
| ½ | teaspoon ground cinnamon |

In a large saucepan, combine the water, barley, rice, oats, dates, raisins, brown sugar, salt, and cinnamon. Bring to a boil over high heat. Reduce the heat to medium, cover, and simmer, stirring occasionally, for 45 minutes. Uncover and simmer, stirring occasionally, for 10 minutes longer, or until all the water is absorbed and the cereal is creamy.

**Makes 6 servings**

*Per serving: 272 calories, 6 g protein, 61 g carbohydrates, 2 g fat, 0.5 g saturated fat, 0 mg cholesterol, 185 mg sodium, 6 g fiber*

*Health Note*

## Soluble Fiber Protects the Heart

*After reviewing 67 studies on the effects of fiber and cholesterol, researchers confirmed that soluble fiber does indeed lower cholesterol. Soluble fiber, as the name suggests, dissolves in water and forms gels. To get the benefits of this type of fiber, eat more oats, beans, whole grains, and apples and other fruits.*

# Nibbles for One or a Crowd

I don't like a lot of fuss when it comes to appetizers. Yet I want something that tastes and looks great, without the excessive fat that is found in so many of the classics. Here are some of the techniques I use for simple, healthy appetizers—both elegant and everyday.

🕯 Try oven-frying instead of deep-frying. This technique works surprisingly well in recipes like Mozzarella Melts, Chicken Nuggets, and Parmesan Zucchini Sticks.

🕯 Blend flavorful cheeses, such as feta and goat cheese, with reduced-fat or fat-free cheese. A good example is the Blue Cheese–Stuffed Mushrooms. Enough blue cheese is blended with fat-free cream cheese so that you can taste the full, pungent flavor of the blue cheese. But there is a lot less fat than there might otherwise be.

🕯 Take advantage of phyllo dough. Any time a recipe calls for a pastry shell, use phyllo instead. This paper-thin dough pinch-hits beautifully for higher-fat doughs and has a delightful crunchy texture when baked. Phyllo is available in the freezer section of most supermarkets. To see just how much it lowers the fat, take a look at the Mini Spring Rolls with Plum Sauce.

🕯 Reach for store-bought doughs. These doughs in a tube save loads of time in the kitchen. Low-fat versions shave fat and calories, too. I use low-fat dinner-roll dough to make Mozzarella Melts. And Corn Dog Bites are only minutes away with cornbread stick refrigerator dough.

# Blue Cheese–Stuffed Mushrooms

This appetizer is quick to throw together when unexpected guests arrive—it doesn't even require cooking! Yet it looks and tastes as elegant as you could want. I reduced the calories, fat, and cholesterol by:

❖ *Replacing butter with fat-free cream cheese*
❖ *Slightly reducing the amount of blue cheese*
❖ *Reducing the amount of chopped olives*

*Photo on page 69*

|   |   |
|---|---|
| 4 | ounces fat-free cream cheese, at room temperature |
| ¾ | cup crumbled blue cheese (3 ounces) |
| ¼ | teaspoon mustard powder |
| 12 | mushrooms (medium or large), stemmed |
| 2 | tablespoons chopped pitted black olives |

In a small bowl, stir together the cream cheese, blue cheese, and mustard powder until creamy. Spoon into the mushroom caps. Sprinkle ½ teaspoon of the olives over the filling in each mushroom. Serve immediately or chilled.

**Makes 12 mushrooms**

*Per mushroom: 43 calories, 3 g protein, 2 g carbohydrates, 3 g fat, 1 g saturated fat, 6 mg cholesterol, 166 mg sodium, 0 g fiber*

# Deviled Eggs

My kids love these. And who would guess that more than half the calories, fat, and cholesterol have been removed! Here's how I did it:

❖ *Eliminating one-third of the egg yolks*
❖ *Pureeing fat-free cottage cheese to use in place of both the mayonnaise and the missing yolks*
❖ *Adding Dijon mustard to boost flavor and deepen the yellow color*

6   hard-cooked eggs

⅓   cup 1% cottage cheese with herbs (2½ ounces)

½   teaspoon Dijon mustard

⅛   teaspoon salt

      Pinch of ground black pepper

      Paprika

Cut the eggs in half lengthwise. Discard 2 of the yolks. Put the remaining 4 yolks in a medium bowl and mash them with a fork until crumbly. Set the whites aside.

In a small food processor or blender, puree the cottage cheese until smooth and creamy (resembling marshmallow creme). Add to the yolks, along with the mustard, salt, and pepper. Stir until mixed. Stuff the egg white halves with the yolk mixture. Sprinkle with paprika.

### Makes 12 servings

*Per serving: 33 calories, 4 g protein, 1 g carbohydrates, 2 g fat, 1 g saturated fat, 71 mg cholesterol, 91 mg sodium, 0 g fiber*

*Homestyle Hint:* To prevent the eggs from slipping and sliding on the serving plate, cut a paper-thin slice off the bottoms so that they sit flat.

## *Profile of an Egg*

Eggs are not *verboten*. It's okay to eat them; just don't go overboard. The profile below shows just where the calories, fat, protein, and cholesterol come from in an egg. Notice that the white is the more healthful part. (All figures have been rounded.)

| Part of the Egg | Calories | Fat (g) | Protein (g) | Cholesterol (mg) |
|---|---|---|---|---|
| 1 whole egg | 76 | 5 | 6 | 213 |
| 1 egg yolk | 59 | 5 | 3 | 213 |
| 1 egg white | 17 | 0 | 3 | 0 |

# Texas Caviar

Some like this bean dip fiery hot, so add more jalapeño if you want to kick up the heat. I use reduced-fat salad dressing here because I have yet to find a fat-free commercial dressing that knocks my socks off (even if the flavor is acceptable, the texture is usually lumpy). Fortunately, the reduced-fat salad dressings are quite good. Calories, fat, and cholesterol were reduced by:

❖ *Reducing the amount of dressing*
❖ *Using reduced-fat dressing*

| | |
|---|---|
| ⅔ | cup reduced-fat Italian dressing (not fat-free) |
| ½ | teaspoon ground cumin |
| 3 | cans black beans (15 ounces each), rinsed and drained |
| 1 | green bell pepper, chopped |
| 1 | onion, chopped |
| ½ | cup chopped fresh chives |
| ¼ | cup chopped jarred pimiento |
| 2 | tablespoons chopped fresh cilantro |
| 1–2 | tablespoons drained, seeded, and minced canned jalapeño chile pepper |
| 3 | garlic cloves, minced |
| 4 | cups reduced-fat tortilla chips (optional) |

In a large bowl, mix the dressing and cumin. Add the beans, bell pepper, onion, chives, pimiento, cilantro, chile peppers, and garlic. Gently toss to coat.

Cover and refrigerate for at least 2 hours. Serve chilled or at room temperature with the tortilla chips, if using.

**Makes 5 cups; forty 2-tablespoon servings**

*Per 2 tablespoons: 36 calories, 1 g protein, 8 g carbohydrates, 0.5 g fat, 0 g saturated fat, 0 mg cholesterol, 61 mg sodium, 2 g fiber*

# Southwest Pinwheels

These tightly rolled burritos are sliced crosswise to reveal an attractive pinwheel design. I cut the calories, fat, and cholesterol and boosted fiber by:

❖ *Replacing full-fat cream cheese with fat-free*
❖ *Using whole wheat tortillas*

| Nutrition Scorecard | | |
|---|---|---|
| (per pinwheel) | | |
| | before | after |
| Calories | 43 | 24 |
| Fat (g) | 2 | 0.5 |

8  ounces fat-free cream cheese, at room temperature

½  cup chopped pitted black olives

1  can diced green chile peppers (4 ounces), drained

3  garlic cloves, minced

⅛  teaspoon hot-pepper sauce

⅛  teaspoon ground cumin

8  whole wheat tortillas (10" diameter)

6  ounces paper-thin smoked turkey or smoked chicken slices

In a medium bowl, combine the cream cheese, olives, chile peppers, garlic, hot-pepper sauce, and cumin. Spread some of the olive mixture on each tortilla. Cover with the turkey or chicken and roll tightly. Wrap in plastic wrap and refrigerate for at least 2 hours or overnight. When ready to serve, remove the plastic wrap and cut each roll on a slight diagonal into 6 slices.

**Makes 48 pinwheels**

*Per pinwheel: 24 calories, 2 g protein, 4 g carbohydrates, 0.5 g fat, 0 g saturated fat, 2 mg cholesterol, 138 mg sodium, 1 g fiber*

## Snacking on the Rise

*On average, Americans snack about twice a day. Instead of noshing on high-calorie munchies like potato chips, cookies, and doughnuts, look for more healthful snacks like pretzels, a whole grain muffin, an apple, or a handful of baby carrots.*

# Festive Cheese Log

This savory spread infused with garlic is the first thing to go at get-togethers. I sometimes use cracked peppercorns for more color. I reduced calories, fat, and cholesterol by:

❖ *Replacing part of the goat cheese with fat-free cream cheese*
❖ *Enhancing the flavor with garlic rather than full-fat cheese*

Photo on page 68

| | |
|---|---|
| 4 | ounces goat cheese |
| 4 | ounces fat-free cream cheese, at room temperature |
| 1 | garlic clove, minced or pressed |
| ⅓ | cup finely chopped fresh basil |
| ½ | teaspoon cracked black pepper |
| ½ | teaspoon poppy seeds or sesame seeds |

In a small bowl, mix together the goat cheese, cream cheese, and garlic until smooth. Scrape onto a sheet of plastic wrap or waxed paper and form into a log about 10" long. Wrap well and chill for at least 2 hours, or until firm.

Sprinkle the basil, pepper, and poppy seeds or sesame seeds evenly over a sheet of waxed paper. Unwrap the cheese log and roll it in the seasoning mixture, pressing gently so that the seasonings adhere on all sides. Wrap the log in plastic wrap or waxed paper again and refrigerate until ready to serve.

**Makes 1 log; sixteen 2-tablespoon servings**

*Per 2 tablespoons: 33 calories, 3 g protein, 1 g carbohydrates, 2 g fat, 2 g saturated fat, 6 mg cholesterol, 71 mg sodium, 0 g fiber*

## Alcohol and Appetizers Don't Mix

*If you are concerned about overeating, avoid this dangerous duo. A study of 52 men and women were served either an alcoholic beverage or nonalcoholic beverage with a meal. Those who drank alcohol ate faster, for longer, and had a greater tendency to keep eating even after their hunger abated. This did not happen if they drank juice, water, or another nonalcoholic drink.*

# Feta Pita Wedges

Fresh rosemary and lemon peel give this spread an enticing aroma that transports you to the fragrant regions along the Mediterranean Sea. Calories, fat, and cholesterol were reduced by:

❖ *Replacing butter with fat-free cream cheese*
❖ *Slightly reducing the amount of feta cheese*

| *Nutrition Scorecard* | | |
|---|---|---|
| *(per wedge)* | before | after |
| Calories | 99 | 49 |
| Fat (g) | 8 | 2 |

|   |   |
|---|---|
| 8 | ounces fat-free cream cheese, at room temperature |
| 4 | ounces feta cheese |
| 3 | tablespoons chopped fresh chives |
| 1 | tablespoon chopped fresh rosemary |
| 1½ | teaspoons finely shredded lemon peel |
| 4 | whole wheat pitas |

In a food processor or blender, mix together the cream cheese, feta cheese, chives, rosemary, and lemon peel. Blend until smooth and transfer to a small bowl.

Stack the pitas and cut the stack into 6 wedges. Serve the spread with the pita wedges.

**Makes 24 wedges**

*Per wedge: 49 calories, 4 g protein, 5 g carbohydrates, 2 g fat, 1 g saturated fat, 7 mg cholesterol, 165 mg sodium, 1 g fiber*

*Health Note*

## Rosemary—Adding More Than Spice to Your Life

*The herb rosemary not only has great flavor, it also has powerful antioxidant and anti-tumor properties. I like to use fresh rosemary on grilled or roasted vegetables, in pasta dishes, and in soups.*

# Hot Spinach-Artichoke Dip

I was originally asked to lighten this dip for my "Recipe Makeover" column in *Shape* magazine. It has since become one of my favorites. I love it with reduced-fat crackers or chips. Most people are pleasantly surprised to learn that it's low in fat. I reduced calories, fat, and cholesterol by:

❖ *Replacing the butter with nonstick cooking spray*
❖ *Using fat-free cream cheese instead of regular*
❖ *Using reduced-fat sour cream instead of regular*
❖ *Using reduced-fat Monterey Jack cheese, and less of it*

*Nutrition Scorecard*

(per ¼ cup)

|  | before | after |
|---|---|---|
| Calories | 181 | 75 |
| Fat (g) | 16 | 3 |

*Photo on page 67*

| | |
|---|---|
| 1 | small onion, finely chopped |
| 2 | packages frozen chopped spinach (10 ounces each), thawed and squeezed dry |
| 8 | ounces fat-free cream cheese |
| 1 | cup reduced-fat sour cream (8 ounces) |
| ¾ | cup freshly grated Parmesan cheese (3 ounces) |
| 1 | can water-packed artichoke hearts (14 ounces), drained and chopped |
| ¼ | teaspoon salt |
| ⅛ | teaspoon ground black pepper |
| ⅛ | teaspoon crushed red-pepper flakes |
| 1 | cup shredded reduced-fat Monterey Jack cheese (4 ounces) |

Lightly coat a large nonstick skillet with nonstick spray and warm over medium heat. Add the onion and cook, stirring, for 5 minutes, or until soft. Stir in the spinach and cook for 5 minutes, or until heated through. Reduce the heat to low and stir in the cream cheese and sour cream just until blended and smooth. Stir in the Parmesan and arti-chokes until blended. Remove from the heat and stir in the salt, black pepper, and red-pepper flakes.

Transfer to a 1½-quart microwaveable bowl and top with the Monterey Jack. Microwave on high power for 2 to 3 minutes, or just until the cheese is melted. Serve warm.

### Makes 5 cups; twenty 1/4-cup servings

*Per ¼ cup: 75 calories, 7 g protein, 5 g carbohydrates, 3 g fat, 2 g saturated fat, 12 mg cholesterol, 211 mg sodium, 2 g fiber*

# Mozzarella Melts

This is one of my family's favorite appetizers, and it's so easy to make that you'll turn to it time and again. Stick with regular (full-fat) string cheese for smooth melting. The low-fat version does not perform nearly as well, and since string cheese is naturally low in fat, the fat and calorie savings would not be great. Look for dinner roll dough (not crescent roll dough) in the refrigerated/dairy section of your supermarket. I reduced calories, fat, and cholesterol by:

❖ *Baking instead of frying*
❖ *Using egg whites instead of whole eggs*

> 4 pieces string cheese (1 ounce each)
> 1 package low-fat refrigerator dinner roll dough (8 rolls)
> 2 egg whites
> ½ teaspoon water
> ⅓ cup seasoned dry bread crumbs
> ½ teaspoon garlic powder
> 1 cup low-fat marinara sauce, heated

Preheat the oven to 375°F. Coat a baking sheet with nonstick spray.

Cut each piece of string cheese into quarters to make 16 bite-size pieces. Separate the bread dough into rolls and then divide each roll in half horizontally to make 16 pieces. Using the palms of your hands, flatten each piece of dough to make a 2½"-diameter disk. Wrap each piece of cheese in dough, encasing the cheese completely and rolling the dough between your palms to smooth the dough. Pinch the seams together to seal.

In a shallow bowl, lightly beat together the egg whites and water.

In another shallow bowl, combine the bread crumbs and garlic powder.

Dip a dough-wrapped cheese piece into the egg whites to coat, then roll it in the bread crumb mixture to coat. Place on the prepared baking sheet. Repeat with the remaining pieces, arranging them on the baking sheet so that there is about ¾" between pieces. Bake for 12 to 15 minutes, or until golden.

Serve warm with the marinara sauce for dipping.

### Makes 16 melts

*Per melt: 93 calories, 5 g protein, 13 g carbohydrates, 2 g fat, 1 g saturated fat, 4 mg cholesterol, 304 mg sodium, 1 g fiber*

# Savory Pita-Cheese Triangles

A savory spread makes these pita triangles real winners—whether served as a hot appetizer or enjoyed as a snack. I reduced the calories, fat, and cholesterol and boosted fiber by:

*Nutrition Scorecard*
(per triangle)

|  | before | after |
|---|---|---|
| Calories | 89 | 42 |
| Fat (g) | 6 | 2 |

❖ *Replacing butter with a mixture of light butter and fat-free cream cheese*

❖ *Using reduced-fat Cheddar cheese*

❖ *Using whole wheat pitas*

|  |  |
|---|---|
| 4 | ounces fat-free cream cheese, at room temperature |
| 2 | tablespoons light butter, at room temperature |
| 1 | teaspoon Worcestershire sauce |
| ¾ | teaspoon paprika |
| ⅛ | teaspoon ground red pepper |
| 1 | garlic clove, minced |
| 12 | whole wheat pitas |
| 2½ | cups shredded reduced-fat sharp Cheddar cheese (10 ounces) |
| ⅔ | cups freshly grated Parmesan cheese (3 ounces) |

Preheat the oven to 350°F. Coat a baking sheet with nonstick spray.

In a small mixing bowl, stir together the cream cheese and butter until smooth. Stir in the Worcestershire sauce, paprika, pepper, and garlic.

Split each pita into 2 flat disks. Spread 2 teaspoons of the cream cheese mixture on the rough side of each. Sprinkle each with about 2 tablespoons Cheddar and top with about 2 teaspoons Parmesan. Cut each disk into quarters and transfer to the prepared baking sheet. Bake for 10 to 12 minutes, or until the cheese is bubbling.

## Makes 96 triangles

Per triangle: 42 calories, 3 g protein, 3 g carbohydrates, 2 g fat, 1 g saturated fat, 6 mg cholesterol, 113 mg sodium, 1 g fiber

# The Cheese-and-Calcium Connection

Cheese is a good source of calcium. Below are the calcium levels of 1½ ounces of some favorites. This amount of cheese is considered a serving according to the Food Guide Pyramid and offers just about as much calcium, on average, as a cup of fat-free milk (302 milligrams).

| Cheese | Calcium (mg) |
| --- | --- |
| Parmesan | 585 |
| Cheddar, reduced-fat | 300 |
| Monterey Jack, reduced-fat | 300 |
| Mozzarella, reduced-fat | 275 |
| Blue | 225 |
| Feta | 209 |
| Goat | 127 |

# Chicken Nuggets

These golden jewels got two thumbs up from one of my staunchest critics: my 11-year-old daughter. I reduced the calories, fat, and cholesterol by:

❖ *Baking instead of frying*
❖ *Relying on crushed cornflakes to provide crunch without the fat*

| Nutrition Scorecard | | |
|---|---|---|
| *(per nugget)* | before | after |
| Calories | 48 | 36 |
| Fat (g) | 3 | 0.5 |

½ cup unbleached or all-purpose flour

1 teaspoon paprika

1 teaspoon salt

¼ teaspoon ground red pepper

3 egg whites

1½ cups finely crushed cornflakes

½ pound boneless, skinless chicken breast, cut into 32 pieces

Barbecue sauce or honey mustard (optional)

Preheat the oven to 375°F. Lightly coat a baking sheet with nonstick spray.

In a shallow bowl, combine the flour, paprika, salt, and pepper. In another shallow bowl, lightly beat the egg whites. In a third shallow bowl, spread the cornflakes in a layer.

Toss the chicken in the flour mixture to coat. Dip in the egg whites and then in the cornflakes to coat. Place on the prepared baking sheet and bake for 25 minutes, or until golden and the chicken is no longer pink. Serve with the sauce or mustard, if using.

**Makes 32 nuggets**

*Per nugget: 36 calories, 3 g protein, 6 g carbohydrates, 0.5 g fat, 0 g saturated fat, 4 mg cholesterol, 131 mg sodium, 0.5 g fiber*

## Fast Food for Kids

*Which is the more healthy fast food: a hamburger? Or chicken nuggets? Surprise! The hamburger is the better choice. It's lower in fat. Once chicken is fried, the breading soaks up loads of fat. The typical fast-food serving of chicken nuggets has about 17 grams of fat, while the kid's meal hamburger has just 10 grams of fat. If your kids absolutely love chicken nuggets, make your own at home by baking them in the oven.*

# Corn Dog Bites

Boy, is this ever a hit with kids *and* adults! The recipe lent itself to much simplification during the makeover process. Now, it uses only two ingredients. How much easier could it get? I reduced calories, fat, and cholesterol by:

❖ *Using packaged dough so that these can be baked, not fried*
❖ *Using low-fat frankfurters*

*Photo on page 66*

1 package cornbread sticks refrigerator dough (8 twists or sticks)

8 low-fat frankfurters (about 5" long), each cut into 4 pieces

Preheat the oven to 375°F. Lightly coat a baking sheet with nonstick spray.

Separate the dough into 16 pieces. Cut each piece in half to make 32 pieces. Roll each into a ball and use the palm of your hand to flatten each into a small circle about ¼" thick.

Encase a frankfurter piece in each circle of dough, enclosing entirely and pinching the seams to seal. Place on the prepared baking sheet and bake for 10 to 13 minutes, or until golden.

**Makes 32 pieces**

Per piece: 50 calories, 2 g protein, 6 g carbohydrates, 2 g fat, 0.5 g saturated fat, 4 mg cholesterol, 184 mg sodium, 0 g fiber

## What's in a Corn Dog?

*Corn dogs get their name from the thick cornmeal breading that surrounds the hot dog. The whole thing is deep-fried, which gives each one about 460 calories and 19 grams of fat.*

# Portobello Pizza

My dad loves mushrooms. For Father's Day a few years ago, I bought him the "king" of mushrooms, king-size portobellos, and made him this appetizer using the mushrooms themselves as the "crust." The delight on his face upon seeing and tasting this pizza was priceless. I reduced calories and fat by:

❖ *Reducing the olive oil and replacing part of it with fat-free chicken broth*
❖ *Using reduced-fat mozzarella cheese*

1   tablespoon fat-free chicken broth

2   teaspoons olive oil

4   garlic cloves, minced

4   portobello mushrooms (4" diameter), stemmed

1   tomato, chopped

2   tablespoons chopped fresh basil or 2 teaspoons dried

2   tablespoons freshly grated Parmesan cheese

1   cup shredded reduced-fat mozzarella cheese (4 ounces)

Preheat the oven to 350°F.

In a small bowl or cup, combine the broth, oil, and garlic. Arrange the mushrooms, gill side up, on a baking sheet. Drizzle the garlic mixture over them. Bake for 10 minutes.

Remove from the oven and scatter the tomato and basil evenly over the mushrooms. Top with the Parmesan and mozzarella.

Bake for 10 minutes, or until the cheese is bubbling. Remove from the oven and let stand for 10 minutes. Cut each mushroom into 4 wedges and serve warm.

### Makes 16 wedges

Per wedge: 21 calories, 2 g protein, 2 g carbohydrates, 1 g fat, 0.5 g saturated fat, 1 mg cholesterol, 26 mg sodium, 1 g fiber

*Homestyle Hint:* Reduced-fat mozzarella cheese may be labeled "skim" or "part-skim."

# Barbecue Chicken Quesadillas

This is one of my daughter's favorite after-school snacks. It also makes great party food. Calories, fat, and cholesterol were reduced and fiber was boosted by:

❖ *Using reduced-fat cheeses*
❖ *Using a skinned chicken breast*
❖ *Using whole wheat tortillas*

*Nutrition Scorecard*
(per wedge)

|  | before | after |
|---|---|---|
| Calories | 96 | 74 |
| Fat (g) | 5 | 2 |

| | |
|---|---|
| 4 | whole wheat tortillas (10" diameter) |
| ½ | cup shredded reduced-fat Monterey Jack cheese (2 ounces) |
| ¼ | pound boneless, skinless chicken breast, cooked and shredded |
| ½ | cup barbecue sauce |
| 2 | tablespoons chopped fresh chives |
| 4 | teaspoons chopped fresh cilantro |
| ½ | cup shredded reduced-fat sharp Cheddar cheese (2 ounces) |

Place 2 tortillas on a work surface and sprinkle evenly with the Monterey Jack. Combine the chicken and the barbecue sauce in a small bowl. Spoon evenly over the tortillas. Top with sprinklings of the chives, cilantro, and Cheddar. Top each tortilla with the remaining 2 tortillas.

Coat a large nonstick skillet with nonstick spray and warm over medium-high heat. Cook 1 quesadilla for 3 to 4 minutes, turning once, or until lightly browned on both sides and the cheese is melted. Transfer to a cutting board. Repeat with the remaining quesadilla. Cut each into 6 wedges and serve warm.

**Makes 12 wedges**

*Per wedge: 74 calories, 7 g protein, 8 g carbohydrates, 2 g fat, 1 g saturated fat, 13 mg cholesterol, 221 mg sodium, 1 g fiber*

# Parmesan Zucchini Sticks

Fried zucchini is a perennial favorite. I made this treat more healthful with simple adjustments to the technique and ingredients. I reduced the calories, fat, and sodium by:

- ❖ *Baking rather than frying*
- ❖ *Using garlic powder rather than garlic salt*
- ❖ *Using egg whites instead of whole eggs*

*Nutrition Scorecard*

| (per stick) | before | after |
|---|---|---|
| Calories | 64 | 33 |
| Fat (g) | 4 | 1 |

3   medium zucchini (about 1 pound), ends trimmed

3   egg whites

½   teaspoon water

½   cup unbleached or all-purpose flour

½   cup freshly grated Parmesan cheese (2 ounces)

½   cup seasoned dry bread crumbs

½   teaspoon garlic powder

¼   teaspoon ground black pepper

Preheat the oven to 375°F. Coat a baking sheet with nonstick spray.

Quarter each zucchini lengthwise and then cut each quarter in half crosswise to make 24 pieces that are each about 3" long.

In a shallow bowl, beat together the egg whites and water.

In another shallow bowl, combine the flour, cheese, bread crumbs, garlic powder, and pepper and toss gently.

Dip the zucchini pieces into the egg white mixture to coat and then roll in the bread crumb mixture to coat. Place the zucchini on the prepared baking sheet. Bake for 20 minutes, or until golden.

**Makes 24 sticks**

*Per stick: 33 calories, 2 g protein, 5 g carbohydrates, 1 g fat, 0.5 g saturated fat, 2 mg cholesterol, 113 mg sodium, 0 g fiber*

# Artichoke Squares

If you like artichoke hearts, you'll love this quiche-like appetizer. Calories, fat, and cholesterol were reduced by:

- ❖ *Using egg whites instead of whole eggs*
- ❖ *Using reduced-fat cheese, and less of it*
- ❖ *Replacing half of the marinated artichoke hearts with water-packed artichokes*

| | |
|---|---|
| 1 | **can water-packed artichoke hearts (6 ounces), drained** |
| 1 | **jar marinated artichoke hearts (6 ounces), drained and marinade reserved** |
| 1 | **small onion, finely chopped** |
| 2 | **garlic cloves, minced** |
| 6 | **egg whites** |
| ¼ | **cup plain dry bread crumbs** |
| ⅛ | **teaspoon salt** |
| ⅛ | **teaspoon dried oregano** |
| ⅛ | **teaspoon black pepper** |
| ⅛ | **teaspoon hot-pepper sauce** |
| 1½ | **cups shredded reduced-fat sharp Cheddar cheese (6 ounces)** |
| 2 | **tablespoons chopped flat-leaf parsley** |

Preheat the oven to 350°F. Lightly coat a 9" × 9" baking dish with nonstick spray.

Chop all of the artichokes into small pieces.

In a large skillet, warm the reserved marinade from the marinated artichokes over medium-high heat. Add the onion and garlic and cook, stirring, for 5 to 6 minutes, or until soft. Remove from the heat.

In a large bowl, beat together the egg whites, bread crumbs, salt, oregano, black pepper, and hot-pepper sauce. Stir in the artichokes, cheese, and parsley. Add the onion mixture and stir until well-mixed. Pour into the prepared baking dish. Bake for 25 minutes, or until golden. When cool, cut into 36 squares.

**Makes 36 squares**

*Per square: 27 calories, 3 g protein, 2 g carbohydrates, 1 g fat, 1 g saturated fat, 3 mg cholesterol, 95 mg sodium, 1 g fiber*

# Mini Broccoli Quiche

Guests love these elegant-looking appetizers. Thankfully, they're easy to make. Calories, fat, and cholesterol were reduced by:

❖ *Using plain bread crumbs instead of pastry crust*
❖ *Using reduced-fat cheese*
❖ *Replacing whole eggs with egg whites*
❖ *Replacing heavy cream with fat-free evaporated milk*

¼ cup plain dry bread crumbs

1 cup shredded reduced-fat Swiss cheese (4 ounces)

1 package frozen chopped broccoli (10 ounces), thawed and well-drained

4 egg whites

½ cup fat-free evaporated milk

1 tablespoon chopped fresh basil or 1 teaspoon dried

⅛ teaspoon salt

Dash of ground red pepper

Dash of ground nutmeg (optional)

Preheat the oven to 400°F. Lightly coat the insides of two 12-cup mini-muffin pans with nonstick spray. Sprinkle ½ teaspoon of the bread crumbs evenly into each muffin cup.

In a food processor or blender, combine the cheese, broccoli, egg whites, milk, basil, salt, pepper, and nutmeg, if using, until well-blended. Spoon about 1 tablespoon into each of the muffin cups so that they are nearly full. Bake for 15 to 17 minutes, or until the eggs are set and golden. Cool in the pans on wire racks for 10 minutes. Carefully remove the quiches and serve warm.

## Makes 24 mini quiches

*Per mini quiche: 25 calories, 3 g protein, 2 g carbohydrates, 0.5 g fat, 0.5 g saturated fat, 2 mg cholesterol, 53 mg sodium, 0 g fiber*

# Mini Pizza Turnovers

These miniature calzones are essentially folded pizzas—with a big-flavor filling that you'll love. I reduced the calories, fat, and cholesterol by:

❖ *Using lean turkey sausage, and less of it*
❖ *Using reduced-fat mozzarella cheese, and less of it*
❖ *Using more mushrooms to compensate for less meat*
❖ *Using reduced-fat refrigerator dough*

*Nutrition Scorecard*
*(per turnover)*

|  | before | after |
|---|---|---|
| Calories | 117 | 92 |
| Fat (g) | 7 | 3 |

*Photo on page 66*

¾ **pound lean Italian turkey sausage, casings removed**

1 **large onion, chopped**

1 **red bell pepper, finely chopped**

8 **ounces mushrooms, sliced (2 cups)**

2 **tablespoons chopped flat-leaf parsley**

¼ **teaspoon crushed red-pepper flakes**

2 **packages low-fat refrigerator dinner roll dough (8 rolls each)**

2 **cups shredded reduced-fat mozzarella cheese (8 ounces)**

Preheat the oven to 375°F. Lightly coat 2 baking sheets with nonstick spray.

Coat a large skillet with nonstick spray and warm over medium-high heat. Add the sausage and onion and cook, stirring to break up the meat, for 5 minutes. Add the bell pepper and mushrooms and cook, stirring, for 5 minutes longer, or until the sausage is cooked through and the vegetables are soft. Using a slotted spoon, transfer to a large bowl. Stir in the parsley and red-pepper flakes.

Separate the bread dough into rolls and divide each roll in half crosswise to make 32 pieces. Using a small rolling pin, roll out each piece to a diameter of about 4" and no more than ¼" thick.

Place a generous tablespoonful of the sausage mixture and 2 teaspoons of the mozzarella off-center on each circle. Fold the dough over the filling, pinch the seams to seal, and press along the edges with the tines of a fork to seal further and make an attractive design.

Place on the prepared baking sheets and bake for 15 to 20 minutes, or until golden.

### Makes 32 turnovers

*Per turnover: 92 calories, 6 g protein, 10 g carbohydrates, 3 g fat, 1 g saturated fat, 9 mg cholesterol, 164 mg sodium, 1 g fiber*

# Mini Spring Rolls
# with Plum Sauce

The filling in these spring rolls is so delicious that sometimes I'll make a meal by doubling the amount of the filling and serving it by itself spooned over rice. The plum sauce is one of the easiest dips to make. Calories, fat, and cholesterol were reduced by:

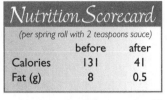

*Nutrition Scorecard*
*(per spring roll with 2 teaspoons sauce)*

|  | before | after |
|---|---|---|
| Calories | 131 | 41 |
| Fat (g) | 8 | 0.5 |

*Photo on page 65*

❖ *Using ground turkey breast instead of ground beef*
❖ *Using phyllo dough instead of traditional egg roll wraps*
❖ *Baking instead of frying*
❖ *Eliminating the oil when cooking the filling*

## PLUM SAUCE

1   jar baby food strained plums with apples (6 ounces)

3   tablespoons packed brown sugar

2   tablespoons rice vinegar

1   piece fresh ginger (1" thick), peeled

1   garlic clove, minced

## SPRING ROLLS

2   tablespoons soy sauce

1   teaspoon sugar

1   cup finely shredded cabbage

1   small carrot, shredded

1   celery rib, finely chopped

2   garlic cloves, minced

½   pound ground turkey breast

8   sheets phyllo dough

TO MAKE THE PLUM SAUCE: In a small saucepan, combine the plums, brown sugar, vinegar, ginger, and garlic. Bring to a boil over medium-high heat, stirring constantly. Remove from the heat and set aside to cool. When cool, remove and discard the ginger.

TO MAKE THE SPRING ROLLS: Preheat the oven to 375°F. Lightly coat 2 baking sheets with nonstick spray. Coat a large skillet with nonstick spray.

In a small bowl, stir together the soy sauce and sugar until smooth. Set aside.

Set the skillet over medium-high heat. Add the cabbage, carrot, celery, and garlic and cook, stirring, for 5 minutes, or until crisp-tender. Remove the vegetables from the skillet and set aside. In the same skillet, cook the turkey, stirring, for 5 minutes, or until no longer pink. Add the soy sauce mixture and mix well. Stir in the cooked vegetables and remove from the heat.

Arrange the sheets of phyllo dough in a single stack. Cut crosswise into 3 strips. Transfer 2 stacks of the strips to waxed paper and cover with plastic wrap to prevent drying out as you work.

Place 1 strip of phyllo on a work surface and lightly coat with nonstick spray. Place 1 tablespoon of the filling at the short end of the strip, centering it between the edges. Roll up the strip and filling one-third of the way. Fold the left and right sides of the phyllo over the filling and continue rolling to the end. Place the roll, seam side down, on a prepared baking sheet. Repeat with the remaining phyllo sheets and filling.

Bake for 15 minutes, or until golden. Serve hot with the sauce.

### Makes 24 spring rolls; 1 cup sauce

*Per spring roll with 2 teaspoons sauce: 41 calories, 3 g protein, 6 g carbohydrates, 0.5 g fat, 0.1 g saturated fat, 6 mg cholesterol, 119 mg sodium, 0.5 g fiber*

# 15-Minute Meals

*I* would love to say that I cook elaborate, healthy meals every night for my family. But the truth is, with two active kids and our busy schedules, I simply don't have time. My husband and I finally reached a point when we designated days of the week for each of us to cook. (I never thought we would get to this, but it has worked out beautifully!) Jeff cooks on Mondays and Wednesdays; I cook on Tuesdays and Thursdays (we leave the other days open). And very rarely does either of us spend a great deal of time in the kitchen. Welcome to real life! Like so many of the meals that we cook for our family, each recipe in this section can be prepared and cooked in 15 minutes or less. This means you can have a meal ready faster than it would take to jump in the car and wait in line for fast food or takeout.

Here are some standby shortcuts to keep in mind for quick weeknight meals.

♨ Check out the fresh produce section and pick up ready-cut vegetables and greens, especially chopped onions, shredded carrots, baby spinach, and other ready-to-eat salad greens.

♨ Round out quick meals with frozen vegetables. Bags of frozen vegetables are just as healthful as fresh and often have an even higher nutrient content. Best of all, they come together faster because they're already cut up.

♨ Invest in some gadgets and tools that make life easier, such as a garlic press and kitchen scissors. Even if you own a standard-size food processor, I find that the mini processors are handy for small batches of chopping (like onions). And they're a lot easier to clean.

# Shortcut Cheddar Soup

This soup tastes like you made it from scratch, but it gets a quick start from condensed cream of celery soup and frozen vegetables. Calories, fat, and cholesterol were reduced by:

### Nutrition Scorecard
(per serving)

|  | before | after |
|---|---|---|
| Calories | 309 | 191 |
| Fat (g) | 20 | 6 |

❖ *Using 1% milk instead of whole milk*
❖ *Using a combination of reduced-fat and fat-free Cheddar cheeses instead of full-fat cheeses*
❖ *Eliminating beer*
❖ *Using canned reduced-fat cream soup*

> 2 cups frozen loose-pack cauliflower, broccoli, and carrot mix
> 2 tablespoons chopped onion
> 1 can reduced-fat condensed cream of celery soup (10¾ ounces)
> 1¼ cups 1% milk
> ¾ cup finely shredded fat-free Cheddar cheese (3 ounces)
> ¾ cup shredded reduced-fat sharp Cheddar cheese (3 ounces)

In a microwaveable bowl, cook the frozen vegetables in the microwave on high power for 3 to 4 minutes, or until nearly tender. Drain and cover to keep warm.

Meanwhile, coat a medium saucepan with nonstick spray and warm over medium heat. Add the onion and cook, stirring, for 2 minutes, or until soft. Add the soup and milk and cook, stirring, for 2 minutes, or until bubbly. Remove from the heat. Add the cheeses and stir until melted. Stir in the vegetables and serve immediately.

**Makes 4 servings**

*Per serving: 191 calories, 19 g protein, 16 g carbohydrates, 6 g fat, 4 g saturated fat, 21 mg cholesterol, 685 mg sodium, 2 g fiber*

## Quick Vegetables

*A typical can of vegetable soup counts as two servings of vegetables, and it takes only a minute or two to heat up in the microwave or on top of the stove. Looking for a super-quick healthy meal? Problem solved!*

# Speedy Tostadas

This meal is a family favorite, especially on late nights when we juggle soccer games with other activities. I prefer to make these with pinto beans that I have cooked myself (and frozen), but to my surprise, canned refried beans work very well, too—my husband's discovery. I reduced calories, fat, and cholesterol by:

**Nutrition Scorecard**
*(per tostada)*

| | before | after |
|---|---|---|
| Calories | 273 | 162 |
| Fat (g) | 14 | 7 |

❖ *Using fat-free beans*
❖ *Using reduced-fat cheese*
❖ *Using chopped bits of avocado rather than guacamole*

|   |   |
|---|---|
| 8 | tostada shells (5" diameter) |
| 1 | can fat-free refried beans (16 ounces) or 2 cups leftover cooked beans |
| ½ | cup shredded reduced-fat Cheddar cheese (2 ounces) |
| 1½ | cups shredded lettuce |
| 2 | tomatoes, chopped |
| ½ | avocado, finely chopped |

Preheat the oven to 375°F.

Arrange the tostada shells on baking sheets. Spread the beans on the tostada shells and sprinkle each with 1 tablespoon of the cheese. Bake for 5 minutes, or until the cheese is melted. Top with the lettuce, tomatoes, and avocado.

**Makes 8 tostadas**

*Per tostada: 162 calories, 7 g protein, 19 g carbohydrates, 7 g fat, 2 g saturated fat, 5 mg cholesterol, 408 mg sodium, 5 g fiber*

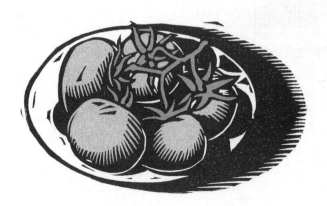

# Pizza Sloppy Joes

My kids love these. And they even have pepperoni! I reduced the calories, fat, and cholesterol and boosted fiber by:

❖ *Replacing the ground beef with ground turkey breast*
❖ *Using low-fat pepperoni*
❖ *Using reduced-fat mozzarella cheese*
❖ *Using whole wheat hamburger buns*

| | |
|---|---|
| 1 | small onion, finely chopped |
| 1 | green or red bell pepper, chopped |
| 1 | pound ground turkey breast |
| 1 | jar low-fat pizza sauce (14 ounces) |
| 1 | jar mushroom stems and pieces (2½ ounces), drained |
| 18 | slices low-fat pepperoni, quartered (1 ounce) |
| ½ | teaspoon dried oregano, crushed |
| 6 | whole wheat hamburger buns, split |
| ¾ | cup shredded reduced-fat mozzarella cheese (3 ounces) |

Coat a large nonstick skillet with nonstick spray and warm over medium-high heat. Add the onion and pepper and cook, stirring occasionally, for 2 minutes, or until soft. Add the turkey and cook, stirring to break up the meat, for 5 minutes, or until browned and no longer pink. Add the pizza sauce, mushrooms, pepperoni, and oregano and cook, stirring, for 2 to 3 minutes, or until heated through. Spoon onto the buns and top with the cheese.

**Makes 12 open-faced sandwiches; 6 servings**

*Per serving: 272 calories, 29 g protein, 26 g carbohydrates, 7 g fat, 2 g saturated fat, 45 mg cholesterol, 705 mg sodium, 2 g fiber*

*Homestyle Hint:* Almost any type of low-fat spaghetti sauce or marinara sauce can stand in for the pizza sauce.

## Teens are Time-Pressed, Too

Adolescents say that time and convenience are among the key factors influencing their food choices. If your teens have trouble eating a healthful diet, help them along by having plenty of healthful grab-and-go foods on hand. Good choices include bags of cut-up veggies, fresh fruit, fruit juice boxes or bottles, frozen fruit bars, and reduced-fat granola bars.

# Open-Faced Ham and Apple Melts

The marriage of ham and fruit is a time-honored one, and it works beautifully here with cheese. I reduced calories, fat, and cholesterol and boosted fiber by:

❖ *Using reduced-fat Swiss cheese*
❖ *Eliminating mayonnaise*
❖ *Using lean ham*
❖ *Using whole wheat English muffins*

| *Nutrition Scorecard* | | |
|---|---|---|
| *(per serving)* | | |
| | before | after |
| Calories | 420 | 221 |
| Fat (g) | 24 | 4 |

4   whole wheat English muffins, split
3   tablespoons Dijon mustard
8   thin slices low-fat ham
1   apple, peeled and cored
4   slices reduced-fat Swiss cheese, halved crosswise

Preheat the broiler. Arrange the muffin halves, cut side up, on a baking sheet. Broil for 1 to 2 minutes, or until the muffins are lightly browned. Remove from the broiler but do not remove from the baking sheet. Do not turn off the broiler.

Spread the mustard on the muffin halves. Top each with 1 slice of ham.

Slice the apple crosswise into 8 rings. Place the rings on the ham. Top with the cheese.

Broil for 1 to 2 minutes, or until the cheese is melted.

**Makes 8 open-faced sandwiches; 4 servings**

*Per serving: 221 calories, 19 g protein, 27 g carbohydrates, 4 g fat, 1 g saturated fat, 29 mg cholesterol, 843 mg sodium, 29 g fiber*

*Homestyle Hint:* I like to use a crisp, juicy apple, such as Cortland, Pippin, or Granny Smith.

## Eating Out Means More Calories and Fat

*In a study of 129 women, those who ate out (or ordered takeout) six or more times per week ate more calories, fat, and sodium than those who ate out five times or less per week and cooked for themselves the rest of the time.*

# Hot Chicken Heroes
# with Roasted Pepper Spread

The secret to these exceptional sandwiches is in the sauce. To make this even faster, use leftover chicken. Just slide the sandwiches under the broiler for a minute or two to melt the cheese and reheat the chicken. Calories, fat, and cholesterol were reduced by:

❖ *Eliminating the oil to cook the chicken*
❖ *Using fat-free mayonnaise in the spread*
❖ *Using reduced-fat cheese*
❖ *Eliminating ham*

### Nutrition Scorecard

| (per hero) | before | after |
|---|---|---|
| Calories | 776 | 410 |
| Fat (g) | 48 | 9 |

Photo on page 120

### SPREAD

1  garlic clove
1  jar roasted red peppers (7 ounces), drained
½  cup fat-free mayonnaise

### SANDWICHES

4  boneless, skinless chicken breast halves (1 pound total)
4  slices reduced-fat provolone cheese or reduced-fat mozzarella cheese
4  French-style sandwich rolls, split
4  teaspoons chopped fresh basil

TO MAKE THE SPREAD: In a small food processor or blender, pulse the garlic until finely chopped. Add the peppers and mayonnaise and puree until smooth.

TO MAKE THE SANDWICHES: Coat a large nonstick skillet with nonstick spray and warm over medium heat. When hot, add the chicken and cook for 4 minutes on each side, or until golden brown. Top each chicken breast half with a slice of cheese. Cover the skillet and remove from the heat to allow the cheese to melt.

Spread both halves of each roll with the pepper spread. Place a chicken breast on the bottom half. Sprinkle with the basil. Top with the top halves of the rolls.

**Makes 4 heroes**

Per hero: 410 calories, 35 g protein, 39 g carbohydrates, 9 g fat, 1 g saturated fat, 79 mg cholesterol, 835 mg sodium, 5 g fiber

# Thai-Style Chicken Pizza

These individual pizzas are a hit. I prefer using leftover chicken, but canned chicken works surprisingly well, thanks to the bold flavor of the peanut sauce. Ready-to-go shredded carrots are easy to find in the produce section of the grocery store. Calories, fat, cholesterol, and sodium were reduced and fiber was boosted by:

*Photo on page 70*

- ❖ *Using less peanut butter*
- ❖ *Using reduced-fat mozzarella cheese*
- ❖ *Using reduced-sodium soy sauce*
- ❖ *Using whole wheat tortillas*

| | |
|---|---|
| 4 | **whole wheat flour tortillas (10" diameter)** |
| ½ | **cup smooth natural-style peanut butter** |
| 3 | **tablespoons low-sodium soy sauce** |
| 2 | **tablespoons honey** |
| 1 | **tablespoon seasoned rice vinegar** |
| 1½ | **cups shredded cooked chicken breast or 1 can white chicken meat (10 ounces)** |
| 1 | **cup bean sprouts, rinsed** |
| 1 | **small carrot, shredded, or ½ cup packaged shredded carrots** |
| 1½ | **cups shredded reduced-fat mozzarella cheese (6 ounces)** |

Preheat the oven to 400°F. Arrange the tortillas on a baking sheet.

In a medium bowl, mix together the peanut butter, soy sauce, honey, and vinegar until smooth. Spread half of the mixture on the tortillas.

Add the chicken to the remaining peanut butter mixture and toss to coat. Spoon the chicken over the tortillas and top with layers of sprouts, carrots, and cheese.

Bake for 10 minutes, or until the cheese is melted. Remove from the oven and cut each pizza into quarters.

### Makes 4 pizzas

*Per pizza: 409 calories, 35 g protein, 40 g carbohydrates, 15 g fat, 5 g saturated fat, 55 mg cholesterol, 921 mg sodium, 4 g fiber*

# Creamy Chicken Curry

With packaged frozen cooked chicken breast meat, this tasty meal is ready in minutes. You don't even need to thaw the chicken. I streamlined the cooking method so that it's all done in one skillet instead of finishing the dish in the oven. I like to serve this over Quick Couscous (page 317). Calories, fat, and cholesterol were reduced by:

❖ *Using fat-free sour cream instead of full-fat sour cream*
❖ *Using reduced-fat Cheddar cheese, and less of it*

> 2   packages frozen cooked, cubed chicken breast (9 ounces each)
>
> 1   pound packaged fresh broccoli florets
>
> 1   can reduced-fat cream of chicken soup (10¾ ounces)
>
> 1   cup fat-free sour cream (8 ounces), without gelatin
>
> 2   teaspoons curry powder
>
> ½   cup shredded reduced-fat Cheddar cheese (2 ounces)

Coat a large nonstick skillet with nonstick spray and warm over medium-high heat.

Add the chicken and cook, stirring occasionally, for 3 minutes, or until heated.

Meanwhile, place the broccoli and a tablespoon or two of water in a microwaveable dish. Cover and microwave on high power for 3 minutes, or just until vibrant green. Add to the skillet.

In a small bowl, stir together the soup, sour cream, and curry powder. Stir into the chicken mixture. Reduce the heat to medium-low and cook, stirring, for 3 minutes, or until heated through, taking care not to let the mixture boil. Scatter the cheese on top, cover, remove from the heat, and let stand for 5 minutes, or until the cheese is melted.

### Makes 4 servings

*Per serving: 372 calories, 44 g protein, 24 g carbohydrates, 10 g fat, 4 g saturated fat, 100 mg cholesterol, 712 mg sodium, 4 g fiber*

*Homestyle Hint:* If your market doesn't carry packaged fresh broccoli florets, buy about 2 pounds of broccoli and use only the florets.

# Skillet Chicken Paprikash

I strongly recommend Sweet Hungarian paprika for this dish. It is available in tins at most grocery stores in the spice aisle. Try this over rice or noodles. I reduced the calories, fat, and cholesterol by:

❖ *Eliminating the oil to cook the onion*
❖ *Using fat-free sour cream instead of full-fat sour cream*

*Nutrition Scorecard*

| (per serving) | | |
|---|---|---|
| | before | after |
| Calories | 385 | 254 |
| Fat (g) | 21 | 6 |

*Photo on page 121*

1   small onion, chopped

2   packages frozen cooked, cubed chicken breast (9 ounces each)

1   cup fat-free sour cream (without gelatin), 8 ounces

1   tablespoon paprika

½   teaspoon salt

Coat a large nonstick skillet with nonstick spray and warm over medium-high heat. Add the onion and cook, stirring occasionally, for 3 minutes, or until soft. Add the chicken and cook, stirring, for 5 minutes, or until heated through. Cover the skillet and reduce the heat to medium.

In a small bowl, stir together the sour cream, paprika, and salt. Stir into the chicken mixture. Cover and cook, stirring, for 3 minutes, or until heated through, taking care not to let the mixture boil. Serve immediately.

**Makes 4 servings**

*Per serving: 254 calories, 36 g protein, 13 g carbohydrates, 6 g fat, 2 g saturated fat, 84 mg cholesterol, 541 mg sodium, 1 g fiber*

 *Health Note*

## Eating Out, Eating Smart

*Over the past two decades, foods eaten away from home have risen from 19 to 34 percent of total caloric intake. And sit-down restaurant foods provide 46 percent of calories from fat in the American diet, more than fast foods or foods eaten at school. That doesn't mean you shouldn't eat out. Just look for healthy options like grilled chicken or broiled fish; ask for salad dressings and other sauces on the side; avoid the butter or olive oil served with bread; limit alcohol consumption; and share dessert.*

# Black Bean Burritos

Not only are the fat and calories dramatically lowered in these burritos but I was also able to cut the sodium level nearly in half. Calories, fat, cholesterol, and sodium were reduced by:

| *Nutrition Scorecard* | | |
|---|---|---|
| (per burrito) | | |
| | before | after |
| Calories | 428 | 209 |
| Fat (g) | 15 | 3 |

❖ *Eliminating the oil used to cook the onion*
❖ *Using reduced-fat cheese, and less of it*
❖ *Using reduced-sodium beans*

1   small onion, chopped

2   cans reduced-sodium black beans (15 ounces each), rinsed and drained

1   cup salsa
   Juice of ½ lime

3   tablespoons chopped fresh cilantro

6   whole wheat tortillas (10" diameter)

¾   cup shredded reduced-fat Cheddar cheese (3 ounces)

Coat a large nonstick skillet with nonstick spray and heat over medium-high heat.

Add the onion and cook, stirring occasionally, for 3 minutes, or until soft. Add the beans, salsa, lime juice, and cilantro. Cook, stirring, for 5 minutes, or until heated through.

Meanwhile, wrap the tortillas in paper towels or microwaveable plastic wrap and cook in the microwave on high power for 30 seconds, or until warmed.

Place the tortillas on 6 individual serving plates. Spoon an even amount of the bean mixture just off-center on each tortilla and top each with 2 tablespoons cheese. Fold in the sides of the tortillas. Roll up from the bottom to enclose the filling.

### Makes 6 burritos

*Per burrito: 209 calories, 14 g protein, 43 g carbohydrates, 3 g fat, 2 g saturated fat, 10 mg cholesterol, 941 mg sodium, 10 g fiber*

*Homestyle Hint:* I like medium salsa for this dish, but use whatever heat level you and your family like best.

**Spicy Garlic Shrimp** *(page 139)*
119

Hot Chicken Heroes with Roasted Pepper Spread *(page 114)*

**Skillet Chicken Paprikash** *(page 117)*

121

Tex-Mex Skillet *(page 136)*

**Broiled Breaded Scallops** *(page 141)* **and Orzo Salad** *(page 277)*

**Chicken-Tortilla Soup** *(page 144)*

Sweet-and-Sour Stew *(page 162)* and Rosemary-Cheddar Scones *(page 54)*

125

**Pumpkin Soup with Apple Croutons** *(page 148)*

**Chili with Cornbread Dumplings** *(page 160)*
127

Red-Pepper Bisque *(page 151)* and Triple-Light Angel Biscuits *(page 50)*

**Potato-Bacon Clam Chowder** *(page 158)* **and Easy Cheesy No-Knead Batter Bread** *(page 47)*

129

**Sweet-and-Sour Pork Kebabs** *(page 202)*

**Beef Pinwheels** *(page 170)* **and Roasted Asparagus** *(page 312)*

131

**Orange Beef Stir-Fry** *(page 172)*

Barbecue Pot Roast *(page 182)*

**Pork and Peppers** *(page 200)*
134

# Jeff's Pronto Pepper Pasta

I have to thank my husband, Jeff, for this household staple. He found that adding frozen chopped bell peppers to our favorite commercial pasta sauce is incredibly tasty. And here's the nutrition bonus: Each serving provides more than 100 percent of your vitamin C needs for a day. Because Jeff developed this recipe as a low-fat, healthful dish, I did not modify it to reduce calories, fat, and cholesterol. This explains the lack of "before" figures in the Nutrition Scorecard.

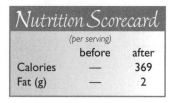

| Nutrition Scorecard | | |
|---|---|---|
| (per serving) | | |
| | before | after |
| Calories | — | 369 |
| Fat (g) | — | 2 |

1   package frozen chopped bell peppers (16 ounces)

1   jar low-fat spaghetti sauce (26 ounces)

1   pound dried angel hair pasta

6   tablespoons freshly grated Parmesan cheese (1¼ ounces)

Coat a large skillet with nonstick spray and warm over medium-high heat.

Add the peppers and cook, stirring occasionally, for 2 minutes, or until thawed and warm. Add the spaghetti sauce and bring to a boil. Reduce the heat to medium-low, cover, and cook gently for 10 minutes, or until the flavors have blended.

Meanwhile, cook the pasta according to the package directions. Divide the pasta among 6 serving plates. Top with the sauce and Parmesan.

**Makes 6 servings**

Per serving: 369 calories, 14 g protein, 71 g carbohydrates, 2 g fat, 0.5 g saturated fat, 3 mg cholesterol, 490 mg sodium, 6 g fiber

## Gender Gap

*Men are starting to cook more, but it seems that women still wear the aprons in the family. In a study of 1,200 couples, researchers found that 36 percent of men were involved in major food shopping, and 27 percent of men usually prepared the food. Younger men and men in households in which the woman worked full-time were more likely to be involved in meal planning and food preparation.*

# Tex-Mex Skillet

The original version of this dish had more than an entire day's worth of sodium, much of it from pork sausage. Using reduced-sodium beans helped lower the sodium, add fiber, and add flavor. I reduced calories, fat, cholesterol, and sodium by:

❖ *Using turkey sausage instead of pork, and using half of the usual amount*
❖ *Adding reduced-sodium black beans to make up for the missing sausage*
❖ *Using reduced-sodium tomato sauce*
❖ *Using reduced-fat cheese, and less of it*

½   pound lean Italian turkey sausage, casings removed

1   tablespoon chili powder

1   can reduced-sodium tomato sauce (15 ounces)

1   can Mexican-style corn, drained, or regular canned corn (12 ounces), drained

½   cup water

1   cup instant white rice

1   can reduced-sodium black beans (15 ounces), rinsed and drained

½   cup shredded reduced-fat Cheddar cheese (2 ounces)

Coat a large skillet with nonstick spray and warm over medium-high heat.

Add the sausage and chili powder and cook, stirring occasionally, for 5 minutes, or until browned. Stir in the tomato sauce, corn, and water. Bring to a boil. Stir in the rice and beans.

Remove from the heat. Scatter the cheese over the top, cover, and let stand for 5 minutes, or until the rice is tender and the cheese is melted.

## Makes 4 servings

*Per serving: 419 calories, 25 g protein, 59 g carbohydrates, 10 g fat, 3 g saturated fat, 41 mg cholesterol, 797 mg sodium, 10 g fiber*

# Cornmeal-Fried Fish

Fish fillets are naturally lean, and a little bit of cornmeal breading gives them body and texture. I reduced the calories, fat, and cholesterol by:

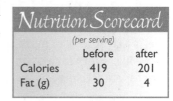

❖ *Using egg whites instead of whole eggs*

| | |
|---|---|
| 1 | **pound fresh fish fillets (½" thick)** |
| 1 | **egg white** |
| 1 | **teaspoon water** |
| ½ | **cup cornmeal** |
| ½ | **teaspoon salt** |
| ⅛ | **teaspoon ground red pepper** |
| 2 | **teaspoons olive oil** |

Cut the fish into 4 equal-size pieces and pat dry.

In a shallow dish, whisk together the egg white and water. In another shallow dish, mix the cornmeal, salt, and pepper. Dip the fish first into the egg white mixture, then coat with the cornmeal mixture.

Warm the oil in a large nonstick skillet over medium heat. Add the fish, raise the heat to medium-high, and cook for 4 to 5 minutes on each side, carefully turning only once, until golden and the fish flakes easily.

**Makes 4 servings**

*Per serving: 201 calories, 26 g protein, 14 g carbohydrates, 4 g fat, 1 g saturated fat, 42 mg cholesterol, 354 mg sodium, 1 g fiber*

*Homestyle Hint:* Any mild, white-fleshed fish can be used for this recipe, such as flounder, sole, halibut, cod, catfish, or snapper.

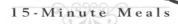

# Broiled Sole
# with Parmesan-Olive Topping

This is a great meal to make at the last minute when company is coming. Every time I serve it, I get rave reviews on the savory topping. Calories, fat, and cholesterol were reduced by:

| Nutrition Scorecard | | |
|---|---|---|
| *(per serving)* | before | after |
| Calories | 340 | 163 |
| Fat (g) | 21 | 6 |

- ❖ *Eliminating the olive oil and using chicken broth in its place*
- ❖ *Reducing the amount of olives and replacing them in part with bread crumbs*

|   |   |
|---|---|
| 1 | garlic clove |
| 1 | jar stuffed green olives (3 ounces), drained |
| ¼ | cup chicken broth |
| ¼ | cup freshly grated Parmesan cheese (1 ounce) |
| 1 | tablespoon plain dry bread crumbs |
| 4 | fresh sole fillets (4 ounces each) |

Coat a broiler pan with nonstick spray. Preheat the broiler.

In a small food processor or blender, pulse the garlic until finely chopped. Add the olives and pulse until chopped. Add the broth, cheese, and bread crumbs and pulse until nearly smooth.

Arrange the fish on the broiler pan in a single layer. Spread the olive paste over each fish fillet in a thin layer. Broil for 4 minutes, or until the fish flakes easily. Do not turn the fillets during cooking.

**Makes 4 servings**

Per serving: 163 calories, 25 g protein, 3 g carbohydrates, 6 g fat, 2 g saturated fat, 59 mg cholesterol, 724 mg sodium, 0 g fiber

## Another Reason to Eat Fish

*Italian researchers reviewed the cases of more than 10,000 cancer patients, comparing their diets with those of nearly 8,000 people who had no cancer. They found that eating just a small amount of fish every week reduced the risk of several cancers, especially of the digestive tract. Fish fillets, shrimp, scallops, and other seafood are all good choices.*

# Spicy Garlic Shrimp

This shrimp sizzles with the flavors of garlic and hot red-pepper flakes. I like to serve it over angel hair pasta or thin spaghetti. I reduced the calories, fat, and cholesterol by:

Nutrition Scorecard

| | before | after |
|---|---|---|
| (per serving) | | |
| Calories | 318 | 178 |
| Fat (g) | 17 | 7 |

*Photo on page 119*

❖ *Reducing the amount of olive oil and adding fat-free chicken broth*

❖ *Reducing the amount of wine*

❖ *Adding a small amount of cornstarch instead of oil so that the sauce clings to the shrimp*

|   |   |
|---|---|
| 4 | garlic cloves, minced |
| 3 | tablespoons white wine or nonalcoholic white wine |
| 2 | tablespoons fat-free chicken broth |
| 4 | teaspoons olive oil |
| ½ | teaspoon salt |
| ½ | teaspoon crushed red-pepper flakes |
| 1 | pound frozen peeled and deveined medium-large shrimp, thawed |
| 1 | red bell pepper, cut into thin strips |
| 1 | teaspoon cornstarch |

In a medium bowl, combine the garlic, wine, broth, oil, salt, and red-pepper flakes. Add the shrimp and toss to coat. Set aside to marinate for 5 minutes.

Coat a large nonstick skillet with nonstick spray and warm over medium-high heat. Add the bell pepper and cook for 1 minute to soften slightly. Add the shrimp and all but 1 tablespoon of the marinade. Cook for 2 minutes, or until the shrimp turn pink on the bottom. Turn the shrimp over and cook for 1 to 2 minutes longer, or until the shrimp are opaque.

In a cup, dissolve the cornstarch in the remaining 1 tablespoon marinade. Push the shrimp to the side of the pan and stir the cornstarch into the sauce in the center of the pan. Cook for 1 minute, or until the sauce is slightly thickened. Mix with the shrimp and serve immediately.

### Makes 4 servings

*Per serving: 178 calories, 23 g protein, 4 g carbohydrates, 7 g fat, 1 g saturated fat, 173 mg cholesterol, 200 mg sodium, 0 g fiber*

# Scallops in Swiss Cheese Sauce

To catch the sauce, serve this dish over a quick-cooking pasta, such as angel hair. Calories, fat, and cholesterol were reduced by:

❖ *Replacing the butter with olive oil, and using less of it*
❖ *Replacing the heavy cream with a mixture of fat-free evaporated milk and fat-free chicken broth*
❖ *Using reduced-fat Swiss cheese*

## SCALLOPS

| | |
|---|---|
| 1 | tablespoon olive oil |
| 3 | garlic cloves |
| 2 | tablespoons chopped fresh chives |
| 1½ | pounds large sea scallops |

## SAUCE

| | |
|---|---|
| ¼ | cup fat-free evaporated milk |
| ¼ | cup white wine or nonalcoholic white wine |
| ¼ | cup fat-free chicken broth |
| ¼ | teaspoon salt |
| 2 | teaspoons cornstarch |
| ½ | cup finely shredded reduced-fat Swiss cheese (2 ounces) |

TO MAKE THE SCALLOPS: Coat a large nonstick skillet with nonstick spray and warm over medium-high heat. Combine the oil, garlic, and chives in the skillet and cook, stirring, for 1 minute. Add the scallops and cook, turning occasionally, for 3 to 4 minutes, or until the scallops are opaque. Transfer to a warm serving dish.

TO MAKE THE SAUCE: In a medium saucepan over medium heat, combine the milk, wine, 3 tablespoons of the broth, and the salt. Cook, stirring, for 2 minutes, or until heated through.

In a small dish, combine the cornstarch and the remaining 1 tablespoon broth. Stir into the milk mixture and cook, stirring, for 1 minute, or until bubbly. Cook for 1 minute longer. Remove from the heat, add the cheese, and stir until the cheese is melted. Pour over the scallops and serve immediately.

**Makes 4 servings**

*Per serving: 238 calories, 34 g protein, 9 g carbohydrates, 6 g fat, 1 g saturated fat, 62 mg cholesterol, 526 mg sodium, 0 g fiber*

# Broiled Breaded Scallops

These skewered scallops are a hit every time. Large sea scallops are easier to find than smaller bay scallops, and they taste wonderful prepared this way. I reduced the calories, fat, and cholesterol by:

❖ *Eliminating the butter*
❖ *Reducing the amount of bread crumbs*

*Photo on page 123*

| | |
|---|---|
| 1 | pound large sea scallops |
| 3 | tablespoons fat-free milk |
| 2 | garlic cloves, minced |
| ⅓ | cup seasoned dry bread crumbs |
| ⅓ | cup freshly grated Parmesan cheese (1½ ounces) |
| 2 | tablespoons finely chopped flat-leaf parsley |

Coat the broiler pan with nonstick spray. Preheat the broiler.

If the scallops are larger than 1", slice them in half crosswise. Thread onto 4 thin metal skewers.

In a shallow bowl, combine the milk and garlic. In another shallow bowl, combine the bread crumbs, cheese, and parsley.

Carefully roll a skewer of scallops in the milk mixture, turning to coat all sides. Then roll in the bread crumb mixture, turning to coat all sides. Lay the skewer on the prepared broiler pan and repeat with the remaining 3 skewers.

Broil, turning once, for 3 to 5 minutes, or until opaque.

**Makes 4 servings**

*Per serving: 178 calories, 24 g protein, 11 g carbohydrates, 3 g fat, 2 g saturated fat, 44 mg cholesterol, 594 mg sodium, 0 g fiber*

# Creamed Tuna on Toast

This dish was a childhood favorite that my family ate at least once a week. I serve it to my own family today, but with some healthful modifications. To save time, I toast the almonds at the same time as I toast the English muffin halves. Calories, fat, and cholesterol were reduced by:

❖ *Replacing the whole milk with 1% milk*
❖ *Using fat-free sour cream instead of full-fat sour cream*
❖ *Using water-packed tuna instead of oil-packed tuna*
❖ *Slightly reducing the amount of almonds and toasting them for more flavor*

> 4 whole wheat English muffins, split
>
> 2 tablespoons sliced almonds
>
> $\frac{1}{4}$ cup chopped fresh chives
>
> $1\frac{1}{3}$ cups 1% milk
>
> 3 tablespoons white wine or nonalcoholic white wine
>
> 5 teaspoons cornstarch
>
> 1 can white tuna packed in water ($9\frac{1}{4}$ ounces), drained and flaked
>
> $\frac{1}{2}$ cup fat-free sour cream (without gelatin), 4 ounces

Preheat the broiler.

Arrange the muffin halves, cut side up, on a baking sheet. Sprinkle the almonds around the muffins. Broil for 1 to 2 minutes, or until the muffins are lightly browned and the nuts are golden and fragrant. Remove from the broiler.

Coat a medium saucepan with nonstick spray and warm over medium-high heat. Add the chives and cook, stirring, for 1 minute. Stir in the milk.

In a small dish, combine the wine and cornstarch until smooth. Add to the milk mixture and cook, stirring, for 2 minutes, or until bubbly. Add the tuna and sour cream. Cook, stirring, for 2 minutes, or until heated through, taking care not to boil. Serve over the muffin halves. Sprinkle with the almonds.

## Makes 4 servings

*Per serving: 327 calories, 28 g protein, 38 g carbohydrates, 6 g fat, 1 g saturated fat, 31 mg cholesterol, 536 mg sodium, 3 g fiber*

# Relax while It Cooks

My family starts to tease me the moment they see a raindrop. They know that whenever it rains, I make a big pot of hearty soup for dinner. I love making soup because you can just throw all the ingredients in a pot and relax while it simmers.

This chapter includes all my favorite soup recipes, one fabulous stew, and a few other dishes that cook unattended. A couple of recipes call for a slow cooker, which is a mighty handy appliance when you're busy doing other things (and who isn't these days!). I also like to use a handheld immersion blender for creamy soups—it beats having to wash a food processor or blender. Not everyone has these gadgets, so I give alternate instructions in the recipes for pureeing soups using food processors or blenders and cooking casseroles in the oven instead of in a slow cooker.

A couple of nutrition notes: First, these soups have stellar nutrition profiles. Butternut Bisque and Gingered Carrot Soup are packed with vitamin A. And the bean-based recipes, like Chili with Cornbread Dumplings and Senate Bean Soup, are loaded with heart-smart fiber. Second, you'll see that I frequently use 1% milk in cream-style soups. With only 2.5 grams of fat per cup, this low-fat milk is a nutrition bargain. The advantage of 1% milk over fat-free for cooking is that it has more body and a solid white color. For a really creamy consistency, I combine 1% milk with fat-free evaporated milk in soups like Wild Mushroom Soup.

# Chicken-Tortilla Soup

I get rave reviews every time I make this soup, which has become a family favorite in our house. I reduced the calories, fat, and cholesterol by:

❖ *Baking the corn tortilla strips instead of frying them*
❖ *Using reduced-fat cheese, and less of it*
❖ *Eliminating the oil for cooking the vegetables*

*Photo on page 124*

|     |     |
|----:|-----|
| 6 | corn tortillas (6" diameter) |
| ¾ | pound boneless, skinless chicken breast, cut into thin strips |
| 1 | green bell pepper, chopped |
| 1 | red bell pepper, chopped |
| 3 | carrots, chopped |
| 1 | small onion, chopped |
| 2 | garlic cloves, chopped |
| 6 | cups fat-free chicken broth |
| 1 | package frozen corn kernels (10 ounces) |
| 1½ | teaspoons ground cumin |
| 3 | large tomatoes, chopped |
| 6 | tablespoons shredded reduced-fat Cheddar cheese (1½ ounces) |

Preheat the oven to 375°F. Coat a baking sheet with nonstick spray.

Cut the tortillas in half and then into short ½" strips. Lay the strips in a single layer on the prepared baking sheet. Coat with nonstick spray (this will help them to crisp) and bake for 10 minutes, or until golden brown. Set aside to cool.

Coat a 4-quart pot with nonstick spray and warm over medium-low heat. Add the chicken, peppers, carrots, onion, and garlic. Cook, stirring occasionally, for 4 minutes, or until the chicken is no longer pink. Add the broth, corn, and cumin. Bring to a boil over high heat. Reduce the heat to low and cook for 30 minutes to blend the flavors.

Divide the tomatoes among 6 soup bowls. Scatter half of the tortilla strips on top of the tomatoes. Ladle the soup into the bowls and top with the remaining tortilla strips and cheese.

**Makes 6 servings**

*Per serving: 275 calories, 27 g protein, 34 g carbohydrates, 4 g fat, 2 g saturated fat, 44 mg cholesterol, 556 mg sodium, 5 g fiber*

# Hominy Soup

This simple soup, which is also called *posole* (poh-SOH-leh), has a rich tradition in my family. My mother made it in vats for special occasions and always for my sister Elaine's birthday. This slimmed-down version passed muster with my mother. I cut the calories, fat, cholesterol, and sodium by:

❖ *Using chicken instead of pork and beef*
❖ *Using reduced-sodium chicken broth*
❖ *Eliminating oil for cooking the vegetables*

|   |   |
|---|---|
| 1 | pound boneless, skinless chicken breasts |
| 1 | onion, chopped |
| 1 | red bell pepper, chopped |
| 4 | garlic cloves, minced |
| 4 | cups reduced-sodium chicken broth |
| 1 | can red enchilada sauce (10 ounces) |
| 2 | cans white hominy (15 ounces each), drained |
| 1 | tomato, chopped |
| ½ | teaspoon dried oregano |
| ½ | cup chopped fresh chives (optional) |
| ½ | cup chopped fresh cilantro (optional) |
| 1 | tablespoon chopped fresh oregano (optional) |

Coat a 4-quart pot with nonstick spray and warm over medium-high heat. Add the chicken to the pot and cook for 3 to 4 minutes on each side. Remove the chicken and set aside.

Add the onion, pepper, and garlic to the pot and cook, stirring occasionally, for 5 to 6 minutes, or until tender.

Meanwhile, cut the chicken into bite-size pieces. Add the chicken, broth, enchilada sauce, hominy, tomato, and dried oregano to the pot. Bring to a boil over high heat. Reduce the heat to medium, cover, and simmer for 30 minutes to blend the flavors. Ladle the soup into bowls to serve. Place the chives, cilantro, and fresh oregano in small bowls and serve alongside the soup as garnishes, if using.

### Makes 6 servings

*Per serving: 234 calories, 22 g protein, 27 g carbohydrates, 4 g fat, 1 g saturated fat, 47 mg cholesterol, 674 mg sodium, 6 g fiber*

*Homestyle Hint:* Hominy is simply dried corn kernels without the hull or germ. In the supermarket, look for it in cans near the other canned vegetables or in the international aisle.

# Matzo Ball Soup

I'll never forget my first experience with this soup. My family loved it, but about an hour after we had eaten, our stomachs were uncomfortably full. I quickly realized this was because I had been in a hurry and had not let the matzo balls fully cook. Now, I always let the matzo balls simmer for at least 15 minutes before serving. The calories, fat, cholesterol, and sodium were reduced by:

❖ Using egg whites instead of whole eggs
❖ Using fat-free vegetable broth
❖ Reducing the amount of salt

## MATZO BALLS

| | |
| --- | --- |
| 7 | large egg whites |
| ¾ | cup 2% buttermilk |
| 1 | tablespoon vegetable oil |
| ½ | teaspoon salt |
| ½ | teaspoon ground black pepper |
| 1¼ | cups matzo meal |
| ¼ | teaspoon baking powder |

## SOUP

| | |
| --- | --- |
| 1 | onion, chopped |
| 2 | celery ribs, chopped |
| 4 | ounces mushrooms, sliced |
| 2 | parsnips, peeled and chopped |
| 1 | large carrot, chopped |
| 4 | cups fat-free vegetable broth |
| 4 | cups water |
| 2 | tablespoons chopped flat-leaf parsley |

TO MAKE THE MATZO BALLS: In a medium bowl, whisk together the egg whites, buttermilk, oil, salt, and pepper. Whisk in the matzo meal and baking powder. Cover and chill for at least 1 hour or overnight.

TO MAKE THE SOUP: Generously coat a 4-quart pot with nonstick spray and warm over medium heat. Add the onion and celery and cook for 4 minutes, or until soft. Add the mushrooms and cook for 5 minutes. Add the parsnips, carrot, broth, and water. Bring to a boil over medium-high heat. Reduce the heat to medium-low, cover, and cook for 15 to 20 minutes, or until the parsnips are almost tender.

Dampen your palms and gently roll the chilled matzo dough by rounded teaspoonfuls between your palms into 42 balls. Drop into the simmering broth as you work. Cover and simmer briskly for 15 minutes. (Do not lift the lid; the broth must remain at a rapid simmer to allow the matzo balls to expand properly). Ladle the soup into bowls and garnish with the parsley.

**Makes 6 servings**

*Per serving: 205 calories, 10 g protein, 34 g carbohydrates, 4 g fat, 0.5 g saturated fat, 1 mg cholesterol, 962 mg sodium, 2 g fiber*

# Pumpkin Soup
# with Apple Croutons

Crispy brown-sugared apple croutons make this soup special. Plus, one serving provides more than twice your vitamin A needs for the day. Calories, fat, and cholesterol were reduced by:

*Photo on page 126*

❖ *Eliminating the oil for cooking the vegetables*
❖ *Using 1% milk instead of heavy cream*
❖ *Using fat-free chicken broth*
❖ *Reducing the amount of sugar for the apple croutons*

## CROUTONS

1   apple, peeled and cored
3   tablespoons brown sugar

## SOUP

1   small onion, chopped
1   celery rib, chopped
1   carrot, chopped
3½  cups fat-free chicken broth
2   cups canned plain pumpkin puree
2   tablespoons maple syrup
½   teaspoon ground cinnamon
¼   teaspoon ground nutmeg
¾   cup 1% milk

TO MAKE THE CROUTONS: Preheat the oven to 300°F. Coat a baking sheet with nonstick spray.

Cut the apple in half lengthwise (from stem-end to blossom-end). Slice the apple crosswise into paper-thin half-moon slices using the 2"-wide slot on a handheld grater, a food processor fitted with a 2-millimeter slicing disk, or a very sharp knife and a steady hand.

Spread the apple slices in a single layer on the prepared baking sheet and sprinkle evenly with the brown sugar. Bake in the middle of the oven for 30 to 35 minutes, or until crisp and golden. Transfer immediately to a rack to cool.

TO MAKE THE SOUP: Coat a 4-quart pot with nonstick spray and warm over medium-high heat. Add the onion, celery, and carrot to the pot and cook, stirring occasionally, for

10 to 15 minutes, or until tender. Stir in the broth, pumpkin puree, maple syrup, cinnamon, and nutmeg and bring to a boil. Reduce the heat to medium, cover, and simmer for 30 minutes.

Puree the soup in a food processor or blender, working in batches if necessary. Return to the pot and stir in the milk. Simmer, uncovered, for 5 minutes, or until heated through. Ladle the soup into bowls and serve. Garnish with the apple croutons.

**Makes 4 servings**

*Per serving: 167 calories, 8 g protein, 34 g carbohydrates, 1 g fat, 0.5 g saturated fat, 2 mg cholesterol, 341 mg sodium, 7 g fiber*

*Homestyle Hints:* Take care to buy plain pumpkin puree, not spiced puree that may be labeled "pie filling."

To make the apple croutons, I like to use tart apples such as Granny Smith. But just about any baking apple will do.

## Be a Pumpkin Eater

*Pumpkin is a significant source of beta-carotene. Just 2 tablespoons of canned pumpkin provide more than half of your vitamin A needs for the day. Try pumpkin any time of year—not just around the holidays.*

# Butternut Bisque

I can think of no better way to enjoy butternut squash than this soup. Fresh orange peel and bits of apple lend a bright, fresh flavor. Calories, fat, and cholesterol were reduced by:

❖ *Eliminating the butter for cooking the vegetables*
❖ *Using 1% milk instead of whole milk*

|  |  |
|---|---|
| 2 | onions, chopped |
| 1 | large butternut squash (about 3 pounds), peeled |
| 1 | apple, peeled and chopped |
| 3 | cups fat-free chicken broth |
| 2 | teaspoons brown sugar |
| 1½ | teaspoons curry powder |
| ½ | teaspoon salt |
| ⅛ | teaspoon ground nutmeg |
| 1 | orange |
| ½ | cup 1% milk |
| ¼ | cup low-fat sour cream (2 ounces), optional |

Coat a 4-quart pot with nonstick spray and warm over medium-high heat. Add the onions to the pot and cook, stirring occasionally, for 5 minutes, or until tender. Cut the squash into small pieces, discarding the seeds and strings. Add the squash, apple, broth, brown sugar, curry powder, salt, and nutmeg to the pot.

Finely grate the orange peel and add to the soup. Squeeze the orange juice into the soup. Bring to a boil. Reduce the heat to medium, cover, and cook for 30 minutes, or until the squash is tender.

Puree the soup in batches in a blender or food processor. Return the soup to the pot. Stir in the milk and heat through. Ladle the soup into 6 bowls. Swirl 2 teaspoons sour cream into each bowl, if using.

### Makes 6 servings

Per serving: 77 calories, 4 g protein, 16 g carbohydrates, 1 g fat, 0.5 g saturated fat, 1 mg cholesterol, 272 mg sodium, 3 g fiber

*Homestyle Hints:* I like to use a tart apple, such as Granny Smith, for this soup.

An easy way to puree the soup in the pot is to use an immersion blender, mixing until the soup is smooth.

# Red-Pepper Bisque

This creamy, colorful soup supplies nearly three-fourths of your vitamin C needs for the day. Calories, fat, and cholesterol were reduced by:

♦ *Eliminating the butter for cooking the vegetables*
♦ *Using a combination of fat-free evaporated milk and 1% milk in place of heavy cream*
♦ *Using fat-free chicken broth*

| | |
|---|---|
| 4 | red bell peppers, chopped |
| 2 | leeks, white part only, chopped |
| 1 | onion, chopped |
| 2 | cups fat-free chicken broth |
| ½ | teaspoon salt |
| ½ | cup fat-free evaporated milk |
| 1 | cup 1% milk |
| ¼ | cup low-fat sour cream (2 ounces), optional |
| 3 | tablespoons chopped fresh basil |

Coat a 4-quart pot with nonstick spray and warm over medium-high heat. Add the peppers, leeks, and onion to the pot and cook, stirring occasionally, for 10 minutes, or until tender. Add the broth and salt. Bring to a boil over high heat. Reduce the heat to medium, cover, and simmer for 30 minutes to blend the flavors.

Puree the soup in batches in a food processor or blender. Return to the pot. Stir in the evaporated milk and 1% milk and cook for 2 minutes, or until heated through. Ladle the soup into 6 bowls. Swirl 2 teaspoons of the sour cream into each bowl, if using. Sprinkle with the basil.

### Makes 6 servings

*Per serving: 91 calories, 5 g protein, 15 g carbohydrates, 2 g fat, 0.5 g saturated fat, 2 mg cholesterol, 568 mg sodium, 3 g fiber*

*Homestyle Hint:* To clean leeks, trim off the white roots and dark green tops. Slice the leeks from top to bottom and rinse under running water to remove any grit between the leaf layers.

# Wild Mushroom Soup

Wild mushrooms impart a rich, earthy flavor to this soup. Any kind will do—try shiitakes, morels, chanterelles, or oyster mushrooms. Use all one kind or mix a few together. You can also use the standard variety of white button mushrooms in a pinch. Note that just a small amount of light butter does wonders for the flavor of this soup. Calories, fat, and cholesterol were reduced by:

❖ *Replacing heavy cream with a combination of fat-free evaporated milk and 1% milk*

❖ *Using light butter instead of regular butter, and much less of it*

❖ *Using cornstarch instead of flour for thickening*

| | |
|---|---|
| 12 | ounces wild mushrooms |
| 2 | tablespoons light butter |
| 1 | onion, chopped |
| 2 | shallots, chopped |
| 2 | cans beef broth (13 ounces each) |
| ¼ | cup fat-free evaporated milk |
| ¼ | cup 1% milk |
| 2 | teaspoons cornstarch |

Cut half of the mushrooms into thin slices. Finely chop the remaining mushrooms.

In a 4-quart pot, melt the butter over medium-high heat and add the onion and shallots. Stir in the sliced and chopped mushrooms and cook, stirring gently, for 2 to 4 minutes, or until tender. Stir in the broth, evaporated milk, and all but 1 tablespoon of the 1% milk.

In a cup, dissolve the cornstarch in the remaining 1 tablespoon milk. Add to the soup. Reduce the heat to medium and cook, stirring, or until bubbly. Cook for 1 minute longer. Ladle into bowls and serve.

## Makes 6 servings

*Per serving: 68 calories, 5 g protein, 8 g carbohydrates, 2 g fat, 0.5 g saturated fat, 6 mg cholesterol, 228 mg sodium, 1 g fiber*

# Gingered Carrot Soup

My daughter Krystin, who is not crazy about vegetables, loves this soup with its slightly sweet flavor offset by the fresh ginger. The carrots provide more than three times the daily vitamin A requirement. Calories, fat, and cholesterol were reduced by:

❖ *Eliminating the butter for cooking the vegetables*
❖ *Using 1% milk instead of heavy cream*
❖ *Using cornstarch instead of flour for thickening*

|   |   |
| --- | --- |
| 1 | large onion, chopped |
| ¼ | cup peeled and grated or minced fresh ginger |
| 4 | cups fat-free chicken broth |
| 2 | cups water |
| 10 | carrots, sliced |
| 1 | teaspoon sugar |
| ¾ | teaspoon dried thyme |
| ½ | teaspoon ground cinnamon |
| 1½ | cups 1% milk |
| 2 | tablespoons cornstarch |

Coat a 4-quart pot with nonstick spray and warm over medium-high heat. Add the onion and ginger to the pot and cook, stirring, for 5 minutes, or until tender. Add the broth, water, carrots, sugar, thyme, and cinnamon. Bring to a boil. Reduce the heat to medium, cover, and simmer for 30 minutes to blend the flavors.

Puree the soup in batches in a food processor or blender. Return to the pot. Stir in all but 2 tablespoons of the 1% milk.

In a cup, dissolve the cornstarch in the remaining 2 tablespoons milk. Add to the soup. Cook, stirring, for 1 minute, or until bubbly. Cook for 1 minute longer. Ladle into bowls and serve.

### Makes 6 servings

*Per serving: 121 calories, 5 g protein, 21 g carbohydrates, 3 g fat, 1 g saturated fat, 2 mg cholesterol, 741 mg sodium, 4 g fiber*

*Homestyle Hint:* The easiest way to prepare fresh ginger is to peel it with a paring knife or the edge of a spoon, then finely grate it on a handheld grater. To get ¼ cup minced or grated ginger, you'll need a piece of ginger that's 4" to 5" long.

# Mulligatawny Soup

This Indian-inspired soup gets its unique flavor from a combination of curry powder and cloves. Calories, fat, and cholesterol were reduced by:

❖ *Eliminating the butter for cooking the vegetables*
❖ *Using cornstarch instead of flour for thickening*
❖ *Using fat-free chicken broth*

| | |
|---|---|
| 1 | onion, chopped |
| 1 | carrot, chopped |
| 1 | green bell pepper, chopped |
| 1 | celery rib, chopped |
| 1 | apple, peeled, cored, and chopped |
| 1 | can diced tomatoes (15 ounces) |
| 1 | cup chopped cooked chicken breast |
| 2 | tablespoons chopped flat-leaf parsley |
| 1 | teaspoon curry powder |
| 2 | whole cloves |
| ⅛ | teaspoon ground nutmeg |
| 3 | cups fat-free chicken broth |
| 2 | tablespoons cornstarch |

Coat a large saucepan with nonstick spray and warm over medium-high heat. Add the onion, carrot, pepper, celery, and apple to the pot and cook, stirring, for 5 minutes, or until tender.

Add the tomatoes (with juice), chicken, parsley, curry powder, cloves, and nutmeg. Add all but 2 tablespoons of the broth. Cook for 30 minutes, or until the flavors are blended.

In a cup, dissolve the cornstarch in the remaining 2 tablespoons broth. Add to the soup. Reduce the heat to medium and cook, stirring, for 1 minute, or until bubbly. Cook for 1 minute longer. Ladle into bowls and serve.

### Makes 4 servings

*Per serving: 143 calories, 16 g protein, 16 g carbohydrates, 2 g fat, 0.5 g saturated fat, 30 mg cholesterol, 480 mg sodium, 3 g fiber*

*Homestyle Hint:* I like to use a tart apple, such as Granny Smith, for this soup.

# Senate Bean Soup

This traditional soup has been on the lunch menu every day on Capitol Hill in both the House and Senate restaurants. My version is healthier than the one served to our Congress. Take a look at the fiber value—18 grams in one serving is nearly 75% of what we need every day. I reduced the calories, fat, cholesterol, and sodium by:

### Nutrition Scorecard
*(per serving)*

|  | before | after |
|---|---|---|
| Calories | 287 | 164 |
| Fat (g) | 10 | 2 |

* ❖ *Replacing ham hocks with diced turkey ham*
* ❖ *Eliminating the butter for cooking the vegetables*
* ❖ *Reducing the amount of salt*

| | |
|---|---|
| 1 | teaspoon olive oil |
| 1 | large onion, chopped |
| 1 | pound dried navy beans, rinsed and sorted |
| 10 | cups water |
| ½ | pound bulk turkey ham (not slices), chopped |
| 1½ | teaspoons salt |
| ½ | teaspoon ground black pepper |

Warm the oil in a 4-quart pot over medium heat. Add the onion to the pot and cook, stirring, for 5 minutes, or until tender. Add the beans, water, and turkey ham. Bring to a boil over high heat. Reduce the heat to medium, cover, and simmer for 1½ to 2 hours, or until the beans are tender. Add the salt and pepper.

Using a potato masher, mash some the beans in the soup. The soup will be lumpy. Ladle into bowls and serve.

## Makes 8 servings

*Per serving: 164 calories, 17 g protein, 35 g carbohydrates, 2 g fat, 1 g saturated fat, 16 mg cholesterol, 683 mg sodium, 18 g fiber*

## *Water: The Forgotten Nutrient*

It has no color and not much flavor, but water is an essential nutrient. The average sedentary adult needs at least 8 to 12 cups of water a day, in the form of noncaffeinated, nonalcoholic beverages, soups, and other foods like fruits and vegetables. Enjoying homemade soup is a great way to meet your water needs.

# Roasted Garlic–Potato Soup

I remember when I was intimidated by the thought of roasting garlic. I have since found that it's incredibly easy, not to mention savory. Don't be alarmed by the amount of garlic used in this soup; roasting mellows the flavor considerably. Calories, fat, cholesterol, and sodium were reduced by:

| *Nutrition Scorecard* | | |
|---|---|---|
| (per serving) | | |
| | before | after |
| Calories | 308 | 187 |
| Fat (g) | 19 | 1 |

* *Replacing some of the olive oil with chicken broth for roasting the garlic*
* *Using a combination of 1% milk and fat-free evaporated milk in place of cream*
* *Reducing the amount of salt*

## ROASTED GARLIC

1   whole head garlic

1   tablespoon fat-free chicken broth

½   teaspoon olive oil

## SOUP

2   onions, chopped

4   potatoes, peeled and finely chopped

3   cups fat-free chicken broth

2   cups water

½   cup fat-free evaporated milk

½   cup 1% milk

¾   teaspoon salt

1   tablespoon chopped flat-leaf parsley

TO MAKE THE ROASTED GARLIC: Preheat the oven to 375°F.

Cut ¼" off the top of the head of garlic, exposing but not separating the individual cloves. Spoon the broth into a small baking dish. Add the garlic head, root end down. Drizzle the oil over the exposed cloves. Cover tightly with foil and roast for 20 minutes. Remove the foil and roast for 5 to 10 minutes longer, or until the cloves soften. Set aside to cool. When cool enough to handle, use a wooden pick or fork tine to remove the individual garlic cloves to a plate. Remove and discard the skins.

TO MAKE THE SOUP: Coat a 4-quart pot with nonstick spray and warm over medium-high heat. Add the onions to the pot and cook, stirring, for 5 minutes, or until golden brown and tender.

Add the potatoes, roasted garlic, broth, and water. Bring to a boil over high heat. Reduce the heat to low, cover, and simmer for 10 minutes, or until the potatoes are tender.

Puree the soup in batches in a food processor or blender. Return to the pot. Stir in the evaporated milk, 1% milk, and salt. Cook for 2 minutes, or until heated through. Ladle the soup into bowls and garnish with the parsley.

**Makes 4 servings**

*Per serving: 187 calories, 10 g protein, 35 g carbohydrates, 1 g fat, 0.5 g saturated fat, 2 mg cholesterol, 716 mg sodium, 3 g fiber*

## The Chicken Soup Rx

*It looks like Mom was right. Chicken soup has long been a popular remedy for colds, and there may be a scientific explanation for it. Researchers found that eating hot chicken soup helps clear the nasal passageways primarily because of the water vapor inhaled while slurping the soup. The researchers also found that chicken soup possesses an additional substance (an aroma or taste mechanism factor) that helps clear nasal passages.*

# Potato-Bacon Clam Chowder

You will find that this chowder is extremely thick, thanks, in part, to my father. He takes his clam chowder very seriously. When I was growing up, we would drive for miles to a restaurant on the ocean pier just for a bowl of thick clam chowder. To this day, my dad still likes his chowder thick, and so do I. You can always thin the soup to the consistency that you prefer, however, by adding a little bit of milk. You'll be surprised how just a little bacon adds big flavor. Calories, fat, and cholesterol were reduced by:

❖ *Reducing the amount of bacon*
❖ *Using 1% milk instead of heavy cream*
❖ *Using a combination of 1% milk and cornstarch instead of heavy cream*

| Nutrition Scorecard | | |
| --- | --- | --- |
| *(per serving)* | before | after |
| Calories | 312 | 274 |
| Fat (g) | 8 | 3 |

*Photo on page 129*

| | |
| --- | --- |
| 2 | slices bacon |
| 2 | onions, chopped |
| 4 | potatoes, peeled and chopped |
| 3 | cans minced clams (6½ ounces each) |
| ¼ | teaspoon ground black pepper |
| 2 | cups 1% milk |
| 2 | tablespoons cornstarch |

Warm a large saucepan over medium-high heat. Add the bacon and cook for 5 minutes, or until crisp. Drain on paper towels, leaving the drippings in the pan. When cool, crumble and set aside.

Using the same saucepan, cook the onions in the bacon drippings, stirring, for 5 minutes, or until tender. Add the potatoes, clams (with juice), and pepper. Bring to a boil. Reduce the heat to medium, cover, and simmer, stirring occasionally, for 10 to 15 minutes, or until the potatoes are tender. Pour all but 2 tablespoons of the milk into the pan.

In a cup, dissolve the cornstarch in the remaining 2 tablespoons milk. Add to the soup. Cook, stirring, or until bubbly. Cook for 1 minute longer. Ladle the soup into bowls and sprinkle with the bacon.

## Makes 4 servings

*Per serving: 274 calories, 17 g protein, 45 g carbohydrates, 3 g fat, 1 g saturated fat, 31 mg cholesterol, 696 mg sodium, 3 g fiber*

# Parmesan-Corn Chowder

Here's a hearty chowder that pairs nicely with a tossed green salad and a crusty roll. The tang of the cheese blends well with the sweetness of the corn. I reduced calories, fat, and cholesterol by:

❖ *Using 1% milk instead of whole milk*
❖ *Using cornstarch as a thickener rather than butter and flour*
❖ *Using fat-free chicken broth*

|   |   |
|---|---|
| 2 | cups fat-free chicken broth |
| 2 | potatoes, peeled and chopped |
| 1 | carrot, chopped |
| 1 | celery rib, chopped |
| 1 | small onion, chopped |
| ¼ | teaspoon ground black pepper |
| 1 | ear corn, shucked |
| 1 | can cream-style corn (17 ounces) |
| 2 | cups 1% milk |
| 2 | tablespoons cornstarch |
| 1 | cup freshly grated Parmesan cheese (4 ounces) |

In a 4-quart pot, combine the broth, potatoes, carrot, celery, onion, and pepper. Bring to a boil over medium-high heat. Reduce the heat to medium, cover, and simmer for 10 minutes, or until the vegetables are tender.

Slice the corn kernels off the cob. Add to the soup along with the cream-style corn. Pour all but 2 tablespoons of the milk into the corn mixture.

In a cup, dissolve the cornstarch in the remaining 2 tablespoons milk. Add to the soup. Cook, stirring, for 1 minute, or until bubbly. Cook for 1 minute longer. Add the cheese and stir until melted. Ladle into bowls and serve.

**Makes 6 servings**

*Per serving: 251 calories, 12 g protein, 35 g carbohydrates, 6 g fat, 4 g saturated fat, 35 mg cholesterol, 744 mg sodium, 3 g fiber*

# Chili with Cornbread Dumplings

This hearty, satisfying meal is packed with fiber, thanks to the kidney beans. One serving provides more than two-thirds of the recommended fiber requirement for a day. Calories, fat, and cholesterol were reduced by:

*Photo on page 127*

❖ *Replacing ground beef with ground turkey breast, and using less of it*
❖ *Adding more kidney beans to make up for less meat*
❖ *Using nonstick spray instead of oil*
❖ *Using a reduced-fat biscuit mix for the dumplings*

## CHILI

1 pound ground turkey breast
2 onions, chopped
3 garlic cloves, minced
1½ tablespoons chili powder
1 teaspoon ground cumin
¼ teaspoon ground red pepper
1 can chopped tomatoes (28 ounces)
3 cans reduced-sodium kidney beans (15 ounces each), rinsed and drained
1 can tomato sauce (8 ounces)
1 can diced green chile peppers (4 ounces)

## DUMPLINGS

1⅓ cups reduced-fat biscuit mix
⅓ cup cornmeal
¼ cup shredded reduced-fat Cheddar cheese (1 ounce)
¼ teaspoon ground cumin
¼ teaspoon chili powder
⅓ cup fat-free milk
¼ cup corn kernels
Paprika

TO MAKE THE CHILI: Coat a 4-quart pot with nonstick spray and warm over medium-high heat. Add the turkey to the pot and cook, stirring to break up the meat, for 5 minutes, or until crumbly and brown. Add the onions and garlic. Cook, stirring, for 5 minutes, or until the onion is soft. Add the chili powder, cumin, and red pepper. Stir in the tomatoes (with juice), beans, tomato sauce, and chile peppers (with juice). Bring to a boil. Reduce the heat to medium-low, cover, and simmer.

TO MAKE THE DUMPLINGS: Meanwhile, in large bowl, stir together the biscuit mix, cornmeal, cheese, cumin, and chili powder.

In a 1-cup measure, combine the milk and corn. Pour into the cornmeal mixture and mix just until moistened.

Drop the dumpling mixture by heaping tablespoons onto the chili, covering the surface but with a little chili showing between the dumplings. Sprinkle with paprika. Cover and simmer gently for 30 minutes, or until a wooden pick inserted in a dumpling comes out clean. Spoon into bowls and serve.

**Makes 6 servings**

*Per serving: 472 calories, 37 g protein, 73 g carbohydrates, 5 g fat, 1 g saturated fat, 38 mg cholesterol, 831 mg sodium, 18 g fiber*

## Tomato Power

*One of America's favorite vegetables may help prevent cancer. A Harvard University study involving nearly 50,000 men found that eating 10 or more servings a week of tomato products was associated with as much as a 34 percent reduced risk of prostate cancer. Tomatoes are a rich source of lycopene, a phytochemical that appears be a potent cancer inhibitor, not only for prostate cancer but for other cancers as well.*

# Sweet-and-Sour Stew

Ooh, this is so good. I reduced calories, fat, cholesterol, and sodium by:

❖ *Using a leaner cut of beef, and less of it*
❖ *Adding more vegetables to compensate for less meat*
❖ *Eliminating the oil for cooking the meat*
❖ *Reducing the amount of salt*

*Photo on page 125*

| | |
|---|---|
| 3 | tablespoons unbleached or all-purpose flour |
| ½ | teaspoon salt |
| ¾ | pound beef round pot roast, cut into ¾" pieces |
| 2½ | cups water |
| ½ | cup ketchup |
| ¼ | cup packed brown sugar |
| ¼ | cup cider vinegar |
| 1 | tablespoon Worcestershire sauce |
| 1 | large onion, chopped |
| 1 | green bell pepper, cut into ¾" pieces |
| 12 | ounces baby carrots, halved |

In a plastic bag, combine the flour and salt. Add a few pieces of meat and shake to coat. Remove the coated meat and add more, shaking to coat. Continue until all the meat is coated with flour.

Coat a large skillet with nonstick spray and warm over medium-high heat. Add the meat to the skillet and cook for 6 to 8 minutes, turning, or until browned.

In a medium bowl, mix together the water, ketchup, brown sugar, vinegar, and Worcestershire sauce. Stir into the meat. Add the onion. Bring to a boil. Reduce the heat to medium, cover, and simmer for 1 hour. Add the pepper and carrots, cover, and continue simmering, stirring occasionally, for 30 minutes longer, or until the vegetables and meat are tender.

**Makes 4 servings**

*Per serving: 321 calories, 21 g protein, 35 g carbohydrates, 11 g fat, 4 g saturated fat, 61 mg cholesterol, 738 mg sodium, 4 g fiber*

# Slow-Cooker Chicken and Stuffing

I love this meal—you toss everything into the slow cooker in the morning, and by dinnertime, you have a complete meal that's ready to eat. No fuss! If you don't have a slow cooker, see the conventional oven directions in the hint below. Calories, fat, and cholesterol were reduced by:

❖ *Eliminating the butter for the stuffing*
❖ *Using reduced-fat cream soup*

*Nutrition Scorecard*

| | before | after |
|---|---|---|
| (per serving) | | |
| Calories | 315 | 261 |
| Fat (g) | 11 | 5 |

| | |
|---|---|
| 1 | package chicken-flavored stuffing mix (6 ounces) |
| ½ | cup water |
| 2½ | cups chopped cooked chicken breast |
| 2 | medium zucchini (about 1 pound total), cut into ½" pieces |
| 8 | ounces mushrooms, sliced |
| 1 | green bell pepper, chopped |
| 1 | onion, chopped |
| 1 | can reduced-fat condensed cream of chicken soup (10¾ ounces) |

In a large bowl, toss together the stuffing mix, flavor packet (if included with the stuffing), and water. (The stuffing will not be completely moistened.) Set aside.

In another large bowl, combine the chicken, zucchini, mushrooms, pepper, and onion. Stir in the soup. Place half in the slow cooker. Top with half of the stuffing. Repeat the layers with the remaining soup and stuffing. Cover and cook on the low-heat setting for 5 to 6 hours or on the high-heat setting for 2½ to 3 hours, or until the vegetables are tender and the flavors are blended.

## Makes 6 servings

*Per serving: 261 calories, 24 g protein, 29 g carbohydrates, 5 g fat, 1 g saturated fat, 54 mg cholesterol, 771 mg sodium, 3 g fiber*

*Homestyle Hint:* To cook this dish in a conventional oven, layer the food in a 2½-quart baking dish, cover, and bake at 350°F for 1 to 1½ hours, or until the vegetables are tender.

# Cheesy Shredded Potatoes and Ham

You can find fresh shredded potatoes in the refrigerator section of the grocery store. They are a great help in recipes such as this delicious cheesy casserole. Calories, fat, and cholesterol were reduced by:

❖ *Using turkey ham instead of regular ham, and less of it*
❖ *Using a combination of reduced-fat cheese and reduced-fat cream soup instead of condensed cheese soup*
❖ *Using 1% milk instead of whole milk*

|  |  |
|---|---|
| 1½ | packages shredded potatoes (24 ounces) |
| 6 | ounces bulk turkey ham (not slices), chopped |
| 1 | jar pimientos (2 ounces), drained |
| 1 | tablespoon chopped flat-leaf parsley |
| ¼ | teaspoon ground black pepper |
| 1 | can reduced-fat cream of chicken soup (10¾ ounces) |
| 1 | cup shredded reduced-fat Cheddar cheese (4 ounces) |
| ¾ | cup 1% milk |

In a slow cooker, combine the potatoes, turkey ham, pimientos, parsley, and pepper.

In a large bowl, whisk together the soup, cheese, and milk until smooth. Pour over the potato mixture in the slow cooker, cover, and cook on the low-heat setting for 7 to 9 hours or on the high-heat setting for 3½ to 4 hours, or until the potatoes are tender and the flavors are blended. Stir before serving.

### Makes 6 servings

Per serving: 243 calories, 18 g protein, 27 g carbohydrates, 7 g fat, 4 g saturated fat, 40 mg cholesterol, 764 mg sodium, 8 g fiber

*Homestyle Hint:* If you don't have a slow cooker, put the food in a 2-quart baking dish, cover, and bake at 350°F for 1 to 1½ hours, or until the potatoes are tender.

# Homestyle Beef and Pork

**H**ere's some good news: You don't have to give up red meat to eat healthfully. The trick is to rely on the leanest cuts, serve reasonably sized portions, and present them in appealing ways.

For instance, to make a 4-ounce serving of meat look more generous and attractive, thinly slice the meat and fan it out on the plate. Likewise, pounding a lean steak to flatten it will expand its surface area and often improve its texture, too. I also like to combine small amounts of meat with other ingredients like vegetables, rice, or pasta. This works great in stir-fries, stews, and casseroles.

When buying beef, look for the word *round*. This lean cut averages about 2 grams of fat per ounce of cooked meat. I regularly use round steak, round roast, eye of round, and top round steak. As for that kitchen staple, ground beef, keep in mind that even lean ground beef is usually pretty fatty. To lower the fat, combine extra-lean ground beef with some ground turkey breast. Adding a bit of grated apple also does wonders for the texture and moisture—and it adds a pleasant flavor. I use these tricks for burgers, meatballs, meat loaves, and other ground beef dishes like Saucy Salisbury Steak.

When pork is on the menu, I stick with tenderloin. It is by far the leanest cut and is comparable to poultry in fat content. Plus, it's incredibly versatile. Pork tenderloin can be roasted whole, cut into medallions, cubed for kebabs and stews, or cut into strips for stir-fries.

# Skillet Steak with Quick Gravy

Here's a quick meal that's sure to please. Pounding the steaks stretches the meat visually, and it speeds up the cooking time. I reduced calories, fat, cholesterol, and sodium by:

- ❖ *Eliminating oil for cooking the meat*
- ❖ *Using reduced-fat cream soup*
- ❖ *Using 1% milk instead of whole milk*
- ❖ *Using fresh mushrooms instead of canned mushrooms for flavor and to reduce the sodium*

*Nutrition Scorecard*

| (per serving) | before | after |
|---|---|---|
| Calories | 573 | 258 |
| Fat (g) | 35 | 7 |

| | |
|---|---|
| 4 | round steaks (4 ounces each), trimmed of fat |
| ¼ | cup unbleached or all-purpose flour |
| 8 | ounces mushrooms, sliced |
| 1 | can reduced-fat cream of mushroom soup (10¾ ounces) |
| 1 | cup 1% milk |
| 1 | teaspoon Worcestershire sauce |
| ⅛ | teaspoon ground black pepper |

Place 1 steak in a heavy-duty plastic bag. Using a mallet or rolling pin, pound the steak from the center outward toward the edges to a thickness of ⅛". Remove the steak and repeat with remaining steaks.

Spread the flour on a plate or in a shallow dish. Dip the steaks in the flour, turning to coat.

Coat a large nonstick skillet with nonstick spray and warm over medium-high heat. Place 2 steaks in the skillet and cook for 2 to 3 minutes on each side, or until tender and no longer pink. Do not overcook. Transfer to a platter. Wipe out the skillet with a paper towel and add a little more nonstick spray. Cook the remaining 2 steaks and transfer to the platter.

Add the mushrooms to the skillet and cook, stirring, for 5 minutes, or until tender. Add the soup, milk, Worcestershire sauce, and pepper. Cook and stir for 8 to 10 minutes, or until bubbly. Pour over the steak and serve immediately.

### Makes 4 servings

*Per serving: 258 calories, 32 g protein, 16 g carbohydrates, 7 g fat, 3 g saturated fat, 80 mg cholesterol, 394 mg sodium, 2 g fiber*

# Beef Stroganoff Bake

Always a crowd pleaser. I reduced calories and fat by:

- ❖ *Using extra-lean ground beef, and less of it*
- ❖ *Adding mushrooms to compensate for less meat*
- ❖ *Using no-yolk egg noodles*
- ❖ *Using light cream cheese instead of full-fat cream cheese*
- ❖ *Using fat-free cottage cheese in place of regular*

| *Nutrition Scorecard* | | |
|---|---|---|
| (per serving) | | |
| | before | after |
| Calories | 562 | 370 |
| Fat (g) | 32 | 13 |

| | |
|---|---|
| 8 | ounces no-yolk egg noodles |
| ¾ | pound extra-lean ground beef |
| 6 | ounces ground turkey breast |
| 2 | onions, chopped |
| 2 | garlic cloves, minced |
| 8 | ounces mushrooms, sliced (2 cups) |
| ½ | teaspoon dried marjoram, crushed |
| ¼ | teaspoon dried thyme, crushed |
| 1 | can tomato sauce (8 ounces) |
| 1 | cup fat-free cottage cheese (8 ounces) |
| 4 | ounces light cream cheese (not fat-free) |
| ½ | teaspoon salt |
| ¼ | teaspoon ground black pepper |
| ½ | cup shredded reduced-fat sharp Cheddar cheese (2 ounces) |

Cook the noodles according to the package directions. Drain and set aside.

Preheat the oven to 350°F. Coat a 2½- to 3-quart baking dish with nonstick spray.

Coat a large nonstick skillet with nonstick spray and warm over medium-high heat. Add the beef, turkey, onions, and garlic. Cook, stirring, for 10 to 15 minutes, or until the meat is no longer pink and the onions are soft. Drain the fat. Add the mushrooms, marjoram, and thyme and cook for 5 minutes. Stir in the tomato sauce, cottage cheese, cream cheese, salt, and pepper. Cook and stir until the cream cheese melts. Stir in the reserved noodles.

Transfer to the prepared baking dish. Sprinkle with the Cheddar. Bake for 25 minutes, or until bubbly.

**Makes 6 servings**

*Per serving: 370 calories, 30 g protein, 34 g carbohydrates, 13 g fat, 6 g saturated fat, 62 mg cholesterol, 697 mg sodium, 2 g fiber*

# Chicken-Fried Steak Italiano

A light bread coating gives this steak the wonderful crunchy texture that you expect with chicken-fried steak—but without the usual fat. The easy Italian-style tomato sauce tops it off for a winning combination. Calories, fat, and cholesterol were reduced by:

❖ *Eliminating the olive oil in the sauce and for frying*
❖ *Using egg whites instead of a whole egg*
❖ *Using nonstick spray for pan-frying*

## SAUCE

2 garlic cloves, minced

1 can diced tomatoes (15 ounces)

1 teaspoon ground oregano

¼ teaspoon salt

¼ teaspoon ground black pepper

## BREADING

2 egg whites

2 teaspoons water

⅔ cup plain dry bread crumbs

3 tablespoons freshly grated Parmesan cheese

2 tablespoons finely chopped flat-leaf parsley

1 teaspoon dried oregano

¼ teaspoon ground red pepper

¼ teaspoon paprika

4 eye of round steaks (4 ounces each), about ¼" thick and trimmed of fat

TO MAKE THE SAUCE: Coat a medium saucepan with nonstick spray and warm over medium heat. Add the garlic and cook for 1 minute, or until fragrant. Add the tomatoes (with juice), oregano, salt, and pepper. Bring to a boil over high heat. Reduce the heat to medium and cook, stirring occasionally, for 10 minutes, or until the sauce is thick and chunky.

TO MAKE THE BREADING: Meanwhile, in a shallow bowl, beat the egg whites with the water.

In another shallow bowl, combine the bread crumbs, cheese, parsley, oregano, pepper, and paprika.

Place 1 steak in a heavy-duty plastic bag. Using a mallet or rolling pin, pound the steak from the center outward toward the edges to a thickness of ⅛". Remove the steak and repeat with remaining steaks.

Dip each steak in the egg white mixture, turning to coat. Then dip each steak in the crumb mixture, turning to coat.

Coat a large nonstick skillet with nonstick spray and heat over medium-high heat. Place 2 steaks in the skillet and cook for 2 to 3 minutes on each side, or until tender and no longer pink. Do not overcook. Transfer to a platter. Wipe out the skillet with a paper towel and add a little more nonstick spray. Cook the remaining 2 steaks. Top with the sauce and serve immediately.

**Makes 4 servings**

*Per serving: 274 calories, 32 g protein, 19 g carbohydrates, 7 g fat, 3 g saturated fat, 75 mg cholesterol, 613 mg sodium, 2 g fiber*

# *Red Meat Trivia*

True or false? To lower your cholesterol, you must cut out red meat. Answer: false. Researchers found that when people with high blood cholesterol levels were put on a diet that included lean red meats (like beef, veal, and pork), they were still able to lower their cholesterol levels. The key was that they followed the National Cholesterol Education Program (NCEP) guidelines of eating no more than 30 percent of calories from fat, taking in less than 300 milligrams of cholesterol a day, and limiting saturated fat to 8 to 10 percent of calories. The bottom line is that lean red meats can be part of a cholesterol-lowering diet. Just make sure that the rest of your diet is healthy, too.

# Beef Pinwheels

These are simple and elegant. To prevent the wooden picks from scorching in the oven, soak them in cold water for 20 minutes before using. I reduced calories and fat by:

❖ *Using a leaner cut of beef*
❖ *Eliminating butter for sautéing and basting*

*Photo on page 131*

## STEAK

1   beef top round steak (1½ pounds), trimmed of fat

¼   teaspoon salt

⅛   teaspoon ground black pepper

## FILLING

8   ounces mushrooms, finely chopped

1   onion, finely chopped

½   cup plain dry bread crumbs

2   tablespoons chopped flat-leaf parsley

¼   teaspoon salt

¼   teaspoon dill seed

2   tablespoons Worcestershire sauce

2   tablespoons fat-free beef broth

TO MAKE THE STEAK: Preheat the oven to 425°F. Place the steak on a countertop or cutting board and cover with plastic wrap. Using a mallet or rolling pin, pound the steak from the center outward to form a rectangle that is about 12" × 8" and ¼" thick. Remove the plastic and season the steak with the salt and pepper on one side.

TO MAKE THE FILLING: Coat a large nonstick skillet with nonstick spray. Add the mushrooms and onion. Cook, stirring, for 5 minutes, or until tender. Stir in the bread crumbs, parsley, salt, and dill seed.

Spread the mushroom mixture over the steak to within 1" of the edges. Roll up the steak, jelly-roll style, starting from one of the short sides. Secure with wooden picks. Place the meat, seam side down, on a rack in a roasting pan. In a cup, stir together the Worcestershire sauce and broth. Brush over the steak.

Roast for 45 to 60 minutes, or until the meat is tender and no longer pink. Brush occasionally with the broth mixture. Cut the roll into 8 slices and serve immediately.

**Makes 8 pinwheels; 4 servings**

*Per serving: 289 calories, 38 g protein, 8 g carbohydrates, 11 fat, 4 g saturated fat, 105 mg cholesterol, 474 mg sodium, 1 g fiber*

# Szechuan Beef

A little sesame oil goes a long way here. If you partially freeze the steak, it'll be easier to slice. I reduced calories and fat by:

❖ *Reducing the amount of oil in the marinade*
❖ *Eliminating most of the oil for stir-frying*

## MARINADE AND STEAK

1 garlic clove, minced

2 tablespoons grated or minced fresh ginger

3 tablespoons sherry or apple juice

3 tablespoons reduced-sodium soy sauce

2 teaspoons dark sesame oil

1 pound round steak, trimmed of fat and cut into thin 2"-long strips

1 cup brown rice

## STIR-FRY

1 teaspoon dark sesame oil

2 carrots, cut into 2" matchsticks

2 celery ribs, cut into 2" matchsticks

3 scallions, white and green parts, cut into 2" lengths

1 teaspoon cornstarch

TO MAKE THE MARINADE AND STEAK: In a shallow bowl, stir together the garlic, ginger, sherry or apple juice, soy sauce, and oil. Add the steak, stir well to coat, cover, and refrigerate for at least 1 hour.

Cook the rice according to the package directions.

TO MAKE THE STIR-FRY: Warm the oil in a large nonstick skillet or wok over high heat. Add the carrots, celery, and scallions and cook, stirring constantly, for 2 minutes, or until crisp-tender.

Add the beef and all but 1 tablespoon of the marinade. Cook, stirring constantly, for 3 minutes, or until the steak is no longer pink.

Dissolve the cornstarch in the remaining marinade. Add to the beef mixture and cook, stirring constantly, for 1 minute, or until the sauce is slightly thickened. Serve immediately with the brown rice.

## Makes 4 servings

*Per serving: 396 calories, 30 g protein, 42 g carbohydrates, 11 g fat, 3 g saturated fat, 70 mg cholesterol, 462 mg sodium, 4 g fiber*

# Orange Beef Stir-Fry

Stir-frys are a satisfying way to enjoy beef. A 3-ounce portion looks a lot less skimpy when mixed with vegetables and other goodies. This stir-fry is particularly flavorful, thanks to fresh oranges and fresh ginger. Calories, fat, and sodium were reduced by:

- ❖ *Eliminating the oil for stir-frying and using nonstick spray instead*
- ❖ *Using reduced-sodium soy sauce*

|   |   |
|---|---|
| 1 | pound beef round steak (about ¾" thick) trimmed of fat |
| 2 | tablespoons reduced-sodium soy sauce |
| 3 | oranges |
| 1½ | teaspoons grated or minced fresh ginger |
| 1 | teaspoon cornstarch |
| 1 | green bell pepper, cut into ½" squares |
| 1 | red bell pepper, cut into ½" squares |
| 3 | scallions, white and green parts, cut into 2" lengths |
| 1 | small head bok choy (about 1½ pounds), cut into 2"-long pieces |

Cut the steak in half lengthwise. Cut each half crosswise into thin ⅛"-thick slices. Transfer to a medium bowl and toss with the soy sauce.

Over a small bowl, grate 1 teaspoon peel from one of the oranges. Set aside.

Juice the same orange over a measuring cup to make ¼ cup orange juice. Set aside. Peel the remaining 2 oranges and trim any white membrane from the fruit. Cut in half lengthwise (from stem end to top) and thinly slice crosswise into half-moon shapes. Set aside.

Add the orange juice, ginger, and cornstarch to the orange peel in the small bowl. Stir to dissolve the cornstarch and set aside.

Coat a large nonstick skillet or wok with nonstick spray and heat over high heat. Add the peppers. Cook, stirring constantly, for 2 minutes, or until crisp-tender. Transfer to a bowl.

In the same skillet, cook the scallions and bok choy, stirring constantly, for 2 minutes, or until crisp-tender. Transfer to the bowl with the peppers.

Add the beef to the skillet, draining the marinade into the bowl with the orange juice mixture. Cook the beef, stirring constantly, for 2 to 3 minutes, or just until the beef loses its pinkness. Return the vegetables to the skillet. Stir in the orange juice mixture and the sliced oranges. Cook, stirring constantly, for 4 to 5 minutes, or until the liquid thickens and is bubbly and the beef is cooked through. Serve immediately.

**Makes 4 servings**

*Per serving: 235 calories, 27 g protein, 16 g carbohydrates, 7 g fat, 3 g saturated fat, 70 mg cholesterol, 345 mg sodium, 3 g fiber*

*Homestyle Hints:* When grating citrus fruits such as oranges, be sure to grate only the colored peel and not the bitter white pith underneath.

The easiest way to prepare fresh ginger is to peel it with a paring knife or the edge of a spoon, then finely grate it on a handheld grater.

## Did You Say B Vitamins?

*Vitamin $B_{12}$ and folate might be to hearing what vitamin A is to eyesight. Researchers found that age-related hearing impairment is linked to low $B_{12}$ and folate intake. To keep your hearing in tact, eat foods high in these nutrients. Vitamin $B_{12}$ is found in most animal products, including meat and dairy. Good sources of folate include dried beans, orange juice, leafy green vegetables, and boysenberries.*

# Swedish Meatballs

Here's a great way to introduce a confirmed red meat–lover to ground turkey breast. This recipe uses a mixture of ground beef and ground turkey breast. The flavor of the meat is very subtle and, once cooked, no one can tell the difference. Calories, fat, and cholesterol were reduced by:

❖ *Using a combination of extra-lean ground beef and ground turkey breast instead of ground beef*
❖ *Adding a shredded apple to the mixture for moisture*
❖ *Using egg whites instead of a whole egg*
❖ *Using fat-free evaporated milk instead of cream*
❖ *Using cornstarch instead of flour for thickening*
❖ *Eliminating the margarine for cooking the meatballs*

| | |
|---|---|
| 1 | onion, finely chopped |
| 1 | cup plain dry bread crumbs |
| ¼ | cup finely chopped flat-leaf parsley |
| 1 | apple, cored, peeled, and shredded |
| 2 | egg whites |
| 1 | teaspoon salt |
| ¼ | teaspoon ground black pepper |
| ¼ | teaspoon ground nutmeg |
| ⅛ | teaspoon allspice |
| 1 | pound extra-lean ground beef |
| ½ | pound ground turkey breast |
| 4 | teaspoons cornstarch |
| ¼ | cup fat-free evaporated milk |
| 1½ | cups fat-free beef broth |

Coat a large skillet with nonstick spray and warm over medium-high heat. Add the onion and cook, stirring occasionally, for 5 minutes, or until softened. Transfer to a large bowl. Set the skillet aside to use to cook the meatballs.

Add the bread crumbs, parsley, apple, egg whites, salt, pepper, nutmeg, and allspice to the bowl and stir gently. Add the beef and turkey and mix well, using your hands or a wooden spoon. Dampen your hands and shape the mixture into about thirty 1½" meatballs.

Recoat the skillet with nonstick spray and warm over medium heat. Add about half the meatballs and cook, turning often, for 10 minutes, or until browned and no longer pink in the center. Transfer to a plate. Recoat the skillet with spray and repeat with the remaining meatballs.

In a small bowl, dissolve the cornstarch in 2 tablespoons of the milk.

Add the broth and the remaining 2 tablespoons milk to the skillet. Stir in the cornstarch mixture and cook, stirring, over medium heat for 3 to 4 minutes, or until bubbly. Cook undisturbed for 1 minute. Return the meatballs to the skillet and cook just until heated through. Serve with sauce spooned over the top.

**Makes 6 servings**

Per serving: 286 calories, 28 g protein, 20 g carbohydrates, 10 g fat, 4 g saturated fat, 66 mg cholesterol, 574 mg sodium, 2 g fiber

*Homestyle Hint:* I like to use a crisp, juicy apple, such as Cortland, Pippin, or Granny Smith, for this recipe.

# Think Zinc, Think Beef

*Beef is the number one food source of zinc for American adults. Zinc helps our immune systems stay healthy and is especially needed for wound-healing. As always, focus on lean cuts of beef, such as round and loin. That way, you'll get the benefits of zinc without all the fat and cholesterol from the beef.*

# Saucy Salisbury Steak

This is really nothing more than a fancy hamburger without the bun. Sound good? It is. I reduced calories, fat, and cholesterol by:

❖ *Using a combination of extra-lean ground beef and ground turkey breast*
❖ *Adding a shredded apple for moisture*
❖ *Eliminating the margarine in the sauce*
❖ *Using less sherry*
❖ *Using cornstarch instead of flour for thickening*

## Nutrition Scorecard

*(per serving)*

|  | before | after |
|---|---|---|
| Calories | 359 | 251 |
| Fat (g) | 25 | 10 |

*Photo on page 184*

## STEAK

¾ pound extra-lean ground beef

¼ pound ground turkey breast

1 small apple, peeled and finely shredded

1 onion, quartered

½ green bell pepper, coarsely chopped

½ celery rib, coarsely chopped

1 tablespoon chopped flat-leaf parsley

1 garlic clove

¼ teaspoon mustard powder

¼ teaspoon dried marjoram, crushed

¼ teaspoon dried thyme, crushed

¼ teaspoon paprika

¼ teaspoon salt

¼ teaspoon ground black pepper

## SAUCE

½ cup fat-free beef broth

2 tablespoons sherry or apple juice

2 teaspoons Worcestershire sauce

½ teaspoon cornstarch

TO MAKE THE STEAK: Preheat the broiler. Coat the broiler pan with nonstick spray.

Place the beef, turkey, and apple in a large bowl, but do not mix.

In a blender or food processor, combine the onion, bell pepper, celery, parsley, garlic, mustard powder, marjoram, thyme, paprika, salt, and black pepper. Process until finely chopped. Add to the meat in the bowl and mix thoroughly.

Shape the meat into 4 patties, each about ¾" thick. Broil for 15 minutes, turning once, or until a thermometer inserted in the center registers 160°F and the meat is no longer pink. Turn once during cooking.

TO MAKE THE SAUCE: In a medium saucepan, combine all but 1 tablespoon of the broth with the sherry or apple juice and Worcestershire sauce. Cook over medium-high heat.

Meanwhile, dissolve the cornstarch in the remaining 1 tablespoon beef broth and add to the saucepan. Cook, stirring, until bubbly and slightly thickened. Cook undisturbed for 1 minute. Serve over the steak.

**Makes 4 servings**

Per serving: 251 calories, 25 g protein, 15 g carbohydrates, 10 g fat, 4 g saturated fat, 70 mg cholesterol, 556 mg sodium, 3 g fiber

*Homestyle Hint:* I like to use a crisp, juicy apple, such as Cortland, Pippin, or Granny Smith, for this recipe.

## Where's the Fat?

*Beef is the number one source of fat among American adults. It's clear we love its taste. But if you want to cut back on fat, concentrate on lean cuts and watch the portion size.*

# Shepherd's Pie

Believe it or not, leftovers led to the development of this classic dish. The traditional recipe uses leftover mashed potatoes and leftover ground beef. Here, I make it with fresh ingredients, but if you have leftovers, by all means, use them. Calories, fat, and cholesterol were reduced by:

- ❖ *Using 1% milk instead of cream for the potatoes*
- ❖ *Replacing full-fat butter with light butter and using less of it for the potatoes*
- ❖ *Using extra-lean ground beef instead of regular ground beef*
- ❖ *Eliminating the oil for cooking the onion in the filling*

## POTATOES

| | |
|---|---|
| 2 | pounds potatoes, peeled and quartered |
| ¼ | teaspoon dried thyme, crushed |
| ¼ | teaspoon dried rosemary, crushed |
| ½ | cup 1% milk |
| 1 | tablespoon light butter |
| ½ | teaspoon salt |
| ¼ | teaspoon ground black pepper |

## MEAT FILLING

| | |
|---|---|
| 1 | pound extra-lean ground beef |
| 1 | onion, chopped |
| ½ | cup fat-free beef broth |
| 2 | tablespoons ketchup |
| 1 | tablespoon Worcestershire sauce |
| 1½ | teaspoons cornstarch |
| ½ | teaspoon salt |
| ¼ | teaspoon ground black pepper |
| 1½ | cups corn kernels |
| 1 | tablespoon chopped flat-leaf parsley |

TO MAKE THE POTATOES: In a medium saucepan, combine the potatoes, thyme, and rosemary. Cover with water and bring to a boil over high heat. Reduce the heat to medium, cover, and simmer for 20 minutes, or until tender. Drain and return to the pot (off the heat). Add the milk, butter, salt, and pepper and, using a fork or potato masher, mash until smooth.

TO MAKE THE MEAT FILLING: Coat a large nonstick skillet with nonstick spray and warm over medium-high heat. Add the beef and onion and cook, breaking up the meat and stirring, for 10 minutes, or until the meat is no longer pink and the onions are softened. Drain the fat.

In a measuring cup, combine the broth, ketchup, Worcestershire sauce, cornstarch, salt, and pepper. Add to the beef and cook, stirring, until bubbly and thickened. Stir in the corn and parsley.

Preheat the oven to 350°F. Transfer the beef to a shallow 2-quart casserole. Drop large spoonfuls of the mashed potatoes on top of the meat mixture so that they are next to each other. Smooth the potatoes over the meat and use the tines of a fork to create ridges in the potatoes. (This makes a nice presentation and the ridges become delightfully crusty when baked.) Bake for 40 minutes, or until the potatoes are golden.

**Makes 6 servings**

*Per serving: 344 calories, 22 g protein, 40 g carbohydrates, 11 g fat, 4 g saturated fat, 64 mg cholesterol, 911 mg sodium, 4 g fiber*

## Best Buy: Retail Ground Beef

*Here's one more reason to grill your own burgers and make your own meatloaf. Ground beef purchased from retail sources is lower in fat (on average) than ground beef sold through food-service sources like restaurants.*

# Pizza Dumpling Bake

This attractive dish is great for potlucks. It gets a head start from refrigerator dinner roll dough to make the dumplings. I reduced the calories, fat, cholesterol, and even the sodium (although the sodium level is still on the high side) by:

❖ *Using extra-lean ground beef instead of regular*
❖ *Using reduced-fat cheese*
❖ *Using low-fat dinner roll dough for the dumplings*
❖ *Using an egg white wash instead of margarine on top of the rolls*

*Photo on page 183*

| | |
|---|---|
| 1 | pound extra-lean ground beef |
| 1 | large onion, chopped |
| 1 | can tomato sauce (8 ounces) |
| 1 | can tomato paste (6 ounces) |
| ¾ | cup water |
| 1½ | teaspoons dried oregano |
| ¾ | teaspoon salt |
| ½ | teaspoon dried rosemary, crushed |
| ¼ | teaspoon ground black pepper |
| 2 | cups shredded reduced-fat mozzarella cheese (8 ounces) |
| 8 | ounces frozen Italian-style vegetables, thawed |
| 1 | package low-fat refrigerator dinner roll dough (8 rolls) |
| 1 | egg white |
| 2 | teaspoons water |
| | Freshly grated Parmesan cheese, optional |

Preheat the oven to 375°F. Coat a 13" × 9" baking dish with nonstick spray.

Coat a large nonstick skillet with nonstick spray and warm over medium-high heat. Add the beef and onion and cook, breaking up the meat and stirring, for 10 to 15 minutes, or until the meat is no longer pink and the onion is softened. Drain any fat.

Add the tomato sauce, tomato paste, water, 1 teaspoon of the oregano, salt, rosemary, and pepper to the skillet. Bring to a boil over high heat. Reduce the heat to medium-low, cover, and cook, stirring occasionally, for 15 minutes, or until well-blended and slightly thickened.

Transfer the mixture to the prepared baking dish. Sprinkle 1 cup of the mozzarella over the beef. Spoon the mixed vegetables evenly over the cheese. Top with the remaining 1 cup mozzarella.

Cut each dinner roll in half horizontally to make 16 halves. Arrange decoratively over the mozzarella.

In a small cup, beat together the egg white and water. Brush over the dinner rolls. Sprinkle with the remaining ½ teaspoon oregano. Bake for 20 minutes, or until the rolls are golden brown. Serve sprinkled with Parmesan, if using.

**Makes 8 servings**

Per serving: 356 calories, 27 g protein, 30 g carbohydrates, 14 g fat, 6 g saturated fat, 57 mg cholesterol, 1,016 mg sodium, 4 g fiber

## The Italians Have Done It Again

*By now, most people know that saturated fat is the chief dietary culprit leading to high cholesterol and clogged arteries. But researchers from Italy give us one more reason to keep saturated fat at bay: gallstone formation. After comparing the diets of people with gallstones and those without, they found that high saturated fat intake (primarily from animal fats) was a risk factor for gallstone formation, especially for men. To limit saturated fat, go easy on full-fat dairy products and choose low-fat and fat-free milk and cheeses instead. Choose poultry more often over red meats. When you do eat red meats, choose the leanest cuts and be sure that they're trimmed of excess fat.*

# Barbecue Pot Roast

My family loves this meal on weekends, and leftovers make terrific sandwiches. Spread your favorite barbecue sauce on a French roll, then top it with some of the thinly sliced beef from this dish. Calories, fat, and cholesterol were reduced by:

❖ *Using a leaner cut of meat, and less of it*
❖ *Using nonstick spray instead of oil to brown the meat*
❖ *Increasing the amount of vegetables*

*Photo on page 133*

| | |
|---|---|
| 2 | pounds beef top round roast, trimmed of fat |
| ½ | teaspoon salt |
| ¼ | teaspoon ground black pepper |
| 2 | onions, sliced and separated into rings |
| 1 | red bell pepper, sliced into rings |
| 4 | ounces mushrooms, sliced (1 cup) |
| 2 | garlic cloves, minced |
| ¾ | cup barbecue sauce |
| ⅓ | cup water |
| 2 | tablespoons molasses |
| 1 | teaspoon chili powder |
| 1 | teaspoon mustard powder |
| 1 | bag peeled small carrots (1 pound) |

Coat a 4-quart flame-proof roasting pan or Dutch oven with nonstick spray and warm over medium-high heat.

Season the meat with the salt and black pepper and place in the prepared pan. Brown the meat, turning, until all sides are browned. Transfer to a plate and set aside.

Add the onions, bell pepper, mushrooms, and garlic to the pan. Reduce the heat to medium and cook, stirring occasionally, for 5 minutes, or until tender. Stir in the barbecue sauce, water, molasses, chili powder, and mustard powder and bring to a boil over high heat. Add the beef, reduce the heat to low, cover, and cook for 1 hour. Add the carrots and cook for 30 to 45 minutes longer, or until the meat is fork-tender and cooked through and the carrots are soft.

**Makes 6 servings**

*Per serving: 241 calories, 28 g protein, 20 g carbohydrates, 5 g fat, 2 g saturated fat, 61 mg cholesterol, 523 mg sodium, 4 g fiber*

**Pizza Dumpling Bake** *(page 180)*
183

Saucy Salisbury Steak *(page 176)* and Roasted Garlic Mashed Potatoes *(page 315)*

Spicy Cashew-Chicken Stir-Fry *(page 207)*
185

Barbecue Chicken Pizza *(page 208)*

**Chicken–Cream Cheese Bundles** *(page 222)* **and Garden Couscous Salad** *(page 276)*

187

**Sesame Chicken** *(page 211)*
188

**Country Captain** *(page 209)*

**Marian's Autumn Chicken with Dijon Cider Sauce** *(page 220)*

**Chicken Saltimbocca** *(page 218)* **and Orzo with Spinach** *(page 318)*

**Polenta Lasagna** *(page 232)*
192

**Mexican Pizza** *(page 235)*

193

**Barley-Stuffed Peppers** *(page 244)*

194

**Crustless Italian Ricotta Pie** *(page 230)* **and Mandarin Spinach Salad with Orange Vinaigrette** *(page 272)*

**Tuna-Noodle Skillet Supper** *(page 262)*

**Spirals with No-Cook Summer Sauce** *(page 252)*
197

**Stuffed Shells Florentine** *(page 270)*
198

# Breaded Pork Tenderloin

This robust pork tenderloin tastes great served with mashed potatoes and a salad. I reduced calories, fat, and cholesterol by:

❖ *Eliminating bacon grease and replacing it with nonstick spray to cook the vegetables*
❖ *Using egg whites instead of a whole egg*
❖ *Eliminating the oil for cooking the pork*

| *Nutrition Scorecard* | | |
|---|---|---|
| *(per serving)* | | |
| | before | after |
| Calories | 337 | 236 |
| Fat (g) | 17 | 6 |

| | |
|---|---|
| 6 | ounces mushrooms, sliced (1½ cups) |
| 2 | onions, thinly sliced |
| ¼ | cup sherry or apple juice |
| 1½ | pounds pork tenderloin |
| ½ | teaspoon salt |
| ½ | teaspoon ground black pepper |
| ¾ | cup plain dry bread crumbs |
| ¼ | teaspoon dried oregano, crushed |
| 2 | egg whites |
| 1 | tablespoon water |

Preheat the oven to 350°F.

Coat a large nonstick skillet with nonstick spray and warm over medium-high heat. Add the mushrooms and onions and cook, stirring, for 8 minutes, or until tender. Add the sherry or apple juice and cook, stirring, for 2 minutes. Spread the vegetables and liquid in an even layer in a 13" × 9" baking dish. Set the skillet aside to use for the pork.

Season the pork with the salt and pepper. In a large shallow dish, mix the bread crumbs and oregano. In another shallow dish, beat together the egg whites and water.

Fold the thin ends of the tenderloin under and secure with wooden picks. Dip the tenderloin in the bread crumbs, turning to coat evenly and patting bread crumbs on the tenderloin if necessary. Dip the tenderloin in the egg whites and turn to coat. Return to the bread crumbs and coat again.

Reheat the skillet over medium-high heat. Add the tenderloin and cook, turning, until brown on all sides. Place on top of the vegetables in the baking dish. Cover with foil and roast for 30 minutes. Uncover and roast for 20 to 25 minutes, or until a thermometer inserted in the tenderloin registers 155°F. Slice and serve.

## Makes 6 servings

*Per serving: 236 calories, 30 g protein, 13 g carbohydrates, 6 g fat, 2 g saturated fat, 80 mg cholesterol, 362 mg sodium, 2 g fiber*

# Pork and Peppers

Red and green bell peppers and bright red tomatoes make this pork dish colorful and tasty. I like it spooned over noodles or rice. Calories and fat were reduced by:

❖ *Using pork tenderloin instead of regular pork loin*
❖ *Eliminating the oil for cooking the pork and vegetables*

*Photo on page 134*

| | |
|---|---|
| 1½ | pounds pork tenderloin, cut into 1" chunks |
| ¾ | teaspoon salt |
| ½ | teaspoon ground black pepper |
| 1 | onion, chopped |
| 1 | red bell pepper, cut into 1" squares |
| 1 | green bell pepper, cut into 1" squares |
| 1 | can diced tomatoes (15 ounces), drained |
| 1 | teaspoon dried basil |
| 1 | tablespoon chopped flat-leaf parsley |

Coat a large saucepan with nonstick spray and warm over medium-high heat. Add the pork and season with the salt and black pepper. Cook, stirring, for 5 minutes, or until lightly browned on all sides.

Add the onion and bell peppers and cook, stirring, for 5 minutes, or until the onion is soft. Add the tomatoes and bring to a boil. Reduce the heat to low, cover, and cook, stirring occasionally, for 20 minutes, or until the pork is tender and no longer pink. Add the basil and parsley, stir gently, and serve.

**Makes 6 servings**

*Per serving: 166 calories, 25 g protein, 6 g carbohydrates, 4 g fat, 2 g saturated fat, 90 mg cholesterol, 423 mg sodium, 1 g fiber*

# Pork Lo Mein

Traditional lo mein begins with moderate amounts of lean pork but loses its healthful promise when copious spoonfuls of oil are poured into the pan. I use just a teaspoon of oil for stir-frying. I reduced the calories and sodium by:

❖ *Using more vegetables and less pasta*
❖ *Using fresh mushrooms instead of canned*

| *Nutrition Scorecard* | | |
|---|---|---|
| *(per serving)* | | |
| | before | after |
| Calories | 500 | 386 |
| Fat (g) | 20 | 6 |

|  |  |
|---|---|
| 8 | ounces dried spaghetti |
| ¾ | pound pork tenderloin, cut into thin bite-size strips |
| 2 | tablespoons reduced-sodium soy sauce |
| 2 | tablespoons oyster sauce |
| 2 | tablespoons sherry or apple juice |
| 1 | teaspoon grated or minced fresh ginger |
| 1 | teaspoon peanut oil or canola oil |
| 1 | small head bok choy (about 1½ pounds), cut into 2"-long pieces |
| 1 | carrot, cut into thin 2" matchsticks |
| 4 | ounces mushrooms, sliced (1 cup) |
| ½ | cup fat-free chicken broth |

Cook the spaghetti according to the package directions. Drain well.

In a medium bowl, combine the pork, soy sauce, oyster sauce, sherry or apple juice, and ginger. Toss well, cover, and set aside.

Heat the oil in a large nonstick skillet or wok over high heat. Add the bok choy, carrot, and mushrooms. Cook, stirring constantly, for 2 minutes, or until crisp-tender.

Add the pork to the skillet, reserving the marinade. Cook the pork, stirring constantly, for 3 minutes, or just until it loses its pinkness and is thoroughly cooked. Stir the broth into the marinade and add to the skillet. Cook for 1 minute. Add the spaghetti and heat through. Serve immediately.

### Makes 4 servings

*Per serving: 386 calories, 29 g protein, 52 g carbohydrates, 6 g fat, 1 g saturated fat, 50 mg cholesterol, 785 mg sodium, 3 g fiber*

*Homestyle Hints:* Oyster sauce can be found in the international or Asian section of most supermarkets. If you can't find it, substitute 2 tablespoons reduced-sodium soy sauce.

To cut a carrot into matchsticks, cut the carrot crosswise into 2" pieces. Cut each piece lengthwise into very thin strips. Stack the strips and cut lengthwise again into matchsticks.

# Sweet-and-Sour Pork Kebabs

These kebabs look wonderful over rice, and it's a great meal to make ahead of time for entertaining. Calories, fat, and cholesterol were reduced by:

❖ *Reducing the amount of oil in the marinade*
❖ *Using a leaner cut of pork, and less of it*
❖ *Adding bell peppers to compensate for less meat*

## Nutrition Scorecard
(per serving)

|  | before | after |
|---|---|---|
| Calories | 550 | 201 |
| Fat (g) | 26 | 5 |

*Photo on page 130*

### MARINADE AND PORK

2 tablespoons red wine vinegar

1 tablespoon dark sesame oil

2 garlic cloves, minced

2 teaspoons crushed red-pepper flakes

½ teaspoon salt

1 pound pork tenderloin, cut into thirty-two 1" chunks

### SAUCE

¼ cup ketchup

2 tablespoons red wine vinegar

2 tablespoons sugar

2 teaspoons reduced-sodium soy sauce

¼ teaspoon dark sesame oil

### KEBABS

2 red or green bell peppers, cut into thirty-two 1" pieces

1 can pineapple chunks (20 ounces)

TO MAKE THE MARINADE AND PORK: In a large bowl, combine the vinegar, oil, garlic, red-pepper flakes, and salt. Stir in the pork, cover, and chill for at least 6 hours or overnight. Drain the pork, reserving the marinade.

TO MAKE THE SAUCE: In a small bowl, combine the ketchup, vinegar, sugar, soy sauce, and oil. Set aside.

TO ASSEMBLE THE KEBABS: Soak eight 10"-long bamboo skewers in water for 30 minutes. Thread a bell pepper chunk followed by a pineapple chunk and a pork chunk onto a skewer. Repeat this sequence 4 times on each skewer.

Coat a grill rack or broiler pan with nonstick spray. Preheat the grill or broiler. Brush the kebabs with some of the reserved marinade. Grill over medium-hot coals or broil them on a rack for 20 minutes, or until the pork is no longer pink but still juicy. Turn the kebabs 3 or 4 times during cooking. Drizzle with the marinade several times during the first 10 minutes of cooking. Discard any remaining marinade; do not serve it with the kebabs.

Just before removing the kebabs from the grill, spoon half of the sweet-and-sour sauce over them. Turn the kebabs, spoon the remaining sauce over them, and grill for 1 minute longer. Serve immediately.

**Makes 8 kebabs; 4 servings**

*Per serving: 201 calories, 17 g protein, 22 g carbohydrates, 5 g fat, 1 g saturated fat, 45 mg cholesterol, 393 mg sodium, 1 g fiber*

*Homestyle Hint:* I soak bamboo skewers in water before making kebabs so that the skewers don't burn during grilling. If you don't have bamboo skewers, use metal ones and skip the soaking step.

## Fruit Makes a Difference for Teens

*Researchers found that teenage girls who ate, on average, a little more than four servings of fruit per day had the best blood lipid levels (including cholesterol and triglycerides), which are beneficial for heart health. It's never too early to develop heathful eating habits and a healthy heart.*

# Glazed Pork Medallions

Garlic-scented apricot jam makes an irresistible glaze for pork. And it's so easy to put together. This meal is ready in minutes because slicing the tenderloin into thin medallions allows it to cook quickly. I reduced calories, fat, and cholesterol by:

❖ *Using chicken broth instead of oil in the glaze*
❖ *Using pineapple juice instead of wine in the glaze*

| | |
|---|---|
| 1 | pound pork tenderloin |
| ½ | teaspoon salt |
| ¼ | teaspoon ground black pepper |
| 1 | garlic clove, minced |
| ¼ | cup pineapple juice |
| 2 | tablespoons apricot jam |
| 2 | teaspoons fat-free chicken broth |

Slice the pork into eight ¾"-thick slices (medallions). Season with the salt and pepper.

Coat a large skillet with nonstick spray and place over medium-high heat until hot. Add the pork to the skillet and cook, turning once, for 6 minutes, or until browned on the outside and no trace of pinkness remains in the center. Transfer to a platter.

Add the garlic to the skillet and cook, stirring, for 30 seconds. Stir in the pineapple juice, jam, and broth. Bring to boil and cook for 1 minute longer, or until slightly thickened. Return the pork to the pan, turn to coat with the glaze, and cook until heated through. Serve immediately.

**Makes 4 servings**

Per serving: 174 calories, 24 g protein, 9 g carbohydrates, 4 g fat, 1 g saturated fat, 67 mg cholesterol, 321 mg sodium, 0 g fiber

## The Not-So-Porky Pork

*The leanest cut of pork is the tenderloin. A 3-ounce serving of cooked pork tenderloin has just 4 grams of fat, which is leaner than a skinless chicken thigh.*

# Finger-Lickin' Chicken and Turkey

*I*t's no secret that poultry is one of the most healthful food choices. However, it's healthfulness can be quickly undermined if the bird is fried, smothered in fatty sauce, or served with its skin. Here are some basics for preparing healthy chicken and turkey.

☕ Instead of deep-fat frying chicken, try oven-frying. The basic method is to remove the skin, coat the chicken in flour, then in beaten egg whites, and finally, in a low-fat coating (for a good coating, see Oven-Fried Chicken Parmesan). If you like your coating extra-crispy, coat the food—instead of the pan—with a liberal amount of nonstick spray before baking. This same technique works on other foods that are traditionally fried, like onion rings and firm fish fillets.

☕ For lean yet rich-tasting sauces, I rely on flavorful ingredients like chicken stock, wine, vegetables, lemon, and herbs. For thickening these sauces, a touch of cornstarch does the trick. I also use soy sauce and a little sesame oil for Asian-style sauces. Even peanuts can be part of healthy chicken dish, as in Chicken Smothered in Peanut Sauce.

☕ When it comes to turkey, cooking a healthful meal is easier than ever. You can now buy turkey as tenderloins, tidbits, and as ground turkey breast. You can even buy whole bone-in turkey breast. I use a whole bone-in breast for Roast Turkey Breast with Apple Stuffing, one of my favorite weekend meals.

# Chicken in Red-Pepper Sauce

This sauce is delicious over just about anything, especially mild-flavored food like chicken. It comes together quickly because I use jarred roasted red peppers from the supermarket, although you could use home-roasted peppers, too. Calories, fat, and cholesterol were reduced by:

❖ *Eliminating butter and oil for cooking the chicken*
❖ *Using chicken broth instead of cream for the sauce*
❖ *Adding fresh basil to boost flavor*

1  onion, chopped
2  garlic cloves, minced
1  jar roasted red peppers (7 ounces), drained
½  cup fat-free chicken broth
4  boneless, skinless chicken breast halves
½  teaspoon salt
¼  teaspoon black pepper
2  tablespoons chopped fresh basil or
  2 teaspoons dried

Generously coat a large nonstick skillet with nonstick spray and warm over medium heat. Add the onion and garlic and cook, stirring, for 5 minutes, or until tender. Transfer to a food processor or blender. Add the roasted peppers and broth. Blend until smooth and set aside.

Recoat the skillet with nonstick spray and warm over medium-high heat. Season the chicken with the salt and black pepper. Add to the skillet and cook for 3 to 4 minutes on each side, or until browned.

Pour the red-pepper sauce over the chicken. Bring to a boil over high heat, stirring frequently. Reduce the heat to medium and stir in the basil. Cover and cook for 2 minutes, or until a thermometer inserted in the thickest portion registers 160°F and the juices run clear. Transfer the chicken to serving plates and spoon the sauce over the chicken.

### Makes 4 servings

*Per serving: 171 calories, 28 g protein, 5 g carbohydrates, 3 g fat, 1 g saturated fat, 73 mg cholesterol, 567 mg sodium, 1 g fiber*

*Homestyle Hint:* To roast a bell pepper, place over a flame or under a broiler until blackened all over, turning occasionally. Set aside in a sealed paper bag for 15 minutes until cool enough to handle. Peel and discard the blackened skin. Discard the core and seeds. Chop and use immediately, or place in an airtight container with just enough water to cover, and refrigerate for up to a week.

# Spicy Cashew-Chicken Stir-Fry

You can find hoisin sauce and chili paste in the international section of most grocery stores. For less heat, use less chili paste. For a change of pace, I serve this over noodles. Calories, fat, and cholesterol were reduced by:

❖ *Using a smaller amount of cashews and using halved nuts, which distributes the nutty flavor*
❖ *Eliminating the vegetable oil for stir-frying*
❖ *Reducing the amount of sesame oil*

2  garlic cloves, minced

1  teaspoon grated or minced fresh ginger

3  boneless, skinless chicken breast halves, cut into 2" strips

3  cups broccoli florets

3  scallions, white and green parts, cut into 2" lengths

2  tablespoons hoisin sauce or reduced-sodium soy sauce

1  tablespoon dark sesame oil

1½  teaspoons Asian chili paste or ½ teaspoon crushed red-pepper flakes

3  tablespoons cashew halves

Coat a large nonstick skillet or wok with nonstick spray and warm over medium-high heat. Add the garlic and ginger and cook for 30 seconds, or until fragrant. Add the chicken and cook, stirring constantly, for 3 to 4 minutes, or until no longer pink. Transfer to a plate.

Add the broccoli and cook, stirring constantly, for 3 minutes, or until crisp-tender. Return the chicken to the skillet and add the scallions.

Meanwhile, in a small bowl, combine the hoisin sauce or soy sauce, oil, and chili paste or red-pepper flakes. Pour into the pan and cook, stirring constantly, for 2 minutes, or until the flavors blend. Stir in the cashews and serve immediately.

### Makes 4 servings

*Per serving: 213 calories, 23 g protein, 10 g carbohydrates, 9 g fat, 2 g saturated fat, 55 mg cholesterol, 233 mg sodium, 2 g fiber*

*Homestyle Hints:* I sometimes add a sliced red bell pepper to this dish.

The easiest way to prepare fresh ginger is to peel it with a paring knife or the edge of a spoon, then finely grate it on a handheld grater.

# Barbecue Chicken Pizza

I'll never forget the first time I made this—it was such a hit that I had to go back to the kitchen and make another pizza! Fortunately, it was easy enough to do because this pizza uses a ready-made crust. I reduced the calories, fat, and cholesterol by:

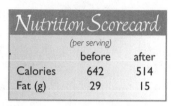

❖ *Using reduced-fat mozzarella cheese instead of gouda cheese and slightly less of it*
❖ *Eliminating olive oil for cooking the chicken*

| Nutrition Scorecard | | |
|---|---|---|
| (per serving) | | |
| | before | after |
| Calories | 642 | 514 |
| Fat (g) | 29 | 15 |

*Photo on page 186*

    2   **boneless, skinless chicken breast halves**
   ½   **cup hickory-flavored barbecue sauce**
    1   **prebaked cheese pizza crust (16 ounces)**
  1½   **cups shredded reduced-fat mozzarella cheese (6 ounces)**
    1   **small red onion, finely chopped**
    1   **tablespoon chopped fresh cilantro**

Position the rack in the center of the oven. Preheat the oven to 450°F.

Coat a nonstick skillet with nonstick spray and warm over medium-high heat. Cook the chicken for 5 minutes on each side, or until a thermometer inserted in the thickest portion registers 160°F and the juices run clear. Transfer to a plate and let cool for 5 minutes. Cut the chicken crosswise into ¼"-wide slices. Transfer to a bowl and toss with ¼ cup of the barbecue sauce.

Place the pizza crust on a baking sheet. Sprinkle with ¾ cup of the cheese. Arrange the chicken over the crust and sprinkle with the onion and cilantro. Drizzle with the remaining ¼ cup barbecue sauce and sprinkle with the remaining ¾ cup cheese.

Bake for 15 minutes, or until the cheese is bubbly. Serve immediately.

### Makes 4 servings

*Per serving: 514 calories, 37 g protein, 59 g carbohydrates, 15 g fat, 7 g saturated fat, 61 mg cholesterol, 1,086 mg sodium, 1 g fiber*

*Homestyle Hint:* Prebaked pizza crusts are available at most grocery stores. One popular brand is Boboli.

# Country Captain

I like to serve this easy, lightly curried chicken dish over rice. Calories, fat, and cholesterol were reduced by:

- ❖ *Eliminating the oil for cooking the vegetables*
- ❖ *Using skinless chicken breasts*
- ❖ *Slightly reducing the amount of almonds*

*Photo on page 189*

| | |
|---|---|
| ¼ | cup unbleached or all-purpose flour |
| ½ | teaspoon paprika |
| 4 | boneless, skinless chicken breast halves |
| 1 | large onion, chopped |
| 1 | green bell pepper, chopped |
| 1 | red bell pepper, chopped |
| 1 | garlic clove, minced |
| 2 | teaspoons curry powder |
| ½ | teaspoon salt |
| ¼ | teaspoon ground black pepper |
| 1 | can chopped tomatoes (14½ ounces) |
| ½ | cup raisins |
| 1 | tablespoon chopped flat-leaf parsley |
| 3 | tablespoons slivered almonds, toasted |

Preheat the oven to 375°F. In a shallow dish, combine the flour and paprika. Dredge the chicken in the flour to coat and shake off any excess.

Coat a Dutch oven or deep 4-quart saucepan with nonstick spray and warm over medium-high heat. Add the chicken and cook, turning several times, for 4 to 6 minutes, or until browned. Remove the chicken and set aside while cooking the vegetables.

Reduce the heat to medium and recoat the pan with nonstick spray. Add the onion, bell peppers, and garlic. Cook, stirring, for 5 minutes, or until the vegetables are tender. Stir in the curry powder, salt, and black pepper. Cook for 1 minute. Add the tomatoes (with juice), raisins, and parsley. Bring to a boil over high heat.

Return the chicken to the pan. Reduce the heat to medium, cover, and simmer for 10 to 15 minutes, or until a thermometer inserted in the thickest portion registers 160°F and the juices run clear. Sprinkle the almonds over the chicken.

### Makes 4 servings

*Per serving: 323 calories, 32 g protein, 35 g carbohydrates, 7 g fat, 1 g saturated fat, 73 mg cholesterol, 521 mg sodium, 4 g fiber*

# Chicken Piccata

This lemony chicken dish has always been one of my favorites—and now that it's more healthful than ever, I can enjoy it more often. I reduced the calories, fat, and cholesterol by:

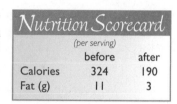

♦ *Eliminating the oil for cooking the chicken*
♦ *Using fat-free chicken broth in place of butter in the sauce*

¼ cup unbleached or all-purpose flour
¾ teaspoon salt
¼ teaspoon ground black pepper
4 boneless, skinless chicken breast halves
¼ cup dry white wine or nonalcoholic white wine
¼ cup fat-free chicken broth
¼ cup lemon juice
1 lemon, thinly sliced
1 tablespoon chopped flat-leaf parsley

In a shallow dish, combine the flour, salt, and pepper. Place each chicken breast between 2 pieces of plastic wrap. Working from the center to the edges, pound lightly with the flat side of a meat mallet or small skillet to an even ¼" thickness. Remove the plastic wrap.

Dredge the chicken in the flour mixture and shake off any excess.

Coat a large nonstick skillet with nonstick spray and warm over medium-high heat. Cook the chicken for 3 to 4 minutes on each side, or until no longer pink in the center and the juices run clear. Transfer to a plate.

Add the wine and broth to the pan. Cook, stirring, for 1 minute, scraping up the browned bits from the bottom of the pan. Add the lemon juice and bring to a boil over high heat.

Reduce the heat to medium-high and return the chicken to the pan. Cover the chicken with the lemon slices and cook for 3 minutes, or until the sauce thickens slightly. Transfer the chicken and lemon slices to serving plates and spoon the pan sauce over them. Sprinkle with the parsley.

**Makes 4 servings**

*Per serving: 190 calories, 28 g protein, 9 g carbohydrates, 3 g fat, 1 g saturated fat, 73 mg cholesterol, 486 mg sodium, 1 g fiber*

*Homestyle Hint:* You will need about 3 lemons for this dish.

# Sesame Chicken

Here's one of my all-time favorite recipes. Just a tiny bit of sesame oil makes all the difference in the sauce. I like to serve it over rice. Calories, fat, and sodium were reduced by:

❖ *Eliminating peanut oil for cooking the chicken*
❖ *Using reduced-sodium soy sauce*
❖ *Toasting the sesame seeds to enhance flavor*
❖ *Using a small amount of dark sesame oil to enhance flavor*

| | |
|---|---|
| ¼ | cup unbleached or all-purpose flour |
| ¼ | teaspoon salt |
| ⅛ | teaspoon ground black pepper |
| 4 | boneless, skinless chicken breast halves, cut into 2"–4" strips |
| ¼ | cup reduced-sodium soy sauce |
| ¼ | cup sugar |
| ½ | teaspoon dark sesame oil |
| 2 | tablespoons sesame seeds, toasted |
| ¼ | cup chopped fresh chives |

In a shallow dish, combine the flour, salt, and pepper. Dredge the chicken in the flour mixture and shake off any excess.

Coat a large nonstick skillet with nonstick spray and warm over medium-high heat. Add the chicken to the skillet in batches and cook, stirring occasionally, for 3 to 4 minutes, or until white and no longer pink. Transfer to a plate.

Reduce the heat to medium. Combine the soy sauce and sugar in the skillet. Cook, stirring occasionally, until the sugar dissolves. Stir in the oil and sesame seeds. Add the chicken and chives. Toss and serve immediately.

### Makes 4 servings

*Per serving: 265 calories, 30 g protein, 22 g carbohydrates, 6 g fat, 1 g saturated fat, 73 mg cholesterol, 703 mg sodium, 1 g fiber*

*Homestyle Hints:* To toast sesame seeds, place in a dry skillet and toast, shaking the pan, over medium-high heat for a minute or so, or until fragrant and lightly browned. I like to do this step first. Then, when the chicken is cooked in the same skillet, it picks up more sesame flavor.

For more crunch and color, cook ½ red bell pepper, cut into strips, and ½ cup trimmed snow peas for 4 minutes in the skillet before adding the chicken. Remove from the skillet and keep warm while you cook the chicken. Add the cooked vegetables at the end with the chives.

# Chicken Smothered in Peanut Sauce

The sauce really makes this dish. Be sure to serve this one with rice or barley to soak up every drop. Calories, fat, and cholesterol were reduced by:

❖ *Eliminating the oil for cooking the chicken*
❖ *Using chicken breast meat only, which is leaner than other chicken meat*
❖ *Slightly reducing the amount of peanut butter*

*Nutrition Scorecard*
(per serving)

|  | before | after |
|---|---|---|
| Calories | 385 | 273 |
| Fat (g) | 21 | 10 |

| | |
|---|---|
| 1 | onion, chopped |
| 4 | boneless, skinless chicken breast halves |
| ½ | teaspoon salt |
| ¼ | teaspoon paprika |
| ⅛ | teaspoon ground black pepper |
| 2 | cans diced tomatoes (15 ounces each), drained and juices reserved |
| 3 | tablespoons creamy peanut butter |
| ¼ | cup packed fresh cilantro |
| 2 | garlic cloves |
| ¼ | teaspoon crushed red-pepper flakes |

Coat a large skillet with nonstick spray and warm over medium-high heat. Add the onion and cook, stirring, for 5 minutes, or until softened.

Season the chicken with ¼ teaspoon of the salt, the paprika, and the black pepper. Add the chicken to the skillet and cook for 3 to 4 minutes on each side, or until browned.

Meanwhile, in a food processor or blender, combine the reserved tomato juice, peanut butter, cilantro, garlic, red-pepper flakes, and the remaining ¼ teaspoon salt. Blend until smooth. Pour over the chicken and add the tomatoes. Bring to a boil over high heat. Reduce the heat to low, cover, and simmer for 25 minutes, or until a thermometer inserted in the thickest portion of a breast registers 160°F and the juices run clear.

## Makes 4 servings

*Per serving: 273 calories, 32 g protein, 17 g carbohydrates, 10 g fat, 2 g saturated fat, 73 mg cholesterol, 839 mg sodium, 5 g fiber*

# Chicken Skin Explained

The simplest way to cut fat and calories from a chicken dish is to remove the skin. Even if you do nothing else, this alone will reduce calories by as much as 50 percent. To keep things healthy from the start, I use skinless chicken breasts quite a bit. But when using other chicken parts, or for dishes that are not cooked in a sauce or liquid, I like to leave the skin on during cooking to keep the meat moist, and then remove the skin before eating. Don't forget to remove skin from drumsticks. This chart illustrates what a big difference a little skin can make.

| Chicken Part | Calories with Skin | Calories without Skin |
| --- | --- | --- |
| Breast | 193 | 142 |
| Drumstick | 112 | 76 |
| Thigh | 153 | 109 |
| Wing | 99 | 43 |

# Oven-Fried Chicken Parmesan

This is such a family favorite that I usually make a double batch. Be sure to use freshly grated Parmesan cheese; it makes a big flavor difference. Calories, fat, and cholesterol were reduced by:

❖ *Using lightly beaten egg white instead of butter for dipping the chicken*

❖ *Using cornflake crumbs instead of bread crumbs for extra crispiness*

| | |
|---|---|
| 1 | teaspoon olive oil |
| 1 | garlic clove, minced |
| 2 | teaspoons water |
| 1 | teaspoon Worcestershire sauce |
| 1 | egg white |
| ¼ | teaspoon salt |
| ⅔ | cup freshly grated Parmesan cheese (3 ounces) |
| ½ | cup finely crushed cornflakes |
| ⅓ | cup chopped flat-leaf parsley |
| 4 | boneless, skinless chicken breast halves |

Preheat the oven to 350°F. Coat a baking sheet with nonstick spray.

In a small microwaveable cup, combine the oil and garlic. Cook in the microwave on high power for 30 seconds, or until fragrant.

In a shallow bowl, beat together the water, Worcestershire sauce, egg white, and salt. Stir in the garlic mixture.

In another shallow bowl, combine the cheese, cornflake crumbs, and parsley.

Dip a chicken breast in the egg white mixture to coat. Dredge in the cornflake crumb mixture to coat completely. Place on the prepared baking sheet. Repeat with the remaining chicken. Lightly coat the chicken with nonstick spray (this will make it crispier when baking).

Bake for 35 minutes, or until a thermometer inserted in the thickest portion registers 160°F and the juices run clear.

## Makes 4 servings

*Per serving: 286 calories, 36 g protein, 14 g carbohydrates, 9 g fat, 4 g saturated fat, 86 mg cholesterol, 682 mg sodium, 1 g fiber*

# Phyllo-Wrapped Chicken

This elegant dish offers a nice surprise when you bite into the pastry covering the chicken: a creamy sauce that tastes complex but is easy to make. The secret is cream of mushroom soup! Calories, fat, and cholesterol were reduced by:

*Nutrition Scorecard*

*(per serving)*

| | before | after |
|---|---|---|
| Calories | 487 | 311 |
| Fat (g) | 31 | 7 |

* ❖ *Replacing puff pastry with phyllo dough*
* ❖ *Eliminating butter to cook the onions*
* ❖ *Using reduced-fat cream soup*

| | |
|---|---|
| 4 | boneless, skinless chicken breast halves |
| 3 | tablespoons lemon juice |
| 1 | onion, chopped |
| 1 | large shallot, chopped |
| 1 | can reduced-fat cream of mushroom soup (10¾ ounces) |
| 2 | tablespoons chopped fresh cilantro |
| ¼ | teaspoon ground black pepper |
| 8 | sheets phyllo dough |

Coat a large nonstick skillet with nonstick spray and warm over medium-high heat. Add the chicken and cook for 3 to 4 minutes on each side, or until browned. Transfer to a plate.

Add the lemon juice, onion, and shallot to the skillet. Cook, stirring, for 5 minutes, or until tender. Stir in the soup, cilantro, and pepper. Cook for 5 minutes, or until well-blended and heated through.

Preheat the oven to 400°F. Coat a baking sheet with nonstick spray.

Place 1 sheet of phyllo dough on a work surface and coat with nonstick spray. Lay another sheet on top and coat it with nonstick spray. Cover the unused phyllo with a damp kitchen towel to prevent drying as you work.

Place a chicken breast onto a short end of the sprayed phyllo stack. Spoon one-quarter of the soup mixture onto the chicken. Fold the long edges of the phyllo over the chicken. Beginning at the short end with the chicken, roll up to enclose. Arrange, seam side down, on the prepared baking sheet. Repeat with the remaining phyllo and chicken. Bake for 10 to 15 minutes, or until the phyllo is golden brown and a thermometer inserted in the thickest portion of the chicken registers 160°F and the juices run clear.

## Makes 4 servings

*Per serving: 311 calories, 31 g protein, 29 g carbohydrates, 7 g fat, 2 g saturated fat, 79 mg cholesterol, 545 mg sodium, 2 g fiber*

# Chicken Kiev

These bundles of breaded chicken are hard to resist—especially now that I have made them more healthful by using Muenster cheese instead of butter for the filling. I also reduced the calories, fat, and cholesterol by:

❖ *Eliminating the butter for cooking the chicken*
❖ *Replacing the egg with egg whites*

2 garlic cloves, minced
4 boneless, skinless chicken breast halves
¼ teaspoon salt
⅛ teaspoon ground black pepper
1 tablespoon chopped flat-leaf parsley
1 tablespoon chopped fresh chives
4 slices (½ ounce each) light Muenster cheese
¼ cup unbleached or all-purpose flour
2 egg whites, lightly beaten
1 tablespoon water
¼ cup plain dry bread crumbs

Preheat the oven to 400°F. Lightly coat an 11" × 7" baking dish with nonstick spray.

Coat a large nonstick skillet with nonstick spray and warm over medium heat. Add the garlic and cook for 5 minutes, or until soft. Remove from the heat.

Meanwhile, place each chicken breast between 2 pieces of plastic wrap. Working from the center to the edges, pound lightly with the flat side of a meat mallet or small skillet to an even ⅛" thickness. Remove the plastic wrap.

Season the chicken with the salt and pepper. Stir the parsley and chives into the skillet with the garlic. Spoon the garlic mixture over the chicken.

Place a cheese slice on each chicken breast. Fold in the long sides of the chicken and roll from a short end, jelly-roll style. Secure with wooden picks.

Spread the flour in a shallow bowl. In another shallow bowl, beat together the egg whites and water. Put the bread crumbs in a third bowl.

Roll the chicken rolls in the flour and then dip into the egg white mixture. Finally, coat with the bread crumbs.

Recoat the skillet with nonstick spray and warm over medium-high heat. Add the chicken rolls and cook for 5 minutes, turning, or until browned.

Arrange the chicken rolls in the prepared baking dish. Bake for 15 to 18 minutes, or until the meat is no longer pink.

**Makes 4 servings**

*Per serving: 247 calories, 34 g protein, 11 g carbohydrates, 6 g fat, 3 g saturated fat, 81 mg cholesterol, 503 mg sodium, 1 g fiber*

# Chicken: White Meat or Dark—What's the Difference?

When it comes to fat and calories, white chicken meat is the healthier choice. Here are the numbers for both a roasted chicken breast and a dark-meat thigh. Note that a chicken breast is larger than a thigh, which is why it's a little higher in calories but still lower in fat.

| Chicken Part | Calories | Fat (g) |
|---|---|---|
| 1 breast, no skin | 142 | 3 |
| 1 breast, with skin | 193 | 8 |
| 1 thigh, no skin | 109 | 6 |
| 1 thigh, with skin | 153 | 10 |

# Chicken Saltimbocca

The classic prosciutto has been replaced with lower-fat turkey ham, but these chicken rolls are still delicious, especially with the sage-scented sherry sauce. Orzo with Spinach (page 318) makes a perfect accompaniment. Calories, fat, and cholesterol were reduced by:

❖ *Eliminating the margarine for cooking the chicken*
❖ *Using turkey ham instead of prosciutto*
❖ *Using reduced-fat Swiss or Provolone cheese*
❖ *Using cornstarch instead of flour and butter to thicken the sauce*

*Nutrition Scorecard*

| (per serving) | before | after |
|---|---|---|
| Calories | 583 | 240 |
| Fat (g) | 33 | 8 |

*Photo on page 191*

## CHICKEN ROLLS

4   boneless, skinless chicken breast halves

4   thin slices turkey ham

4   slices reduced-fat Swiss or Provolone cheese

1   tomato, chopped

## SAUCE

1   tablespoon olive oil

2   garlic cloves, minced

1   cup fat-free chicken broth

2   teaspoons cornstarch

¼   teaspoon salt

2   tablespoons chopped fresh sage or 1 teaspoon dried

2   tablespoons dry sherry or apple juice

TO MAKE THE CHICKEN ROLLS: Rinse the chicken and pat dry. Place each breast between 2 pieces of plastic wrap. Working from the center to the edges, pound lightly with the flat side of a meat mallet or small skillet to an even ⅛" thickness. Remove the plastic wrap.

For each roll, place 1 slice of turkey ham and 1 slice of cheese on each chicken breast. Top with one-quarter of the chopped tomato. Fold in the long sides of the chicken and roll up from a short side, jelly-roll style. Secure with wooden picks.

Coat a large skillet with nonstick spray and warm over medium-low heat. Cook the chicken rolls, turning occasionally, for 25 to 30 minutes, or until the meat is no longer pink and they are evenly browned. Remove from the heat, cover, and keep warm.

TO MAKE THE SAUCE: Heat the oil a medium saucepan over medium-high heat. Add the garlic and cook, stirring occasionally, for 5 minutes, or until soft. Add the broth and cook for 5 minutes.

In a small bowl, combine the cornstarch, salt, sage, and sherry or apple juice. Add to the pan and stir until bubbly. Add the chicken and cook for 2 minutes, spooning the sauce over the chicken.

Place a chicken roll on each serving plate. Spoon the sauce over the rolls and serve.

**Makes 4 servings**

*Per serving: 240 calories, 35 g protein, 4 g carbohydrates, 8 g fat, 2 g saturated fat, 86 mg cholesterol, 463 mg sodium, 1 g fiber*

## *Safe Poultry Handling*

The best place to defrost chicken or turkey is in the refrigerator. Put the poultry on the bottom shelf of the fridge so that the juices won't drip onto other foods. Even if time is short, avoid defrosting on the kitchen counter because bacteria love to grow at room temperature. That's why it's also best to marinate poultry in the refrigerator, even if it's only for an hour or two.

# Marian's Autumn Chicken with Dijon Cider Sauce

My friend Marian inaugurates every fall season with this in-credible chicken dish. The fragrant sauce is served over sautéed apple rings and a simple skillet chicken. Don't be alarmed by the 2 tablespoons of butter—this amount is minis-cule compared with the ½ cup in the original recipe. And Marian doesn't miss the fat at all. She gave this lighter version two thumbs up. Calories, fat, and cholesterol were reduced by:

| *Nutrition Scorecard* | | |
|---|---|---|
| (per serving) | | |
| | before | after |
| Calories | 762 | 329 |
| Fat (g) | 55 | 7 |

*Photo on page 190*

❖ *Replacing cream with a combination of 1% milk and cornstarch*
❖ *Reducing the amount of butter*

### SAUCE

- 2 cups apple cider
- 1½ cups 1% milk
- 2 tablespoons cornstarch
- 2 tablespoons Dijon mustard
- ¼ teaspoon salt
- ¼ teaspoon ground black pepper
- ⅛ teaspoon ground red pepper

### APPLES

- 2 tablespoons butter
- 2 large apples, with peel, cored and cut into ¼"-thick rings

### CHICKEN

- ⅓ cup unbleached or all-purpose flour
- ¾ teaspoon salt
- ½ teaspoon ground black pepper
- 6 boneless, skinless chicken breast halves
- 1 tablespoon dry sherry or apple juice

TO MAKE THE SAUCE: In a medium saucepan, bring the cider to a boil over medium-high heat and cook for 15 minutes, or until reduced to ½ cup. Transfer to a cup and let cool.

In the same saucepan, add all but 2 tablespoons of the milk. In a cup, dissolve the cornstarch in the remaining 2 tablespoons milk and add to the pan. Stir in the mustard, salt, black pepper, and red pepper. Cook and stir over medium heat for 3 to 5 minutes, or until the mixture begins to thicken. Stir in the cooled reduced cider. Cook and stir until bubbly. Remove from the heat and set aside.

TO MAKE THE APPLES: Preheat the oven to 200°F. Melt the butter in a large skillet. Add the apples and cook over medium heat for 3 minutes per side, or just until tender. Transfer to an oven-safe platter and place in the oven to keep warm. Leave the butter in the skillet for cooking the chicken.

TO MAKE THE CHICKEN: In a shallow dish, combine the flour, salt, and pepper.

Place the chicken breasts between 2 pieces of plastic wrap and, using a mallet, pound each to ½" thickness. Dredge the chicken in the flour mixture and shake off any excess.

Place the chicken in the skillet that contains the butter. Cook over medium-high heat for 5 minutes per side, or until a thermometer inserted in the thickest portion registers 160°F and the juices run clear. Transfer to the apple platter and keep warm in the oven.

Add the sherry or apple juice to the skillet. Cook and stir over medium heat for 1 minute, scraping up the browned bits from the bottom of the pan. Add the cider sauce and cook for 4 minutes, or until heated through.

Arrange the chicken and apple slices on 6 dinner plates. Top with the sauce.

**Makes 6 servings**

*Per serving: 329 calories, 32 g protein, 33 g carbohydrates, 7 g fat, 4 g saturated fat, 83 mg cholesterol, 741 mg sodium, 2 g fiber*

*Homestyle Hint:* I like to use a crisp, juicy apple, such as Cortland or Granny Smith, for this recipe.

# Chicken–Cream Cheese Bundles

Wrapped in bacon, these chicken bundles make an attractive meal. The filling satisfies my cravings for something rich and creamy. Calories, fat, and cholesterol were reduced by:

* *Replacing cream cheese with a combination of light and fat-free cream cheeses*
* *Using turkey bacon instead of pork bacon*
* *Eliminating the butter in the cream cheese mixture*

### Nutrition Scorecard
(per serving)

| | before | after |
|---|---|---|
| Calories | 544 | 294 |
| Fat (g) | 36 | 12 |

Photo on page 187

### CHICKEN

4   boneless, skinless chicken breast halves

4   ounces light cream cheese

4   ounces fat-free cream cheese

2   tablespoons chopped fresh chives

1   teaspoon unbleached or all-purpose flour

1   garlic clove, minced

4   slices turkey bacon

### SAUCE

1   ounce mushrooms, thinly sliced (¼ cup)

½   small onion, finely chopped

1   tablespoon cornstarch

¾   cup chicken broth

1   tablespoon chopped flat-leaf parsley

2   teaspoons dry sherry or apple juice

TO MAKE THE CHICKEN: Preheat the oven to 400°F. Coat a baking sheet with nonstick spray.

Rinse the chicken and pat dry. Place each breast between 2 pieces of plastic wrap. Working from the center to the edges, pound lightly with the flat side of a meat mallet or small skillet to an even ¼" thickness. Remove the plastic wrap.

In a bowl, stir together the light cream cheese, fat-free cream cheese, chives, flour, and garlic. Spread one-quarter of the mixture on each chicken breast. Fold in the long sides of the chicken and roll up from a short side, jelly-roll style. Wrap 1 slice of bacon around each roll. Arrange the rolls, seam-side down, on the prepared baking sheet. Secure with wooden picks.

Bake for 40 minutes, or until a thermometer inserted in the thickest portion registers 160°F and the juices run clear. Turn on the broiler and broil for 3 minutes, or until the bacon browns.

TO MAKE THE SAUCE: Meanwhile, coat a medium saucepan with nonstick spray and warm over medium heat. Add the mushrooms and onion. Cook, stirring often, for 10 minutes, or until tender.

In a small bowl, dissolve the cornstarch in ¼ cup of the broth. Add to the mushrooms along with the parsley, sherry or apple juice, and the remaining ½ cup broth. Bring to a boil over high heat, stirring constantly. Reduce the heat to low and cook for 1 minute. Serve with the chicken.

**Makes 4 servings**

Per serving: 294 calories, 36 g protein, 7 g carbohydrates, 12 g fat, 6 g saturated fat, 109 mg cholesterol, 500 mg sodium, 0 g fiber

## How Much Protein Is Enough?

*The average woman needs 44 to 50 grams of protein a day. The average man needs 59 to 63 grams a day. Good sources of protein include lean beef, pork, poultry, seafood, whole grains, beans, nuts, eggs, and reduced-fat dairy products like milk, cheese, and yogurt.*

# Turkey Romano Bake

This one-dish meal works well with leftover turkey or chicken. I reduced calories, fat, and cholesterol by:

❖ *Using cornstarch instead of flour and butter to thicken the cheese sauce*

❖ *Replacing whole milk with 1% milk*

❖ *Using reduced-fat Swiss or Provolone cheese*

| Nutrition Scorecard | | |
|---|---|---|
| *(per serving)* | before | after |
| Calories | 429 | 264 |
| Fat (g) | 22 | 6 |

## *TURKEY*

1 bag washed spinach (10 ounces)

2 tablespoons water

½ pound mushrooms, sliced

1¾ cups 1% milk

2 tablespoons cornstarch

¾ teaspoon salt

¼ teaspoon ground black pepper

¼ teaspoon ground nutmeg

½ cup shredded reduced-fat Swiss or Provolone cheese (2 ounces)

½ cup freshly grated Romano or Parmesan cheese (2 ounces)

2 cups cooked, chopped turkey breast

## *TOPPING*

2 tablespoons freshly shredded Romano or Parmesan cheese

1 tablespoon seasoned dry bread crumbs

TO MAKE THE TURKEY: Preheat the oven to 350°F.

Remove the thick stems and coarsely chop the spinach leaves. Put in a large saucepan and add the water. Cover and cook over medium-high heat for 3 minutes, or until the spinach wilts. Drain and then press between paper towels to squeeze out excess water. Spread in an 11" × 7" baking dish.

Wipe out the saucepan and coat with nonstick spray. Warm over medium heat, add the mushrooms, and cook for 6 minutes, or until the juices are rendered. Remove to a plate.

In a small bowl, combine ¼ cup of the milk, the cornstarch, salt, pepper, and nutmeg. Set aside.

Pour the remaining 1½ cups milk into the saucepan. Cook, stirring, over medium-high heat. Add the cornstarch mixture and cook for 1 minute, or until bubbly. Cook for 1 minute longer.

Reduce the heat to low and add the Swiss or Provolone and Romano or Parmesan. Cook, stirring, for 4 minutes, or until the cheese melts. Remove the sauce from the heat.

Stir in the turkey and mushrooms. Pour over the spinach in the baking dish.

TO MAKE THE TOPPING: Stir together the cheese and bread crumbs in a cup. Sprinkle over the turkey mixture. Bake for 20 minutes, or until bubbly and lightly browned on top.

**Makes 4 servings**

Per serving: 264 calories, 36 g protein, 16 g carbohydrates, 6 g fat, 3 g saturated fat, 77 mg cholesterol, 812 mg sodium, 3 g fiber

*Homestyle Hint:* Spinach is now sold prewashed. If you buy it unwashed, remove any grit by swishing the spinach thoroughly in a sinkful of water, then letting it rest for 2 minutes. The grit will settle to the bottom.

## Ground Turkey Tips

*Turkey breast is the leanest ground meat available, with only 1 gram of fat for 3 ounces (uncooked). Be sure to buy 100 percent ground turkey breast. If the label just says "ground turkey," the package may contain more fatty parts of the bird, including the skin. Because the breast meat is so low in fat, it can be somewhat dry. I like to mix it with a handful of finely chopped apples, bread crumbs, or chopped zucchini to boost the moisture content. For burgers and meatballs, I usually mix ground turkey breast with extra-lean ground beef.*

# Roast Turkey Breast
# with Apple Stuffing

I love to make this on Sundays. Nearly half of the fat has been slashed in this homey meal—but no one will ever know. Calories, fat, and cholesterol were reduced by:

❖ *Eliminating the butter for basting the turkey and replacing it with spiced apple juice concentrate*
❖ *Replacing the butter in the stuffing with additional apple juice*
❖ *Removing the turkey skin before serving*

## STUFFING

2 tart, firm apples, peeled and chopped
1 large onion, chopped
¾ cup apple juice
2 cups plain dry bread cubes
¼ cup currants
1 tablespoon lemon juice
½ teaspoon salt
¼ teaspoon ground nutmeg
¼ teaspoon allspice
⅛ teaspoon ground cinnamon

## TURKEY

1 bone-in turkey breast (5 pounds)
¼ cup thawed frozen apple juice concentrate
⅛ teaspoon ground cinnamon
Pinch of ground nutmeg
Pinch of ground allspice
Pinch of salt

TO MAKE THE STUFFING: Coat a Dutch oven or deep 4-quart saucepan with nonstick spray and warm over high heat. Add the apples and onion and cook, stirring, for 1 minute. Add ¼ cup of the apple juice and bring to a boil. Reduce the heat to medium, cover, and cook for 5 minutes, or until the apples are tender. Stir in the bread cubes, cover, and remove from the heat.

In a small saucepan, stir together the currants and the remaining ½ cup apple juice. Bring to a boil over high heat. Reduce the heat to low, cover, and cook for 5 minutes, or until the currants are plump. Stir in the lemon juice, salt, nutmeg, allspice, and cinnamon. Add to the apples and toss well.

Transfer the stuffing to a 1½-quart baking dish. Cover with foil and set aside.

TO ROAST THE TURKEY: Preheat the oven to 325°F. Coat a shallow roasting pan with nonstick spray.

Rinse the turkey and pat it dry with paper towels. Place the turkey, breast side up, in the prepared roasting pan. Cut several small slits all over the skin.

In a 1-cup measuring cup, mix the apple juice concentrate, cinnamon, nutmeg, allspice, and salt. Brush or spoon evenly over the turkey. Roast the turkey for a total of 2 hours, or until a thermometer inserted in the thickest portion registers 170°F. (Do not let the thermometer touch bone.) During roasting, baste the skin with the apple juice mixture about every 20 minutes. (As you work, collect any pan juices and combine them with the apple juice mixture for basting.)

During the final 30 minutes of roasting, put the stuffing in the oven for 15 minutes. Uncover and bake for 15 minutes longer, or until the top is lightly golden.

Remove the turkey and stuffing from the oven. Let the turkey stand for 15 minutes at room temperature to allow the juices to redistribute throughout the meat.

Remove the skin before slicing the turkey. Serve with the stuffing.

### Makes 8 servings

*Per serving: 311 calories, 34 g protein, 21 g carbohydrates, 10 g fat, 3 g saturated fat, 82 mg cholesterol, 156 mg sodium, 2 g fiber*

*Homestyle Hint:* I like to use a tart apple, such as Granny Smith, for this recipe.

# Turkey: White Meat or Dark—What's the Difference?

Don't assume that white meat is automatically the best choice for turkey. The biggest factor is the skin. For example, dark turkey meat without the skin is lower in calories and fat than white meat with the skin. Here's how the numbers shake out for a 3½-ounce serving of roasted turkey.

| Turkey Part | Calories | Fat (g) |
| --- | --- | --- |
| White meat, no skin | 157 | 3 |
| White meat, with skin | 197 | 8 |
| Dark meat, no skin | 187 | 7 |
| Dark meat, with skin | 221 | 12 |

# Baked Chicken Burritos

We used to call these wet burritos when I was growing up. They are topped with a sauce and baked, so they are really a cross between enchiladas and burritos. If you've never tried whole wheat tortillas, this recipe is a great initiation. I reduced calories, fat, and cholesterol and boosted fiber by:

- *Using light cream cheese instead of full-fat cream cheese*
- *Using reduced-fat Cheddar cheese, and less of it*
- *Replacing red-meat chili with chicken chili*
- *Using whole wheat tortillas*

3   boneless, skinless chicken breast halves
1   can diced green chile peppers (4 ounces), drained
4   ounces light cream cheese (not fat-free)
¼   teaspoon ground cumin
6   whole wheat tortillas (8" diameter)
1   cup salsa
1   can chicken or turkey chili without beans (15 ounces)
½   cup shredded reduced-fat Cheddar cheese (2 ounces)
1   tablespoon chopped fresh cilantro

Preheat the oven to 350°F. Lightly coat a 13" × 9" baking dish with nonstick spray.

Coat a nonstick skillet with nonstick spray and warm over medium-high heat. Add the chicken and cook for 5 minutes on each side, or until a thermometer inserted in the thickest portion registers 160°F and the juices run clear. Transfer to a plate and cool for 5 minutes. Shred the chicken with a fork.

In a medium bowl, stir together the chile peppers, cream cheese, and cumin. Stir in the shredded chicken, mixing until well-combined.

Wrap the tortillas in paper towels or microwaveable plastic wrap and microwave on high power for 30 seconds, or until warmed. Spoon about ⅓ cup of the chicken mixture just off-center on a tortilla. Fold the side that is nearest the filling over the filling. Fold in one of the adjacent sides and roll up from the short side, leaving one end open. Transfer, seam side down, to the prepared baking dish. Repeat with the remaining filling and tortillas.

In another medium bowl, combine the salsa and chili. Pour over the burritos and sprinkle with the cheese. Bake for 20 minutes, or until hot and bubbly. Remove from the oven and garnish with the cilantro before serving.

### Makes 6 servings

*Per serving: 353 calories, 26 g protein, 29 g carbohydrates, 14 g fat, 6 g saturated fat, 73 mg cholesterol, 812 mg sodium, 2 g fiber*

# Family-Pleasing Meatless Meals

ome of my favorite dishes are in this chapter—not because they don't have meat, but because they taste so good! And my family loves them. They can't get enough Mexican Pizza, Polenta Lasagna, or Crustless Italian Ricotta Pie.

Most of these dishes are easy, too. Cheesy Green Enchiladas have just seven ingredients and bake in only 30 minutes. Mexican Pizza is ready from start to finish in 25 minutes thanks to a store-bought prebaked pizza shell. In my house, this surefire meal is always at the ready for those really busy nights.

I also like these meatless meals because they sneak in the vegetables without anybody noticing. By turning the spotlight away from meat and toward the other ingredients in the dish, you get double health benefits from vegetables, beans, and other plant foods. That means more fiber, less fat, and, most important, more phytochemicals.

Phytochemicals are natural compounds in plant foods that have a wide range of healing properties. Researchers have identified hundreds of plant compounds that do everything from help lower cholesterol to help reduce the risk of cancer. Finally, we're figuring out why vegetables are so good for us. For more on phytochemicals, see page 15.

Fortunately, you don't have to eat a pure vegetarian diet to get the health benefits of plant foods. You just need to eat plenty of fruits, vegetables, and grains. These meals are a great start.

# Crustless Italian Ricotta Pie

Smoked-garlic cream cheese and artichoke hearts make this savory pie hard to resist. The cheese browns on the bottom forming a natural "crust." Yum! I reduced calories and fat by:

❖ *Using egg whites in place of whole eggs*
❖ *Using light cream cheese instead of heavy cream*
❖ *Replacing some mayonnaise with artichoke marinade*
❖ *Using reduced-fat mozzarella and ricotta cheeses*
❖ *Eliminating a pastry crust*

| | |
|---|---|
| 4 | egg whites, lightly beaten |
| 1 | cup reduced-fat ricotta cheese (8 ounces) |
| 4 | ounces light smoked-garlic cream cheese, softened |
| ⅓ | cup freshly grated Parmesan cheese (1½ ounces) |
| ¼ | teaspoon ground black pepper |
| 1½ | cups shredded reduced-fat mozzarella cheese (6 ounces) |
| 1 | jar marinated artichoke hearts (14 ounces), marinade reserved |
| ¾ | cup canned chickpeas, rinsed, drained, and coarsely chopped |
| 1 | can sliced black olives (2½ ounces), drained |
| 1 | jar chopped pimientos (2 ounces), drained |
| ¼ | cup chopped flat-leaf parsley |

Preheat the oven to 350°F. Lightly coat a 9" pie plate or quiche dish with nonstick spray.

In a large mixing bowl, stir together the egg whites, ricotta, cream cheese, Parmesan, and pepper until smooth. Stir in the mozzarella and ¼ cup of the reserved artichoke marinade.

Coarsely chop the artichoke hearts. Add to the cheese mixture with the chickpeas, olives, pimientos, and parsley and stir to mix. Scrape into the prepared pie plate. Bake for 45 minutes, or until set and golden. Let stand for 10 minutes. Slice into 8 wedges.

## Makes 8 servings

Per serving: 270 calories, 18 g protein, 14 g carbohydrates, 16 g fat, 8 g saturated fat, 40 mg cholesterol, 810 mg sodium, 1 g fiber

*Homestyle Hint:* Light smoked-garlic cream cheese is sold in 8-ounce tubs in supermarkets. You can also use other varieties of flavored cream cheese, such as scallion cream cheese.

# Baked Eggplant and Provolone

While I have never been a fan of bottled fat-free salad dressings, I have found that they work effectively as marinades. This dish, inspired by traditional eggplant parmigiano, is simple to make and as satisfying as its inspiration. I reduced the calories, fat, and cholesterol by:

❖ *Using fat-free Italian dressing mixed with marinara sauce*
❖ *Using reduced-fat provolone cheese*
❖ *Reducing the amount of Parmesan cheese*

|  |  |
|---|---|
| ¼ | cup fat-free Italian dressing |
| 1 | eggplant (about 2 pounds), washed |
| 1 | tablespoon dried rosemary, crushed |
| 1 | teaspoon dried oregano |
| 1½ | cups fat-free marinara sauce |
| 12 | slices reduced-fat provolone cheese |
| ¼ | cup freshly grated Parmesan cheese (1 ounce) |

Lightly coat a baking sheet with nonstick spray. Spread half of the dressing on the baking sheet.

Slice the eggplant crosswise into twelve ½"-thick rounds and arrange on the prepared baking sheet. Brush with the remaining dressing. Sprinkle with the rosemary and oregano. Let stand at room temperature for no longer than 30 minutes, or cover and chill overnight.

Preheat the broiler. Broil the eggplant for 10 minutes, turning once, or until browned and cooked through. Remove from the broiler. Turn off the broiler and adjust the oven temperature to 450°F.

Top each eggplant slice with 2 tablespoons of the sauce and top with a slice of provolone. Sprinkle each with 1 teaspoon of the Parmesan. Bake for 5 minutes, or until the cheese is melted.

**Makes 4 servings**

*Per serving: 326 calories, 30 g protein, 19 g carbohydrates, 14 g fat, 7 g saturated fat, 66 mg cholesterol, 902 mg sodium, 5 g fiber*

# Polenta Lasagna

My family asks for this meal over and over again. It resembles lasagna, but I use polenta instead of noodles, and the tomato sauce is served on the side. Polenta is the Italian equivalent of grits, only much thicker and made with yellow cornmeal. If you've never tried it, this recipe is a great introduction. Calories, fat, and cholesterol were reduced by:

| *Nutrition Scorecard* | | |
|---|---|---|
| (per serving) | | |
| | before | after |
| Calories | 338 | 249 |
| Fat (g) | 17 | 8 |

*Photo on page 192*

❖ *Eliminating the margarine in the polenta*
❖ *Eliminating the margarine for cooking the vegetables*
❖ *Using reduced-fat cheese, and less of it*

## POLENTA

- 4 cups water
- 1 cup yellow cornmeal
- ½ teaspoon salt
- 1½ cups shredded reduced-fat mozzarella cheese (6 ounces)
- ½ cup freshly grated Parmesan cheese (2 ounces)
- 2 tablespoons chopped fresh basil

## SAUCE

- 1 onion, chopped
- 3 garlic cloves, minced
- 1 can Italian-style diced tomatoes (28 ounces)
- ⅓ cup tomato paste
- ½ teaspoon sugar
- ¼ teaspoon dried oregano
- ¼ teaspoon salt
- ⅛ teaspoon ground black pepper
- ¼ cup chopped fresh basil

TO MAKE THE POLENTA: In a medium saucepan, bring 3 cups of the water to a boil over high heat.

In a medium bowl, stir together the cornmeal, salt, and the remaining 1 cup water. Slowly add to the boiling water, stirring constantly. Cook and stir until the mixture returns to a boil. Reduce the heat to low, cover, and cook, stirring occasionally, for 15 to 20 minutes, or until very thick. (The mixture is thick enough when a spoon inserted in the center stands upright.) Remove from the heat.

Lightly coat an 8" × 8" baking dish with nonstick spray. Dollop one-third of the polenta into the prepared dish and spread in an even layer. In another medium bowl, combine the mozzarella, Parmesan, and basil. Sprinkle half over the polenta. Dollop and spread another third of the polenta over the cheese mixture and sprinkle with the remaining cheese mixture. Top with the remaining polenta in an even layer. Let the dish stand until completely cool. Cover with foil and refrigerate for at least 1 hour or overnight, or until firm.

Preheat the oven to 350°F. Uncover and bake for 40 minutes, or until lightly golden and heated through. Let stand for 10 minutes before cutting.

TO MAKE THE SAUCE: Meanwhile, lightly coat a medium saucepan with nonstick spray and warm over medium heat. Add the onion and garlic and cook for 5 minutes, or until tender. Stir in the tomatoes (with juice), tomato paste, sugar, oregano, salt, and pepper. Bring to a boil over high heat. Reduce the heat to medium-low and cook, stirring occasionally, for 15 to 20 minutes, or until the flavors are well-blended. Stir in the basil and cook for 2 minutes longer. Serve with the polenta.

**Makes 6 servings**

*Per serving: 249 calories, 14 g protein, 32 g carbohydrates, 8 g fat, 5 g saturated fat, 23 mg cholesterol, 690 mg sodium, 5 g fiber*

# Enchilada Strata

Thanks to the buttermilk, this egg-and-cheese casserole has a wonderfully creamy texture. Calories, fat, and cholesterol were reduced by:

* *Replacing whole eggs with egg whites*
* *Using reduced-fat cheese, and less of it*

| | |
| --- | --- |
| 8 | corn tortillas (6" diameter), torn into bite-size pieces |
| 1¼ | cups shredded reduced-fat Monterey Jack cheese (5 ounces) |
| 1 | cup whole kernel corn |
| ½ | cup chopped scallions |
| 1 | egg |
| 2 | egg whites |
| 1 | cup 2% buttermilk |
| 1 | can diced green chile peppers (4 ounces), drained |
| ¼ | teaspoon chili powder |
| ¼ | teaspoon salt |

Preheat the oven to 325°F. Lightly coat a shallow 2-quart baking dish with nonstick spray. Arrange half of the tortilla pieces in the prepared baking dish. Top with half of the cheese, ½ cup of the corn, and ¼ cup of the scallions. Scatter the remaining tortilla pieces over the filling. Top with the remaining cheese, ½ cup corn, and ¼ cup scallions.

In a medium bowl, mix together the egg, egg whites, buttermilk, chile peppers, chili powder, and salt. Drizzle evenly over the tortilla mixture. Bake for 30 minutes, or until a knife inserted in the center comes out almost clean.

## Makes 4 servings

*Per serving: 329 calories, 22 g protein, 42 g carbohydrates, 10 g fat, 5 g saturated fat, 81 mg cholesterol, 725 mg sodium, 5 g fiber*

# Mexican Pizza

Eating this quick meal is like eating seven layers of fiesta dip on a pizza crust—delicious! I reduced the calories, fat, and cholesterol by:

❖ *Eliminating the oil in the beans*
❖ *Using reduced-fat cheeses, and less of them*
❖ *Eliminating the sour cream topping*

| *Nutrition Scorecard* | | |
|---|---|---|
| *(per serving)* | | |
| | before | after |
| Calories | 392 | 268 |
| Fat (g) | 21 | 8 |

*Photo on page 193*

|   |   |
|---|---|
| 2 | garlic cloves |
| 2 | tablespoons coarsely chopped fresh cilantro |
| 1 | can black beans (15 ounces), rinsed and drained |
| 1 | teaspoon ground cumin |
| 1 | prebaked pizza crust (16 ounces) |
| ⅓ | cup salsa |
| 1 | cup shredded reduced-fat Monterey Jack cheese (4 ounces) |
| ½ | cup shredded reduced-fat Cheddar cheese (2 ounces) |
| 1 | can sliced black olives (2½ ounces), drained |
| 1 | red bell pepper, chopped |
| ¼ | cup chopped fresh chives |

Preheat the oven to 425°F.

In a food processor or blender, combine the garlic and cilantro and pulse until chopped. Add the beans and cumin and process until pureed. Spread evenly over the pizza crust. Spread the salsa over the top. Scatter with the Monterey Jack, Cheddar, olives, pepper, and chives. Bake for 15 to 20 minutes, or until the cheese is melted and bubbly.

**Makes 8 servings**

*Per serving: 268 calories, 16 g protein, 34 g carbohydrates, 8 g fat, 4 g saturated fat, 15 mg cholesterol, 858 mg sodium, 3 g fiber*

*Homestyle Hint:* Baked pizza crusts are available at the supermarket. One popular brand is Boboli.

# Mixed Bean Tamale Pie

This southwest meal is one of my son's favorites—and a great example of how easy it is to use cornmeal instead of packaged cornbread for the topping. I reduced the calories, fat, and cholesterol by:

❖ *Using cornmeal instead of packaged cornbread topping*
❖ *Eliminating the oil for cooking the vegetables*
❖ *Using reduced-fat cheese*

## FILLING

1   red or green bell pepper, chopped
1   onion, chopped
2   garlic cloves, chopped
1   can black beans (15 ounces), rinsed and drained
1   can red kidney beans (15 ounces), rinsed and drained
1   can vegetable juice cocktail (6 ounces)
¼   cup chopped fresh cilantro
1   teaspoon chili powder
1   teaspoon ground cumin

## TOPPING

3   cups water
1   cup cornmeal
2   teaspoons sugar
¾   teaspoon salt
1   can water-packed corn kernels (11 ounces), drained
½   cup shredded reduced-fat Cheddar cheese (2 ounces)

TO MAKE THE FILLING: Coat a large nonstick skillet with nonstick spray and warm over medium-high heat. Add the pepper, onion, and garlic and cook, stirring, for 5 minutes, or until tender. Stir in the black beans, kidney beans, vegetable juice, cilantro, chili powder, and cumin and cook for 5 minutes, or just until heated through.

TO MAKE THE TOPPING: In a medium saucepan, bring 2 cups of the water to a boil.

In a medium bowl, stir together the cornmeal, sugar, salt, and the remaining 1 cup water. Slowly add to the boiling water, stirring constantly. Cook, stirring, for 3 minutes, or until the mixture returns to a boil. Reduce the heat to low, cover, and cook, stirring occasionally, for 15 minutes, or until very thick. (The mixture is thick enough when a spoon inserted in the center stands upright.) Stir in the corn and ¼ cup of the cheese. Remove from the heat.

Preheat the oven to 400°F. Spray a 10" quiche dish or a 2-quart shallow baking dish with nonstick spray. Spoon the bean filling into the prepared dish and spread the cornmeal topping over it. Top with the remaining ¼ cup cheese. Bake, uncovered, for 20 minutes, or until golden.

**Makes 6 servings**

*Per serving: 274 calories, 14 g protein, 49 g carbohydrates, 4 g fat, 1 g saturated fat, 7 mg cholesterol, 886 mg sodium, 11 g fiber*

# Meatless Sources of Protein

If you're eating less meat these days, look to the foods below to help you meet your protein needs. It's not too difficult. Take cottage cheese, for instance. One cup has almost as much protein as a cooked chicken breast half (about 25 grams).

| Food | Protein (g) |
| --- | --- |
| Grilled reduced-fat cheese sandwich with bun | 22 |
| 1 cup baked beans | 14 |
| ½ cup low-fat cottage cheese | 14 |
| Peanut butter and jelly sandwich | 14 |
| 1 vegetarian burger | 19 |
| 1½ cups meatless spaghetti | 13 |
| 1 cup fat-free refried beans | 13 |
| 1 cup lentil soup | 8 |
| 1 cup reduced-fat fruited yogurt | 10 |

# Cheesy Green Enchiladas

You would never know by tasting these cheesy enchiladas that ricotta cheese gives the filling its creaminess. One serving (two enchiladas) provides more than three-fourths of your daily calcium needs, thanks to the calcium-rich cheeses. Calories, fat, and cholesterol were reduced by:

❖ *Using reduced-fat cheeses and slightly less of them*
❖ *Softening the corn tortillas by dipping them in taco sauce rather than softening them in oil*

| | |
|---|---|
| 2½ | cups mild green taco sauce |
| 1 | container reduced-fat ricotta cheese (15 ounces) |
| 3 | cups shredded reduced-fat Monterey Jack cheese (12 ounces) |
| 1 | can diced mild green chile peppers (4 ounces), drained |
| ½ | cup chopped fresh chives |
| ¼ | cup chopped fresh cilantro |
| 12 | corn tortillas (6" diameter) |

Preheat the oven to 350°F. Spread 1¼ cups of the taco sauce evenly in a 13" × 9" baking dish.

In a large bowl, mix together the ricotta, 2 cups of the Monterey Jack, ½ cup of the remaining taco sauce, chile peppers, chives, and cilantro.

In a large skillet, warm the remaining ¾ cup taco sauce.

Wrap the tortillas in paper towels or microwaveable plastic wrap and microwave on high power for 30 seconds, or until warmed. Using tongs, carefully place 1 tortilla in the warmed sauce, submerging it completely so that it softens enough to roll without cracking. Lift from the pan, letting the excess sauce drip back into the pan. Place the tortilla on a plate. Spoon about ¼ cup filling down the center. Roll the tortilla around the filling and transfer, seam side down, to the baking dish. Repeat with the remaining tortillas and filling.

Pour any remaining sauce over the enchiladas. Top with the remaining 1 cup Monterey Jack. Cover with foil and bake for 30 minutes, or until the cheese is melted.

**Makes 12 enchiladas; 6 servings**

*Per serving: 266 calories, 27 g protein, 8 g carbohydrates, 13 g fat, 9 g saturated fat, 61 mg cholesterol, 540 mg sodium, 1 g fiber*

# Sour Cream Taco Bake

When I want a meatless meal that's rich and creamy, I turn to this recipe. It's like a cheese enchilada casserole with taco seasoning for more flavor. Calories, fat, sodium, and cholesterol were reduced by:

*Nutrition Scorecard*

(per serving)

| | before | after |
|---|---|---|
| Calories | 503 | 328 |
| Fat (g) | 33 | 9 |

- ❖ *Eliminating the oil for cooking the onions*
- ❖ *Using fat-free sour cream*
- ❖ *Using reduced-fat Monterey Jack cheese, and less of it*
- ❖ *Using sodium-free canned tomatoes*

2   onions, chopped

1   can sodium-free chopped tomatoes
    (28 ounces), drained

1   package taco seasoning mix (1¼ ounces)

12  corn tortillas (6" diameter)

3   cups reduced-fat Monterey Jack cheese
    (12 ounces)

1   container fat-free sour cream (without gelatin),
    16 ounces

1   teaspoon sodium-free seasoned salt

    Paprika

Coat a large nonstick skillet with nonstick spray and warm over medium-high heat. Add the onions and cook, stirring, for 5 minutes, or until tender. Add the tomatoes and taco seasoning mix. Bring to a boil. Reduce the heat to medium-low, cover, and cook, stirring occasionally, for 10 minutes, or until well-blended. Remove from the heat.

Preheat the oven to 325°F. Lightly coat a 13" × 9" baking dish with nonstick spray. Spread a little of the tomato sauce in the dish. Arrange 4 of the tortillas on top of the sauce, tearing them to fit. Top with one-third of the remaining sauce and one-third of the cheese. Repeat the layering two more times.

In a small bowl, combine the sour cream and seasoned salt. Spread over the cheese to the edges of the dish. Sprinkle with paprika. Bake for 25 to 30 minutes, or until bubbly.

## Makes 8 servings

*Per serving: 328 calories, 21 g protein, 42 g carbohydrates, 9 g fat, 6 g saturated fat, 30 mg cholesterol, 871 mg sodium, 4 g fiber*

# Crustless Garden Quiche

I like to serve this quiche with brown rice and a tossed green salad. Calories, fat, and cholesterol were reduced by:

❖ *Using reduced-fat cheeses*
❖ *Replacing some of the whole eggs with egg whites*
❖ *Using fat-free evaporated milk instead of whole milk*

| | |
|---|---|
| 1 | onion, chopped |
| 1 | garlic clove, chopped |
| 1 | cup tiny broccoli florets |
| 2 | medium yellow summer squash, chopped |
| 1 | tomato, chopped |
| ¼ | teaspoon dried basil |
| ¼ | teaspoon dried marjoram |
| ½ | cup shredded reduced-fat Swiss cheese (2 ounces) |
| ½ | cup shredded reduced-fat smoked gouda or Swiss cheese (2 ounces) |
| 2 | eggs |
| 4 | egg whites |
| ¾ | cup fat-free evaporated milk |
| 1 | tablespoon unbleached or all-purpose flour |
| ½ | teaspoon salt |

Preheat the oven to 375°F. Lightly coat a 9" quiche dish or pie plate with nonstick spray.

Coat a large nonstick skillet with nonstick spray and warm over medium-high heat. Add the onion, garlic, broccoli, and squash and cook, stirring, for 5 minutes, or until tender. Add the tomato, basil, and marjoram and cook for 1 minute longer. Transfer to the prepared pan, spreading the mixture evenly. Sprinkle the cheeses over the vegetables.

In a medium bowl, beat together the eggs, egg whites, evaporated milk, flour, and salt until well-blended. Pour over the vegetables. Bake for 40 minutes, or until the top is golden and a wooden pick inserted in the center comes out clean. Let stand for 10 minutes before cutting into 4 wedges.

## Makes 4 servings

*Per serving: 171 calories, 20 g protein, 13 g carbohydrates, 4 g fat, 2 g saturated fat, 118 mg cholesterol, 492 mg sodium, 2 g fiber*

# Baked Zucchini with Dill Seed

Many years ago on my husband's birthday, I offered to pre-pare any meal he chose from any cookbook. A true labor of love! He selected a version of this recipe, and it was incred-ibly flavorful and easy to make. To this day, it remains one of his favorite meals in this lightened form. I reduced calories, fat, and cholesterol by:

*Nutrition Scorecard*

| | (per serving) | |
|---|---|---|
| | before | after |
| Calories | 212 | 136 |
| Fat (g) | 11 | 6 |

❖ *Replacing most of the whole eggs with egg whites*
❖ *Using 1% cottage cheese in place of full-fat cottage cheese*
❖ *Using Parmesan cheese as the topping instead of a mixture of butter and bread crumbs*

   2   **pounds zucchini**
   1   **cup 1% cottage cheese (8 ounces)**
   1   **cup shredded reduced-fat Monterey Jack cheese (4 ounces)**
   1   **egg**
   2   **egg whites**
   1   **teaspoon dill seed**
  ¼   **teaspoon salt**
   3   **tablespoons freshly grated Parmesan cheese**

Preheat the oven to 350°F. Lightly coat a 13" × 9" baking dish or shallow casserole with nonstick spray.

Lightly coat a large nonstick skillet with nonstick spray and warm over medium-high heat. Quarter the zucchini lengthwise, then slice crosswise. Add to the skillet and cook, stirring, for 3 minutes, just until tender. Do not overcook.

In a large bowl, stir together the cottage cheese, Monterey Jack, egg, egg whites, dill seed, and salt until well-mixed. Fold in the zucchini. Transfer to the prepared baking dish. Sprinkle with the Parmesan. Bake for 35 to 40 minutes, or until golden and a wooden pick inserted in the center comes out clean.

**Makes 6 servings**

*Per serving: 136 calories, 16 g protein, 6 g carbohydrates, 6 g fat, 3 g saturated fat, 53 mg cholesterol, 482 mg sodium, 2 g fiber*

# Lentil-Cheddar Casserole

Easy to make, this lentil bake also is loaded with nutrients. One serving provides 150 percent of your daily vitamin A requirement, three-fourths of the folic acid, and more than a third of the calcium, iron, and vitamin C. Wow! I call that a nutritious meal. Calories, fat, and cholesterol were reduced by:

| *Nutrition Scorecard* | | |
|---|---|---|
| (per serving) | | |
| | before | after |
| Calories | 416 | 348 |
| Fat (g) | 14 | 6 |

❖ *Using reduced-fat Cheddar cheese and reducing the amount*
❖ *Enhancing the flavor by cooking the lentils in broth instead of relying on oil*

| | |
|---|---|
| 2 | cups lentils, rinsed |
| 2 | cups hot water |
| 1 | cup fat-free chicken broth or vegetable broth |
| 4 | carrots, finely chopped |
| 1 | large onion, finely chopped |
| 1 | green bell pepper, chopped |
| 1 | can Italian-style diced tomatoes (15 ounces) |
| 2 | garlic cloves, chopped |
| 1 | bay leaf |
| ¾ | teaspoon salt |
| ¾ | teaspoon dried marjoram |
| ¼ | teaspoon ground black pepper |
| 1½ | cups shredded reduced-fat sharp Cheddar cheese (6 ounces) |

Preheat the oven to 375°F.

In a large bowl, mix together the lentils, water, broth, carrots, onion, bell pepper, tomatoes (with juice), garlic, bay leaf, salt, marjoram, black pepper, and ¾ cup of the cheese. Pour into a 13" × 9" baking dish.

Cover tightly with foil. Bake for 1 hour, or until the lentils are tender. Remove and discard the bay leaf. Sprinkle with the remaining ¾ cup cheese. Return to the oven and bake, uncovered, for 10 minutes longer, or until bubbling and golden.

## Makes 6 servings

*Per serving: 348 calories, 29 g protein, 48 g carbohydrates, 6 g fat, 4 g saturated fat, 20 mg cholesterol, 636 mg sodium, 11 g fiber*

# Feta-Spinach Rice Bake

I love how the brown rice gives this meal such a pleasing, chewy texture. In a pinch, you can substitute instant brown rice; cook it according to the package directions, but use chicken broth in place of water. Calories, fat, and cholesterol were reduced by:

*Nutrition Scorecard*
(per serving)

| | before | after |
|---|---|---|
| Calories | 306 | 246 |
| Fat (g) | 13 | 7 |

❖ *Cooking the rice in chicken broth for flavor rather than relying on olive oil*
❖ *Reducing the amount of feta cheese*
❖ *Using 1% milk*
❖ *Replacing the whole egg with egg whites*
❖ *Eliminating the oil for cooking the vegetables*

2  cups fat-free chicken broth or vegetable broth
1  cup brown rice
1  onion, chopped
1  red bell pepper, chopped
2  packages frozen chopped spinach (10 ounces each), thawed and squeezed dry
4  ounces feta cheese, finely chopped
1  cup 1% milk
3  egg whites, lightly beaten
¼  cup freshly grated Parmesan cheese (1 ounce)

In a medium saucepan over high heat, bring the broth to a boil. Stir in the rice, reduce the heat to medium-low, cover, and simmer for 35 minutes, or until tender and the broth is absorbed. Remove from the heat and fluff the rice with a fork.

Preheat the oven to 375°F. Coat a 2½-quart shallow baking dish with nonstick spray.

Coat a large nonstick skillet with nonstick spray and warm over medium-high heat. Add the onion and pepper and cook, stirring, for 5 minutes, or until tender. Remove from the heat. Stir in the spinach, feta, and rice. Spoon into the prepared baking dish and spread evenly.

In a medium bowl, mix together the milk and egg whites. Pour evenly over the spinach mixture. Sprinkle with the Parmesan. Cover with foil and bake for 30 minutes, or until set and bubbling around the edges.

## Makes 6 servings

*Per serving: 246 calories, 15 g protein, 33 g carbohydrates, 7 g fat, 4 g saturated fat, 22 mg cholesterol, 522 mg sodium, 4 g fiber*

# Barley-Stuffed Peppers

Barley is right up there with potatoes on my comfort-food scale. It has such a filling, satisfying taste and texture, especially in this dish. Be sure to boil the peppers for a few minutes so that they will cook thoroughly when baked with the stuffing. I reduced calories, fat, and cholesterol by:

❖ *Eliminating the oil for cooking the onion*
❖ *Using reduced-fat cheese, and less of it*
❖ *Using fat-free chicken broth*

| Nutrition Scorecard | | |
|---|---|---|
| (per pepper) | | |
| | before | after |
| Calories | 405 | 233 |
| Fat (g) | 15 | 4 |

*Photo on page 194*

|  |  |
|---|---|
| 2⅔ | cups fat-free chicken broth or vegetable broth |
| 1 | cup pearl barley |
| 6 | red, green, and/or yellow bell peppers |
| 1 | large onion, chopped |
| 3 | carrots, finely chopped or shredded |
| 2 | celery ribs, finely chopped |
| ½ | teaspoon salt |
| 2 | tablespoons chopped flat-leaf parsley |
| 1 | cup shredded reduced-fat Cheddar cheese (4 ounces) |

In a 3-quart saucepan over medium-high heat, bring the broth and barley to a boil. Reduce the heat to low, cover, and cook for 40 minutes, or until the liquid is absorbed.

Preheat the oven to 375°F. Lightly coat a 13" × 9" baking dish with nonstick spray.

Slice off the top stem ends from the peppers and scrape out the seeds and membranes, keeping the peppers intact.

Bring a large stockpot of water to a boil over high heat. Submerge the peppers in the water and cook for 3 minutes, just to soften. Lift from the water with tongs and drain, inverted, on paper towels.

Coat a large nonstick skillet with nonstick spray and warm over medium-high heat. Add the onion, carrots, and celery and cook, stirring occasionally, for 5 minutes, or until tender. Remove from the heat. Stir in the salt, parsley, barley and all but 6 tablespoons of the cheese. Spoon into the peppers, filling each evenly. Top each with 1 tablespoon of the remaining cheese.

Place the peppers in the prepared baking dish, standing them shoulder to shoulder. Bake for 10 minutes, or just until the cheese melts. Serve immediately.

## Makes 6 peppers

*Per pepper: 233 calories, 13 g protein, 38 g carbohydrates, 4 g fat, 3 g saturated fat, 13 mg cholesterol, 511 mg sodium, 8 g fiber*

*Homestyle Hints:* To keep the peppers upright, slice a small piece off the bottom of each pepper before stuffing.

Pearl barley has had the bran removed and the grain steamed and polished. This is a common type of barley that is widely available in the grain aisles of supermarkets.

# Pick a Peck of Vitamin C

Bell peppers are loaded with vitamin C. Just one pepper of any color meets the daily recommendation of vitamin C for adults (60 milligrams a day). Snack on crispy fresh peppers or cook them in soups, stews, and casseroles. Roasted red and yellow peppers are sweet and smoky tasting—just the thing to jazz up a salad, pasta dish, or sandwich.

| Bell Pepper (1 whole) | Vitamin C (mg) |
|---|---|
| Yellow | 341 |
| Red | 141 |
| Green | 66 |

# Zucchini-Potato Pancakes

These savory patties are ultra-low in calories and fat, mainly because I changed the cooking technique. Instead of frying in oil, the cakes are pan-fried in nonstick spray. Calories, fat, and cholesterol were further reduced by:

❖ *Replacing the whole egg with egg whites*
❖ *Eliminating the oil*

| *Nutrition Scorecard* | | |
|---|---|---|
| *(per serving)* | | |
| | before | after |
| Calories | 310 | 224 |
| Fat (g) | 21 | 2 |

2½ pounds zucchini (about 4 medium), grated
2 potatoes, peeled and grated
6 tablespoons unbleached or all-purpose flour
½ small onion, grated
¼ cup freshly grated Parmesan cheese (1 ounce)
4 egg whites, lightly beaten
1 teaspoon dried basil
1 teaspoon salt
¼ teaspoon ground black pepper

In a large bowl, combine the zucchini and potatoes. Using a paper towel, lightly squeeze to remove excess moisture. Stir in the flour, onion, Parmesan, egg whites, basil, salt, and pepper.

Lightly coat a nonstick griddle or large skillet with nonstick spray and warm over medium-high heat. Using a ¼-cup measuring cup, scoop out the batter and drop onto the griddle. Flatten with a spatula to make pancakes that are approximately 4" in diameter. Cook for 3 minutes on each side, or until golden brown. Add a little more spray if necessary to prevent sticking.

**Makes 16 pancakes; 4 servings**

*Per serving: 224 calories, 12 g protein, 44 g carbohydrates, 2 g fat, 1 g saturated fat, 3 mg cholesterol, 667 mg sodium, 7 g fiber*

# Fresh Corn Tamales

Here is one of my favorite meatless recipes. It begins with ordinary corn and doesn't rely on any exotic ingredients. You need to buy corn on the cob, however, to get the husks necessary to make the tamales. I reduced calories, fat, and cholesterol by:

❖ *Replacing cream with low-fat buttermilk*
❖ *Using reduced-fat Muenster cheese*
❖ *Using light butter instead of regular butter*
❖ *Replacing the shortening with applesauce*

| Nutrition Scorecard | | |
|---|---|---|
| *(per serving)* | | |
| | before | after |
| Calories | 384 | 242 |
| Fat (g) | 20 | 7 |

| | |
|---|---|
| 6 | large ears corn, shucked, husks reserved |
| ⅓ | cup cornmeal |
| 2 | tablespoons unsweetened applesauce |
| 1 | tablespoon cornstarch |
| 2 | tablespoons light butter, melted |
| 1 | tablespoon 2% buttermilk |
| 2 | teaspoons sugar |
| ½ | teaspoon salt |
| 6 | slices reduced-fat Muenster cheese, halved |

Cut the corn kernels from the cobs and transfer the kernels to a food processor. Discard the cobs. Add the cornmeal, applesauce, cornstarch, butter, buttermilk, sugar, and salt. Pulse until the texture resembles a coarse paste or wet cookie dough.

For each tamale, overlap 2 corn husks lengthwise. Spread about 3 tablespoons of the corn mixture onto the husks, leaving at least a 1" border on all sides. Place ½ slice of cheese in the center of the dough. Pick up the 2 long sides of the husk and bring them together (this will cause the dough to surround the filling). Fold up the short sides of the husk to form a tightly closed package. Secure by loosely tying it closed with kitchen twine.

Carefully transfer the tamales to a steamer or steaming rack set over 1" to 2" of water in a large pan. Bring the water to a simmer, cover the pot, and steam for 40 minutes, or until cooked through. Serve in the husks. (Do not eat the husks.)

### Makes 12 tamales; 6 servings

*Per serving (2 tamales): 242 calories, 10 g protein, 40 g carbohydrates, 7 g fat, 2 g saturated fat, 15 mg cholesterol, 348 mg sodium, 4 g fiber*

*Homestyle Hint:* For a bit more spice, add a can of chopped mild green chile peppers (4 ounces), drained, along with the cornmeal.

# Parmesan Spinach–Stuffed Potatoes

This is an easy dish to whip up. It's also substantial and satisfying. Calories, fat, and cholesterol were reduced by:

❖ *Eliminating the oil for cooking the spinach*
❖ *Using fat-free cottage cheese in place of full-fat cottage cheese*
❖ *Eliminating the butter*

| | |
|---|---|
| 4 | large potatoes |
| 3 | garlic cloves, minced |
| 1 | package frozen chopped spinach (10 ounces), thawed and squeezed dry |
| 1 | cup fat-free cottage cheese |
| ½ | cup freshly grated Parmesan cheese (2 ounces) |

Preheat the oven to 450°F. Pierce the potatoes in several places with a fork. Bake for 45 minutes, or until tender.

Lightly coat a large skillet with nonstick spray and warm over medium-high heat. Add the garlic and cook for 1 minute. Add the spinach and cook, stirring frequently, for 2 minutes, or until wilted. Stir in the cottage cheese and Parmesan and cook, stirring, for 2 minutes, or until the Parmesan melts.

Cut a 1" to 2" X in each potato and squeeze to open slightly. Divide the stuffing among the potatoes.

**Makes 4 servings**

*Per serving: 351 calories, 19 g protein, 64 g carbohydrates, 3 g fat, 2 g saturated fat, 9 mg cholesterol, 373 mg sodium, 7 g fiber*

## No Protein Shortage Here

*Americans have doubled their animal protein intake since the early 1900s. Meat, fish, and poultry now account for 42 percent of the protein eaten in the United States.*

# Cajun Red Beans and Rice

Canned beans make this dish a snap. And they are just as fiber-rich as the dried beans that you cook from scratch. A single serving of this recipe meets nearly two-thirds of the recommended fiber levels for the day. Serve with cornbread and collards to make a Southern-style meal. I reduced calories, fat, and cholesterol and boosted fiber by:

| *Nutrition Scorecard* | | |
|---|---|---|
| *(per serving)* | | |
| | before | after |
| Calories | 601 | 373 |
| Fat (g) | 16 | 3 |

* *Eliminating the oil for cooking the vegetables*
* *Eliminating sausage and using more bell peppers*
* *Using brown rice instead of white rice*

| | |
|---|---|
| 1 | large onion, chopped |
| 2 | garlic cloves |
| 2 | cans red kidney beans (15 ounces each), rinsed and drained |
| 1 | can tomato sauce (8 ounces) |
| 2 | green and/or red bell peppers, chopped |
| 1 | teaspoon dried oregano |
| 1 | teaspoon dried thyme |
| 1 | teaspoon hot-pepper sauce |
| 2 | cups brown rice |
| ⅓ | cup chopped fresh chives or scallions |

Coat a large nonstick skillet with nonstick spray and warm over medium-high heat. Add the onion and garlic and cook, stirring, for 5 minutes, or until tender. Stir in the beans, tomato sauce, bell peppers, oregano, thyme, and hot-pepper sauce. Bring to a boil. Reduce the heat to low, cover, and cook, stirring occasionally, for 15 minutes, or until the flavors are blended.

Cook the rice according to the package directions. Serve the beans over the rice. Garnish with the chives or scallions.

## Makes 6 servings

*Per serving: 373 calories, 14 g protein, 75 g carbohydrates, 3 g fat, 0.5 g saturated fat, 0 mg cholesterol, 741 mg sodium, 17 g fiber*

# Pastabilities

Not long ago, Americans were in love with the notion of eating any amount of fat-free foods. As a naturally fat-free food, pasta topped the list of good choices. But our waistlines began to expand anyway, and pasta fell into disrepute. It must be the culprit, many decided.

Such thinking is akin to throwing out the baby with the bathwater. Contrary to popular belief, eating carbohydrates like pasta does not kick-start the fat-making machinery in our bodies. The truth is that pasta provides much-needed energy.

Of course, overeating pasta—or any food—can cause you to put on pounds. But pasta itself is not the problem; gigantic servings are. The key to keeping pasta healthy is limiting portion sizes and serving it with healthy sauces.

Most of the recipes in this chapter rely on 3 ounces of dried pasta per serving, an amount that is neither skimpy nor off the scale. I have cut the fat in the sauces by reducing the amounts of oil, using lean cuts of meat, and employing a few other tricks explained throughout the recipes.

When it comes to Parmesan cheese, however, I must confess that I cannot compromise. It is the crowning glory of so many pasta dishes. Nothing beats freshly grated Parmesan for last-minute flavor. If you hesitate to keep a block of Parmesan in your fridge, at the least, I recommend deli-style Parmesan (the tubs of freshly grated cheese in the delicatessen or the cheese section of the supermarket). This is crucial because, when trimming the fat, you have to get extra flavor from somewhere else. For my money, good-quality Parmesan cheese is worth every gram of fat.

# Spirals with No-Cook Summer Sauce

This sauce is bursting with flavor and is one of my all-time favorites. And the beauty is that you don't even cook it! You can make this sauce year-round, but it tastes best when tomatoes are in season in the summer. I reduced calories and fat by:

❖ *Greatly reducing the amount of olive oil*
❖ *Reducing the amount of Parmesan cheese*

*Photo on page 197*

| | |
|---|---|
| 3 | garlic cloves, chopped |
| 2 | teaspoons olive oil |
| 2 | teaspoons white wine vinegar |
| 6 | tomatoes, chopped |
| 1 | large yellow bell pepper, chopped |
| ⅓ | cup chopped fresh basil leaves |
| 2 | tablespoons chopped flat-leaf parsley |
| ¾ | teaspoon salt |
| 1 | can sliced black olives (3.8 ounces), drained |
| ⅓ | cup freshly grated Parmesan cheese (1½ ounces) |
| 12 | ounces dried spiral pasta, such as rotelle |

In a large bowl, combine the garlic, oil, and vinegar. Add the tomatoes, pepper, basil, parsley, salt, olives, and cheese and toss gently. Set aside at room temperature for at least 15 minutes so that the tomatoes can release their juices.

Meanwhile, cook the pasta according to the package directions. Drain. Transfer to the bowl and gently toss with the sauce. Serve immediately.

## Makes 4 servings

*Per serving: 459 calories, 15 g protein, 79 g carbohydrates, 10 g fat, 2 g saturated fat, 7 mg cholesterol, 808 mg sodium, 4 g fiber*

# Linguine with Peppers and Sausage

Made with red, green, and yellow bell peppers, this colorful dish is a staple in our house, especially on busy nights. The turkey sausage gives it robust flavor. Calories, fat, and cholesterol were reduced by:

❖ *Using turkey sausage, and less of it*
❖ *Eliminating the wine*
❖ *Slightly reducing the amount of Parmesan cheese*
❖ *Increasing the amount of peppers to make up for less sausage*

| | |
|---|---|
| 12 | ounces dried linguine |
| ½ | pound hot or sweet lean Italian turkey sausage, casings removed |
| 1 | yellow bell pepper, chopped |
| 1 | red bell pepper, chopped |
| 1 | green bell pepper, chopped |
| 1 | onion, chopped |
| 3 | garlic cloves, chopped |
| ½ | teaspoon salt |
| ⅛ | teaspoon ground black pepper |
| ⅓ | cup freshly grated Parmesan cheese |

Cook the linguine according to the package directions. Drain.

Meanwhile, lightly coat a large nonstick skillet with nonstick spray and warm over medium-high heat. Add the sausage and cook, breaking up the meat and stirring, for 5 minutes, or until no longer pink.

Add the bell peppers, onion, garlic, salt, and black pepper. Cook, stirring, for 5 minutes, or until tender.

Add the linguine to the skillet and toss to mix. Stir in the cheese and serve immediately.

**Makes 4 servings**

*Per serving: 476 calories, 23 g protein, 73 g carbohydrates, 10 g fat, 3 g saturated fat, 73 mg cholesterol, 789 mg sodium, 2 g fiber*

# Sun-Dried Tomato Pesto Pasta

Mamma mia! The original version of this pasta dish oozed with oil. But now it has about half the calories and a fifth of the fat. The flavor is still rich and satisfying. I reduced calories, fat, and cholesterol by:

❖ *Using chicken broth in place of most of the olive oil*
❖ *Using dry-packed sun-dried tomatoes instead of oil-packed*
❖ *Using less cheese*
❖ *Reducing the amount of nuts*

*Nutrition Scorecard*

(per serving)

|  | before | after |
|---|---|---|
| Calories | 847 | 483 |
| Fat (g) | 53 | 12 |

| | |
|---|---|
| 12 | ounces dried spaghetti |
| 3 | ounces dry-packed sun-dried tomatoes |
| 1½ | cups fat-free chicken broth, heated |
| ⅓ | cup freshly grated Parmesan cheese (1½ ounces) |
| ⅓ | cup chopped fresh basil leaves |
| 2 | tablespoons chopped walnuts |
| 3 | garlic cloves |
| 4 | teaspoons olive oil |

Cook the spaghetti according to the package directions. Drain and place in a serving bowl.

Meanwhile, place the tomatoes in a small bowl and pour the hot broth over them. Cover and let soak for 10 minutes, or until soft.

In a food processor or blender, combine the tomatoes, the tomato soaking liquid, cheese, basil, walnuts, and garlic. Process until finely chopped. With the motor running, slowly add the oil. Process until smooth.

Add to the bowl with the spaghetti and toss to coat.

## Makes 4 servings

*Per serving: 483 calories, 18 g protein, 78 g carbohydrates, 12 g fat, 3 g saturated fat, 7 mg cholesterol, 727 mg sodium, 3 g fiber*

# Fettuccine with Spicy Spinach and Tomatoes

This sauce is absolutely delicious. Crumbled goat cheese is the crowning touch. I reduced calories and fat by:

❖ *Eliminating the oil for cooking the vegetables*
❖ *Eliminating the bacon*
❖ *Reducing the amount of Parmesan cheese*
❖ *Reducing the amount of goat cheese*

## Nutrition Scorecard
(per serving)

|  | before | after |
|---|---|---|
| Calories | 424 | 276 |
| Fat (g) | 22 | 8 |

| | |
|---|---|
| 10 | tomatoes, chopped |
| 1 | tablespoon balsamic vinegar |
| 1 | tablespoon chopped fresh rosemary or 1 teaspoon dried |
| ½ | teaspoon salt |
| 2 | leeks, finely chopped |
| 6 | garlic cloves, chopped |
| ½ | teaspoon crushed red-pepper flakes |
| 1 | bag washed baby spinach (6 ounces), chopped |
| 18 | ounces fresh fettuccine or 12 ounces dried |
| ¼ | cup freshly grated Parmesan cheese (1 ounce) |
| 1 | log goat cheese (3½ ounces), sliced into 6 rounds |

In a large bowl, combine the tomatoes, vinegar, rosemary, and salt. Set aside at room temperature for at least 15 minutes so that the tomatoes can release their juices.

Meanwhile, coat a large nonstick skillet with nonstick spray and warm over medium-high heat. Add the leeks, garlic, and red-pepper flakes and cook, stirring, for 5 minutes, or until tender. Add the tomato mixture and cook for 5 minutes, or until the tomatoes are softened. Stir in the spinach, cover, and cook for 2 minutes, or until the spinach is wilted. Reduce the heat to low, stir, cover, and simmer for 10 to 15 minutes, or until the flavors are blended.

Cook the fettuccine according to the package directions. Transfer to a large bowl. Add the spinach mixture and Parmesan. Toss gently and serve. Crumble one round of goat cheese over each serving.

**Makes 6 servings**

Per serving: 276 calories, 14 g protein, 40 g carbohydrates, 8 g fat, 5 g saturated fat, 44 mg cholesterol, 409 mg sodium, 6 g fiber

# Creamy Pesto Pasta

I was thrilled when I figured out how to cut the fat by three-fourths in this richly satisfying pesto sauce. Calories, fat, and cholesterol were reduced by:

❖ *Using pureed 1% cottage cheese in place of cream*
❖ *Using fat-free chicken broth*

| *Nutrition Scorecard* | | |
|---|---|---|
| (per serving) | | |
| | before | after |
| Calories | 674 | 433 |
| Fat (g) | 40 | 11 |

| | |
|---|---|
| 1 | pound dried fusilli, rotini, or any curly pasta |
| 1½ | cups packed fresh basil leaves |
| 3 | tablespoons pine nuts |
| 4 | garlic cloves |
| 1½ | cups 1% cottage cheese (12 ounces) |
| ½ | cup fat-free chicken broth |
| 4 | teaspoons olive oil |
| ¾ | cup freshly grated Parmesan cheese (3 ounces) |
| ⅛ | teaspoon ground black pepper |

Cook the pasta according to the package directions. Drain.

Meanwhile, place the basil, pine nuts, and garlic in a food processor or blender and process until finely chopped. Add the cottage cheese and puree until smooth. With the machine running, slowly add the broth and oil. When completely incorporated, add the Parmesan and pepper. Pulse just to mix.

Warm a large skillet over low heat. Transfer the mixture to the skillet and cook, stirring, just until heated through. Do not boil. Remove from the heat.

Add the pasta to the pesto and toss to coat.

## Makes 6 servings

*Per serving: 433 calories, 24 g protein, 60 g carbohydrates, 11 g fat, 4 g saturated fat, 12 mg cholesterol, 495 mg sodium, 1 g fiber*

# Egg Noodles
# with Wild Mushroom Sauce

Lightening up this dish actually made it easier to prepare.
This version starts with cream of mushroom soup rather than
heavy cream and sliced fresh mushrooms. Calories, fat, and
cholesterol were reduced by:

❖ *Replacing heavy cream with reduced-fat cream of mushroom
soup*
❖ *Using no-yolk egg noodles instead of traditional egg noodles*
❖ *Eliminating the wine*

| | |
|---|---|
| 1 | ounce dried wild mushrooms |
| 1 | cup boiling water |
| 8 | ounces dried no-yolk egg noodles |
| 1 | can reduced-fat cream of mushroom soup (10¾ ounces) |
| 2 | tablespoons 1% milk |
| 1 | teaspoon lemon juice |
| ¾ | teaspoon dried tarragon |
| ½ | cup chopped fresh chives |

In a small bowl, combine the mushrooms and water. Set aside for 15 minutes, or until the
mushrooms are soft. Drain, reserving the soaking liquid. Coarsely chop the mushrooms.

Cook the noodles according to the package directions. Drain.

Meanwhile, in a medium saucepan, combine the soup, milk, lemon juice, and tarragon.
Slowly pour the mushroom soaking liquid into the pan, taking care to leave any gritty
sediment in the bowl. Add the chopped mushrooms. Cook, stirring, over medium heat
for 8 minutes, or until bubbling and the flavors are blended. Spoon over the noodles and
serve sprinkled with the chives.

**Makes 4 servings**

*Per serving: 289 calories, 12 g protein, 52 g carbohydrates, 3 g fat, 1 g saturated fat, 6 mg cholesterol, 327 mg sodium, 3 g fiber*

*Homestyle Hint:* Most supermarkets carry mixtures of dried wild mushrooms in cellophane
bags. The bags usually include chanterelles, shiitakes, and morels. For this sauce, you can use any
mix of dried mushrooms or any single kind of dried mushroom.

# Garlicky Fusilli with Broccoli and Dried Tomatoes

I firmly believe that you never can go wrong with lots of garlic. Calories, fat, and cholesterol were reduced by:

❖ *Eliminating the olive oil*
❖ *Reducing the amount of oil from the sun-dried tomatoes*
❖ *Reducing the amount of Parmesan cheese*

## Nutrition Scorecard

| (per serving) | before | after |
|---|---|---|
| Calories | 836 | 496 |
| Fat (g) | 35 | 11 |

*Photo on page 280*

| | |
|---|---|
| 12 | ounces dried fusilli, rotini, or any curly pasta |
| 4 | ounces oil-packed sun-dried tomatoes |
| 12 | garlic cloves, chopped |
| ¼ | teaspoon crushed red-pepper flakes |
| 4 | cups tiny broccoli florets |
| 3 | large tomatoes, chopped |
| ⅓ | cup chopped fresh basil |
| ¼ | teaspoon salt |
| ½ | cup freshly grated Parmesan cheese (2 ounces) |

Cook the pasta according to the package directions. Drain.

Meanwhile, lightly coat a large nonstick skillet with nonstick spray and warm over medium heat. Drain the sun-dried tomatoes, reserving 2 teaspoons of the oil. Finely chop the sun-dried tomatoes and add to the skillet along with the reserved oil, the garlic, and red-pepper flakes. Cook for 2 minutes, or until the garlic is tender. Add the broccoli and cook, stirring occasionally, for 3 minutes. Add the chopped tomatoes, basil, and salt. Cook, stirring occasionally, for 2 minutes longer, or until the tomatoes begin to give up their juice.

Gently stir in the cooked pasta. Top each serving with 2 tablespoons cheese.

## Makes 4 servings

*Per serving: 496 calories, 19 g protein, 82 g carbohydrates, 11 g fat, 3 g saturated fat, 10 mg cholesterol, 457 mg sodium, 5 g fiber*

*Homestyle Hint:* To get 1 cup of tiny broccoli florets, you'll need about 2 stalks or 1 large head of fresh broccoli.

# Linguine with Eggplant-Basil Sauce

Here's a great way to enjoy eggplant. As it cooks, the eggplant absorbs the flavors of the sauce and becomes deliciously soft. The finished sauce tastes somewhat like ratatouille. It's even better the next day. Calories and fat were reduced by:

❖ *Reducing the amount of olive oil*
❖ *Reducing the amount of nuts*
❖ *Using less Parmesan cheese*

| | |
|---|---|
| 12 | ounces dried linguine |
| 2 | teaspoons olive oil |
| 1 | small eggplant, cut into ½" cubes |
| 2 | red and/or yellow bell peppers, chopped |
| 1 | large onion, chopped |
| 3 | garlic cloves, chopped |
| ½ | cup chopped fresh basil |
| 2 | tablespoons pine nuts, toasted |
| 1 | teaspoon chopped fresh thyme leaves or ½ teaspoon dried |
| 1 | teaspoon chopped fresh rosemary or ½ teaspoon dried |
| 1 | cup fat-free chicken broth |
| ¼ | teaspoon salt |
| ⅛ | teaspoon ground black pepper |
| ¾ | cup freshly grated Parmesan cheese (3 ounces) |

Cook the linguine according to the package directions. Drain and place in a large bowl.

Meanwhile, warm the oil in a 4-quart Dutch oven over medium-high heat. Add the eggplant, bell peppers, onion, and garlic and cook, stirring occasionally, for 8 minutes, or until softened. Add the basil, pine nuts, thyme, and rosemary. Cook, stirring occasionally, for 10 minutes, or until the flavors are blended. Stir in the broth, salt, and black pepper. Reduce the heat to medium-low and simmer for 15 minutes, or until the sauce begins to thicken.

Spoon the sauce over the pasta and toss to coat. Sprinkle with the Parmesan.

### Makes 4 servings

*Per serving: 496 calories, 20 g protein, 80 g carbohydrates, 12 g fat, 4 g saturated fat, 15 mg cholesterol, 739 mg sodium, 5 g fiber*

# Spicy Peanut Penne

Creamy peanut butter makes a bold-flavored sauce when mixed with fresh ginger, lime juice, and soy sauce. Calories, fat, and cholesterol were reduced by:

<table>
<tr><td colspan="3">Nutrition Scorecard</td></tr>
<tr><td colspan="3">(per serving)</td></tr>
<tr><td></td><td>before</td><td>after</td></tr>
<tr><td>Calories</td><td>610</td><td>392</td></tr>
<tr><td>Fat (g)</td><td>12</td><td>8</td></tr>
</table>

- *Using 1% milk thickened with cornstarch instead of heavy cream*
- *Using slightly less peanut butter*
- *Replacing pork with chicken breasts*

Photo on page 279

| | |
|---|---|
| 1 | pound dried penne or other tubular pasta |
| 3 | boneless, skinless chicken breast halves, chopped |
| ½ | teaspoon salt |
| 1 | green or red bell pepper, chopped |
| 1 | tablespoon cornstarch |
| ⅔ | cup 1% milk |
| ¼ | cup creamy peanut butter |
| | Juice of 2 limes |
| 2 | tablespoons reduced-sodium soy sauce |
| 2 | tablespoons honey |
| 2 | garlic cloves, chopped |
| 1 | teaspoon grated or minced fresh ginger |
| ¼ | teaspoon ground red pepper |
| ¼ | cup chopped fresh chives |
| 3 | tablespoons chopped fresh cilantro |

Cook the pasta according to the package directions. Drain.

Coat a large nonstick skillet with nonstick spray and warm over medium-high heat. Add the chicken and sprinkle with the salt. Cook, stirring, for 4 to 5 minutes, or until the chicken is no longer pink. Add the bell pepper and cook for 2 minutes longer, or until tender. Remove the chicken and pepper from the pan and set aside.

In a small bowl, dissolve the cornstarch in 2 tablespoons of the milk. Stir in the remaining milk and add to the skillet. Cook, stirring, for 1 minute, or until thick and bubbly. Cook for 1 minute longer. Reduce the heat to low.

In another small bowl, stir together the peanut butter, lime juice, soy sauce, honey, garlic, ginger, and ground red pepper. Stir into the milk mixture until smooth. Add the chicken and bell pepper along with the chives and cilantro. Add the cooked pasta and toss to coat. Serve immediately.

**Makes 6 servings**

*Per serving: 392 calories, 25 g protein, 55 g carbohydrates, 8 g fat, 1 g saturated fat, 38 mg cholesterol, 597 mg sodium, 1 g fiber*

*Homestyle Hint:* The easiest way to prepare fresh ginger is to peel it with a paring knife or the edge of a spoon, then finely grate it on a handheld grater.

# Pasta: The Right Amount

*Most restaurants serve huge portions of pasta—four to five servings' worth, according to the USDA's Food Guide Pyramid. The pyramid counts ½ cup cooked pasta as one serving in the grain-products group. When cooking pasta at home, remember that 2 ounces of dried pasta will generally yield about 1 cup cooked, or two servings.*

# Tuna-Noodle Skillet Supper

Such a comforting and easy meal to make, this is as good as any tuna-noodle casserole you remember from your childhood—and better for you. Calories, fat, and cholesterol were reduced by:

*Photo on page 196*

❖ *Eliminating the butter for cooking the vegetables*
❖ *Using reduced-fat Cheddar cheese*
❖ *Using no-yolk noodles instead of regular egg noodles*
❖ *Using 1% milk instead of whole milk*
❖ *Replacing the butter and flour with cornstarch for thickening*

| | |
|---|---|
| 6 | ounces dried no-yolk egg noodles |
| 4 | ounces mushrooms, sliced (1 cup) |
| 1 | small onion, finely chopped |
| ½ | red or green bell pepper, finely chopped |
| 3 | tablespoons cornstarch |
| 2½ | cups 1% milk |
| 1 | cup shredded reduced-fat Cheddar cheese (4 ounces) |
| 2 | cans white tuna packed in water (6 ounces each), drained and flaked |
| ¼ | cup chopped flat-leaf parsley |
| ¼ | teaspoon salt |
| ⅛ | teaspoon ground black pepper |

Cook the noodles according to the package directions.

Meanwhile, coat a large nonstick skillet with nonstick spray and warm over medium-high heat. Add the mushrooms, onion, and bell pepper and cook, stirring, for 5 minutes, or until tender.

In a small bowl, dissolve the cornstarch in ¼ cup of the milk. Stir into the remaining 2¼ cups milk and add to the mushroom mixture. Cook, stirring, for 1 minute, or until bubbly. Cook for 1 minute longer, stirring constantly. Stir in the cheese and cook until melted. Stir in the tuna, parsley, salt, and black pepper. Add the noodles and toss to coat. Serve immediately.

**Makes 6 servings**

Per serving: 303 calories, 29 g protein, 31 g carbohydrates, 7 g fat, 3 g saturated fat, 41 mg cholesterol, 526 mg sodium, 1 g fiber

# Cincinnati Chili

This satisfying meal consists of a robust chili spooned over pasta—a tradition in Cincinnati and a crowd pleaser in my family. Calories, fat, and cholesterol were reduced by:

Nutrition Scorecard

(per serving)

|  | before | after |
|---|---|---|
| Calories | 986 | 540 |
| Fat (g) | 42 | 5 |

❖ *Using ground turkey breast instead of ground beef or pork*
❖ *Eliminating the oil for cooking the vegetables*

1 large onion, chopped

3 garlic cloves, minced

1 pound ground turkey breast

2 tablespoons unsweetened cocoa powder

2 tablespoons chili powder

2 teaspoons ground cumin

¼ teaspoon ground cinnamon

¼ teaspoon ground allspice

1 can crushed tomatoes (28 ounces)

2 cans reduced-sodium kidney beans (14 ounces each), rinsed and drained

1 tablespoon red wine vinegar

2 teaspoons sugar

½ teaspoon salt

1 pound dried spaghetti

½ cup chopped fresh chives

¼ cup shredded reduced-fat Cheddar cheese (1 ounce)

Coat a large nonstick skillet with nonstick spray and warm over medium-high heat. Cook the onion, garlic, and turkey, breaking up the meat and stirring, for 10 minutes, or until it is no longer pink. Stir in the cocoa, chili powder, cumin, cinnamon, and allspice. Cook for 1 minute. Reduce the heat to medium-low and add the tomatoes, beans, vinegar, sugar, and salt. Cover and simmer, stirring occasionally, for 30 minutes, or until the flavors are well-blended.

Meanwhile, cook the spaghetti according to the package directions. Drain. Top the pasta with the chili, chives, and cheese.

## Makes 6 servings

*Per serving: 540 calories, 37 g protein, 90 g carbohydrates, 5 g fat, 1 g saturated fat, 41 mg cholesterol, 510 mg sodium, 11 g fiber*

# Italian Macaroni and Cheese

This dish is a snap to make. It may not be classic macaroni and cheese with a traditional cheese sauce, but my kids love it—yours will, too. I reduced the calories, fat, and cholesterol by:

❖ *Using reduced-fat mozzarella cheese, and less of it*
❖ *Replacing pepperoni with sliced black olives*
❖ *Using low-fat spaghetti sauce*

> 12 ounces dried elbow macaroni
>
> 2 cups shredded reduced-fat mozzarella cheese (8 ounces)
>
> 1 jar low-fat garden vegetable spaghetti sauce (26 ounces)
>
> 1 can sliced black olives (3.8 ounces), drained
>
> 3 tablespoons freshly grated Parmesan cheese

Preheat the oven to 350°F. Lightly coat a 13" × 9" baking dish with nonstick spray.

Cook the macaroni according to the package directions. Drain.

In a large bowl, combine the macaroni, mozzarella, spaghetti sauce, and olives. Toss lightly to mix. Transfer to the prepared baking dish. Top with the Parmesan. Bake for 25 minutes, or until browned and bubbly. Remove from the oven and let stand for 10 minutes before serving.

**Makes 6 servings**

*Per serving: 441 calories, 21 g protein, 57 g carbohydrates, 14 g fat, 6 g saturated fat, 27 mg cholesterol, 1,009 mg sodium, 4 g fiber*

*Homestyle Hint:* For richer tomato flavor, add ½ cup coarsely chopped dry-packed sun-dried tomatoes to the pasta water for the last 5 minutes of cooking. Drain along with the pasta and proceed with the recipe.

# Pierogi Lasagna

This dish is sometimes called lazy pierogies because it's a lot easier to make than umpteen potato dumplings. I usually use leftover mashed potatoes. The taste is pure comfort food. Calories, fat, and cholesterol were reduced by:

❖ *Replacing whole eggs with egg whites*
❖ *Using reduced-fat cottage cheese instead of full-fat cottage cheese*
❖ *Using reduced-fat Cheddar cheese*
❖ *Replacing regular butter with light butter and using less of it*

| | |
|---|---|
| 12 | dried lasagna noodles |
| 2 | cups 2% cottage cheese (16 ounces); do not substitute with fat-free |
| 2 | egg whites |
| 1½ | cups shredded reduced-fat sharp Cheddar cheese (6 ounces) |
| 2 | cups cooked and mashed potatoes |
| ¾ | teaspoon salt |
| ¼ | teaspoon ground black pepper |
| 2 | tablespoons light butter |
| 1 | large onion, chopped |

Cook the lasagna according to the package directions. Drain.

Meanwhile, coat a 13" × 9" baking dish with nonstick spray. Line the bottom of the pan with 4 noodles.

In a medium bowl, combine the cottage cheese and egg whites. Spoon over the noodles, spreading evenly. Top with a second layer of 4 noodles.

Using the same bowl, combine 1 cup of the Cheddar with the mashed potatoes, salt, and pepper. Spoon over the noodles, spreading evenly. Top with a third layer of noodles.

Preheat the oven to 350°F.

Melt the butter in a medium nonstick skillet over medium heat. Add the onion and cook, stirring, for 5 minutes, or until soft. Spoon over the noodles and top with the remaining ½ cup Cheddar. Cover and bake for 30 minutes, or until heated through.

## Makes 8 servings

*Per serving: 293 calories, 21 g protein, 36 g carbohydrates, 7 g fat, 4 g saturated fat, 25 mg cholesterol, 789 mg sodium, 3 g fiber*

# Easy Red, White, and Green Lasagna

This lasagna is extra easy to make because it uses no-boil noodles, which you can find in the pasta section of most supermarkets. They're great—but be sure to cover them completely with sauce or cheese so that they will soften in the oven. I reduced calories, fat, and cholesterol by:

❖ *Replacing regular ricotta cheese with a mixture of fat-free ricotta and flour*
❖ *Using reduced-fat mozzarella cheese, and less of it*

| | |
|---|---|
| 1½ | pounds broccoli |
| 3 | large red bell peppers, finely chopped |
| 3 | garlic cloves, chopped |
| 1 | container fat-free ricotta cheese (15 ounces) |
| 1 | tablespoon unbleached or all-purpose flour |
| ⅛ | teaspoon ground black pepper |
| 1 | jar low-fat marinara sauce (26 ounces) |
| 9 | dried no-boil lasagna noodles (7" × 3½" each) |
| 2 | cups shredded reduced-fat mozzarella cheese (8 ounces) |
| 1 | cup freshly grated Parmesan cheese (4 ounces) |

Preheat the oven to 375°F.

Trim the broccoli, discarding the tough part of the stem. Cut the florets and the tender parts of the stem into ¾" pieces.

Coat a large nonstick skillet with nonstick spray and warm over medium-high heat. Add the broccoli, bell pepper, and garlic and cook for 5 minutes, or until crisp-tender. Remove from the heat.

In a large bowl, combine the ricotta, flour, and black pepper. Using a slotted spoon, lift the broccoli mixture from the pan and transfer it to the bowl. Mix well.

Spread 1 cup of the marinara sauce over the bottom of a 13" × 9" baking dish. Place 3 noodles crosswise (not lengthwise) in the dish, making sure that they do not touch each other because they expand during baking. Drop half of the ricotta mixture by spoonfuls onto the noodles and spread evenly. Sprinkle one-third of the mozzarella and one-third of the Parmesan over the top. Repeat layering with the noodles, ricotta mixture, and cheeses, ending with the noodles.

Pour the remaining cups of sauce over the noodles. Top with the remaining mozzarella and Parmesan. Cover tightly with foil, making sure that the foil does not touch the sauce. Bake for 30 minutes. Remove the foil and bake for 10 minutes longer, or until bubbly. Let stand for 10 minutes before serving.

**Makes 6 servings**

*Per serving: 445 calories, 37 g protein, 48 g carbohydrates, 14 g fat, 8 g saturated fat, 44 mg cholesterol, 985 mg sodium, 7 g fiber*

## Eat Noodles for Folate

*Folate is an important B vitamin that helps prevent birth defects and high homocysteine levels, which are related to heart disease. Folate is so important that since January 1998, enriched grain products sold in the United States—such as cereals and pasta—are required to be fortified with folic acid (folate). One cup of pasta provides 100 micrograms of folate, 25 percent of the daily recommendation for this nutrient. Another good reason to eat pasta!*

# Chicken Manicotti

I find it easier to work with egg-roll wrappers than manicotti shells. When the wrappers are boiled, they have the soft texture of noodles. So many of us are accustomed to eating them fried that we forget they are really a form of pasta. Calories, fat, and cholesterol were reduced by:

### Nutrition Scorecard
(per serving)

| | before | after |
|---|---|---|
| Calories | 394 | 289 |
| Fat (g) | 20 | 7 |

❖ *Using low-fat marinara sauce*
❖ *Relying on fat-free ricotta cheese and flour instead of regular ricotta*

| | |
|---|---|
| 2 | boneless, skinless chicken breast halves, finely chopped or ground |
| ½ | small onion, chopped |
| 2 | garlic cloves, chopped |
| ⅛ | teaspoon ground black pepper |
| 2 | cups low-fat marinara sauce |
| 1 | container fat-free ricotta cheese (15 ounces) |
| 2 | egg whites |
| 1 | tablespoon unbleached or all-purpose flour |
| 1 | package frozen chopped spinach (10 ounces), thawed and squeezed dry |
| 18 | egg-roll wrappers |
| ⅔ | cup freshly grated Parmesan cheese (3 ounces) |

Coat a medium nonstick skillet with nonstick spray and warm over medium-high heat. Add the chicken, onion, garlic, and pepper and cook for 7 minutes, or until the chicken is no longer pink. Remove from the heat and set aside for 5 minutes to cool slightly.

Preheat the oven to 375°F. Spread 1 cup of the marinara sauce over the bottom of a 13" × 9" baking dish.

In a medium bowl, combine the ricotta, egg whites, and flour. Mix well. Stir in the spinach and chicken.

Place an egg-roll wrapper on a work surface and spoon about ⅓ cup filling in a column down the center. Fold one side of the wrapper over the filling and continue rolling the wrapper to enclose (the short sides will be open). Place, seam side down, in the baking dish. Repeat with the remaining filling and wrappers. Top with the remaining 1 cup sauce and sprinkle with the Parmesan.

Cover tightly with foil, making sure that the foil does not touch the sauce. Bake for 25 to 30 minutes, or until bubbly and heated through.

**Makes 18 manicotti; 6 servings**

Per serving: 289 calories, 28 g protein, 31 g carbohydrates, 7 g fat, 2 g saturated fat, 41 mg cholesterol, 893 mg sodium, 3 g fiber

*Homestyle Hints:* Egg-roll wrappers are sold in the refrigerated section of supermarkets.

If you have leftover cooked chicken, chop it up and use it in this recipe. You will need about 1½ cups chopped chicken. Cook the onion, garlic, and pepper for a few minutes, then add the cooked chicken and warm through.

## Is Pasta Fattening?

*No, pasta does not make you fat. Of course, sauces and toppings can make a huge calorie difference. So can eating too much. But there is nothing inherently fattening about pasta. Two ounces, or 1 cup of cooked pasta, has an average of 210 calories and only 1 gram of fat.*

# Stuffed Shells Florentine

This has become one of my favorite meals because the filling is so flavorful and quick to make. It's also loaded with calcium. A single serving provides 75 percent of your calcium needs for the day. Calories, fat, and cholesterol were reduced by:

- ❖ *Using a combination of fat-free ricotta cheese and flour instead of full-fat ricotta*
- ❖ *Using reduced-fat mozzarella cheese*
- ❖ *Reducing the amount of Parmesan cheese*

| | |
|---|---|
| 12 | ounces jumbo shells (about 30 shells) |
| 2 | cups low-fat marinara sauce |
| 1 | package frozen chopped spinach (10 ounces), thawed and squeezed dry |
| 3 | cups fat-free ricotta cheese (24 ounces) |
| ½ | cup freshly grated Parmesan cheese (2 ounces) |
| 3 | tablespoons chopped fresh basil |
| 2 | tablespoons unbleached or all-purpose flour |
| 2 | garlic cloves, chopped |
| ½ | teaspoon fennel seeds |
| ½ | cup shredded reduced-fat mozzarella cheese (2 ounces) |

Cook the shells according to the package directions. Drain.

Meanwhile, preheat the oven to 375°F. Spread ½ cup of the marinara sauce over the bottom of a 13" × 9" baking dish.

In a large bowl, combine the spinach, ricotta, Parmesan, basil, flour, garlic, and fennel seeds. Mix well. Spoon some of the filling into each shell. Place the shells, filling side up, in the baking dish. Spoon the remaining 1½ cups sauce over the shells and top with the mozzarella. Cover loosely with foil and bake for 30 minutes, or until the cheese is melted and the filling is hot.

**Makes 6 servings**

*Per serving: 437 calories, 31 g protein, 68 g carbohydrates, 6 g fat, 3 g saturated fat, 24 mg cholesterol, 711 mg sodium, 2 g fiber*

# Salads Big and Small

**S**alads are the great conundrum of healthy eating. They seem like the perfect way to eat vegetables, grains, and fruits, yet so many are loaded with fat—usually from the dressing and other toppings.

Since we "eat" with our eyes as much as we do with our tastebuds, one solution is to put smaller quantities of the fattier ingredients, such as avocados or nuts, right on top of the salad so they are the first thing you see.

When it comes to using oils in dressings, stick with those that have strong flavors, such as olive oil, dark sesame oil, and walnut oil (available in most supermarkets). That way, you'll be sure to taste (and enjoy) every gram of fat. To scale back on the amount of oil used, I often replace some of it with pineapple juice. If extra thickening is needed in simple dressings like a vinaigrette, a touch of plain gelatin does the trick, without adding any fat.

Notice that many of the dressings in this chapter call for the liquid to be whisked together in a measuring cup. I find a measuring cup a lot easier for mixing and pouring, but a small bowl will do, too.

If you make only one recipe from this chapter, I recommend the Asian Super Slaw. Hands down, it is my family's favorite, thanks to the bold-flavored Asian dressing. The dressing is so good that I use it to baste grilled chicken, too.

# Mandarin Spinach Salad with Orange Vinaigrette

The citrus juice in this dressing makes the salad especially refreshing. Plain gelatin thickens the dressing just enough to make it more texturally pleasing, without adding calories. Calories, fat, and cholesterol were reduced by:

❖ *Reducing the amount of walnuts*

❖ *Reducing the amount of oil and replacing it in part with additional lime juice and orange juice*

❖ *Thickening the dressing with gelatin rather than more oil*

*Photo on page 195*

### VINAIGRETTE

¼ cup orange juice

2 tablespoons lime juice

1 tablespoon honey

2 teaspoons walnut or peanut oil

½ teaspoon salt

¼ teaspoon plain gelatin

⅛ teaspoon ground black pepper

### SALAD

1 bag washed torn or baby spinach (6 ounces)

1 can mandarin oranges (15 ounces), drained

1 avocado, chopped

½ red onion, thinly sliced

2 tablespoons chopped walnuts, toasted

TO MAKE THE VINAIGRETTE: In a small glass measuring cup, whisk together the orange juice, lime juice, honey, oil, salt, gelatin, and pepper. Let stand for 5 minutes for the gelatin to soften.

TO MAKE THE SALAD: Divide the spinach among 6 plates. Top with the oranges, avocado, onion, and walnuts. Whisk then drizzle the vinaigrette over the salad before serving.

## Makes 6 servings

*Per serving: 149 calories, 3 g protein, 17 g carbohydrates, 9 g fat, 1 g saturated fat, 0 mg cholesterol, 230 mg sodium, 4 g fiber*

*Homestyle Hint:* To toast walnuts, place them in a dry skillet over medium heat. Cook, shaking the pan often, for 2 minutes, or until lightly browned and fragrant.

# Caesar Salad

I like to stock anchovy paste instead of anchovy fillets. The paste is easier to use, and it keeps in the refrigerator for weeks after opening. Look for it near the anchovy fillets in your market. Anchovy paste is salty, so there is no need to use extra salt in this recipe. Calories, fat, and cholesterol were reduced by:

- ❖ *Using low-fat mayonnaise in place of regular mayonnaise*
- ❖ *Reducing the amount of olive oil*
- ❖ *Using fat-free garlic croutons*
- ❖ *Using anchovy paste instead of anchovy fillets, and less of it*

## DRESSING

- 2  garlic cloves
- ½  cup low-fat mayonnaise
- 2  tablespoons freshly grated Parmesan cheese
- 1  tablespoon lemon juice
- 1  tablespoon olive oil
- 2  teaspoons anchovy paste
- 1  teaspoon Worcestershire sauce
- 1  teaspoon Dijon mustard

## SALAD

- 1  head romaine lettuce, torn into bite-size pieces
- ⅓  cup freshly grated Parmesan cheese (1½ ounces)
- 1½  cups fat-free garlic croutons

TO MAKE THE DRESSING: Chop the garlic in a food processor. Add the mayonnaise, cheese, lemon juice, oil, anchovy paste, Worcestershire sauce, and mustard. Process until smooth.

TO MAKE THE SALAD: Place the lettuce in a large bowl. Add the dressing and toss to coat. Top with the cheese and croutons. Toss gently to blend.

**Makes 6 servings**

Per serving: 147 calories, 7 g protein, 17 g carbohydrates, 5 g fat, 2 g saturated fat, 12 mg cholesterol, 583 mg sodium, 1 g fiber

# Apple-Raisin Picnic Slaw

Sunflower seeds and raisins give this coleslaw wonderful texture. Flecks of shredded apple add a mellow sweetness. Calories, fat, and cholesterol were reduced by:

* *Reducing the amount of sunflower seeds*
* *Reducing the amount of oil and using more flavorful olive oil*

| Nutrition Scorecard | | |
| --- | --- | --- |
| *(per serving)* | | |
| | before | after |
| Calories | 120 | 87 |
| Fat (g) | 6 | 3 |

## DRESSING

1 cup fat-free plain yogurt (8 ounces)
3 tablespoons white vinegar
1 tablespoon olive oil
¾ teaspoon salt
½ teaspoon celery seed
¼ teaspoon ground black pepper

## SLAW

1 head green cabbage, shredded (10 cups)
2 carrots, shredded
1 large green apple, with peel, shredded
½ cup raisins
¼ cup sunflower seeds

TO MAKE THE DRESSING: In a 2-cup glass measuring cup, whisk together the yogurt, vinegar, oil, salt, celery seed, and black pepper.

TO MAKE THE SLAW: In a large bowl, combine the cabbage, carrots, apple, raisins, and sunflower seeds. Whisk the dressing and add to the salad. Toss to coat.

## Makes 12 servings

*Per serving: 87 calories, 3 g protein, 14 g carbohydrates, 3 g fat, 0.5 g saturated fat, 0 mg cholesterol, 163 mg sodium, 2 g fiber*

*Homestyle Hint:* I like to use a tart apple, such as Granny Smith, for this recipe.

# Asian Super Slaw

I'll never forget the first time I made this salad. My family loved it so much that they polished it off as a snack and it never made it to the dinner table. The secret is the flavorful dressing. I reduced calories, fat, and cholesterol by:

Photo on page 282

❖ *Eliminating the vegetable oil and replacing it in part with pineapple juice*
❖ *Slightly reducing the amount of peanut butter*
❖ *Relying on a small amount of sesame oil for flavor instead of vegetable oil*

## ASIAN DRESSING

- ⅓ cup seasoned rice vinegar
- ¼ cup creamy peanut butter
- 3 tablespoons reduced-sodium soy sauce
- 3 tablespoons brown sugar
- 2 tablespoons pineapple juice
- 1 tablespoon dark sesame oil
- 1 teaspoon finely chopped fresh ginger
- 2 garlic cloves, chopped

## SLAW

- 5 cups shredded green cabbage (½ head)
- 2 cups shredded red cabbage (¼ head)
- 2 carrots, shredded
- ½ cup chopped fresh cilantro
- ½ cup chopped fresh chives

TO MAKE THE DRESSING: In a large glass measuring cup, whisk together the vinegar, peanut butter, soy sauce, brown sugar, pineapple juice, sesame oil, ginger, and garlic.

TO MAKE THE SLAW: In a large bowl, combine the green and red cabbage, carrots, cilantro, and chives. Whisk the dressing and add to the salad. Toss to coat.

**Makes 8 servings**

*Per serving: 108 calories, 4 g protein, 12 g carbohydrates, 6 g fat, 1 g saturated fat, 0 mg cholesterol, 405 mg sodium, 3 g fiber*

*Homestyle Hint:* The easiest way to prepare fresh ginger is to peel it with a paring knife, or the edge of a spoon, then finely grate it on a handheld grater.

# Garden Couscous Salad

I generally find that fat-free dressings work well for grain-based salads. The firm texture of the grain compensates for the lack of body in the dressing. Calories, fat, and sodium were reduced by:

❖ *Using fat-free Italian dressing instead of regular Italian dressing*

❖ *Using chicken broth instead of sodium-heavy bouillon cubes*

| | |
|---|---|
| 2 | cups fat-free chicken broth |
| 1 | package plain couscous (10 ounces) |
| 1 | carrot, shredded |
| 1 | red bell pepper, chopped |
| 1 | large zucchini, chopped |
| 1 | large yellow squash, chopped |
| 1 | tomato, chopped |
| 1 | cup fat-free Italian dressing |

Bring the broth to a boil in a medium saucepan over high heat. Stir in the couscous and remove from the heat. Cover and let stand for 5 minutes, or until the liquid is absorbed. Transfer to an extra-large bowl and fluff with a fork.

Add the carrot, pepper, zucchini, squash, and tomato to the bowl. Mix well. Pour the dressing over the salad and toss to coat.

**Makes 8 servings**

Per serving: 164 calories, 6 g protein, 34 g carbohydrates, 1 g fat, 0 g saturated fat, 0 mg cholesterol, 434 mg sodium, 3 g fiber

## *If Vegetables Had a Big Advertising Budget*

Most of food advertising is spent on highly processed and packaged foods, to the tune of $7 billion a year. The dollars spent on advertising healthful items such as fruits and vegetables are negligible in comparison. But why buy the hype? Fresh fruits and veggies are almost always a better choice than packaged foods. And, pound for pound, they're usually less expensive.

# Orzo Salad

Tomato, basil, and garlic are always a winning combination. Here, they flavor up orzo, a tiny pasta that is shaped like rice. I reduced calories, fat, and cholesterol by:

❖ *Using less olive oil*
❖ *Slightly reducing the amount of Parmesan cheese*

*Photo on page 123*

## SALAD

1½  cups dried orzo
2  tomatoes, chopped
1  can sliced black olives (2½ ounces), drained
½  cup freshly grated Parmesan cheese (2 ounces)
⅓  cup chopped fresh basil

## DRESSING

2  tablespoons lemon juice
2  teaspoons olive oil
2  garlic cloves, finely chopped
¾  teaspoon salt
⅛  teaspoon ground black pepper

TO MAKE THE SALAD: Cook the orzo according to the package directions. Rinse with cold water and drain. Transfer to a large bowl and add the tomatoes, olives, cheese, and basil.

TO MAKE THE DRESSING: In a small glass measuring cup, whisk together the lemon juice, oil, garlic, salt, and pepper. Pour over the salad and toss to coat.

**Makes 4 servings**

*Per serving: 234 calories, 9 g protein, 35 g carbohydrates, 6 g fat, 2 g saturated fat, 7 mg cholesterol, 524 mg sodium, 2 g fiber*

# Asian Noodle Salad

Just add a grilled chicken breast, and this makes a terrific main-dish salad. It's a great side dish, too. Calories and fat were reduced by:

❖ *Using reduced-fat Asian dressing*
❖ *Eliminating the peanuts*

| Nutrition Scorecard | | |
|---|---|---|
| *(per serving)* | | |
| | before | after |
| Calories | 595 | 332 |
| Fat (g) | 32 | 9 |

| | |
|---|---|
| 12 | ounces dried linguine |
| 1 | cup thinly sliced red cabbage |
| 2 | carrots, cut into 2" matchsticks |
| 1 | red bell pepper, thinly sliced |
| 1 | cup chopped fresh chives |
| ½ | cup chopped fresh cilantro |
| 1 | batch Asian Dressing (in Asian Super Slaw, page 275) |

Cook the linguine according to the package directions. Rinse with cold water and drain. Transfer to a large bowl and add the cabbage, carrots, pepper, chives, and cilantro. Add the dressing and toss to coat.

**Makes 6 servings**

Per serving: 332 calories, 10 g protein, 54 g carbohydrates, 9 g fat, 1 g saturated fat, 0 mg cholesterol, 521 mg sodium, 2 g fiber

*Homestyle Hint*: To cut a carrot into matchsticks, cut the carrot crosswise into 2" pieces. Cut each piece lengthwise into very thin strips. Stack the strips and cut lengthwise again into matchsticks.

## What's a Serving of Salad?

*You can't really eat too many greens—they're so good for you. But in case you've wondered, 1 cup of fresh leafy greens is considered one serving of vegetables. To get the most nutrients, make your salads with a variety of greens and look for dark greens like spinach.*

**Spicy Peanut Penne** *(page 260)*

Garlicky Fusilli with Broccoli and Dried Tomatoes *(page 258)*

Cranberry Holiday Gelatin *(page 303)*

281

**Asian Super Slaw** *(page 275)*

**Fruit Salad with Honey–Poppy Seed Dressing** *(page 304)*
283

Layered Taco Salad with Sour Cream Dressing *(page 300)*

Apple-Carrot Cake *(page 332)* with Best-Ever Light Cream Cheese Frosting *(page 334)*

**Upside-Down German Chocolate Snack Cake** *(page 328)*

**Strawberry Cheesecake** *(page 340)*
287

Aunt Boojie's Chocolate Box Cake *(page 326)*

**Mom's Rich Double-Chocolate Pudding** *(page 351)*

**Chocolate-Dipped Cookies** *(page 352)* **and Jam-Filled Cookies** *(page 353)*

**Lemon Heaven Meringue Squares** *(page 346)*

**Chocolate Tiramisu** *(page 335)*

Hummingbird Cake *(page 338)*

**Peanut Butter Pie** *(page 344)*
294

# Barley Salad

I love the chewy texture of barley. It's a great source of fiber, too—even better than brown rice. If you're in a time crunch, fat-free Italian dressing can stand in for the dressing below. Calories and fat were reduced by:

- ❖ *Reducing the amount of oil*
- ❖ *Relying on parsley and cucumber for moistness and flavor*

## SALAD

| | |
|---|---|
| ½ | cup pearl barley |
| 1½ | cups vegetable broth or fat-free chicken broth |
| 2 | tomatoes, chopped |
| ½ | cucumber, chopped |
| ⅓ | cup chopped flat-leaf parsley |
| ¼ | cup chopped fresh chives |

## DRESSING

| | |
|---|---|
| 1 | tablespoon lemon juice |
| 2 | teaspoons olive oil |
| ¼ | teaspoon salt |
| ⅛ | teaspoon ground black pepper |

TO MAKE THE SALAD: In a medium saucepan, combine the barley and broth. Bring to a boil over high heat. Reduce the heat to medium-low, cover, and cook for 30 minutes, or until the barley is tender and the broth is absorbed. Transfer to a large bowl and fluff with a fork. Set aside to cool.

Add the tomatoes, cucumber, parsley, and chives to the cooled barley.

TO MAKE THE DRESSING: In a glass measuring cup, whisk together the lemon juice, oil, salt, and pepper. Pour over the salad and toss to coat.

**Makes 4 servings**

*Per serving: 137 calories, 4 g protein, 25 g carbohydrates, 3 g fat, 0.5 g saturated fat, 0 mg cholesterol, 520 mg sodium, 5 g fiber*

# Festive Black Bean Salad

I always get compliments on this salad. It's especially good for parties and potlucks because you can make it the night before. Calories, fat, and cholesterol were reduced by:

❖ *Reducing the amount of oil and replacing it in part with pineapple juice*
❖ *Reducing the amount of sugar*

| *Nutrition Scorecard* | | |
|---|---|---|
| (per serving) | | |
| | before | after |
| Calories | 236 | 155 |
| Fat (g) | 12 | 3 |

## DRESSING

2  tablespoons cider vinegar

2  tablespoons pineapple juice

4  teaspoons olive oil

2  garlic cloves, chopped

1  teaspoon ground cumin

½  teaspoon sugar

¼  teaspoon salt

⅛  teaspoon ground red pepper

## SALAD

3  cans black beans (15 ounces each), rinsed and drained

1  can water-packed corn (15 ounces), drained

1  red bell pepper, chopped

½  red onion, chopped

½  cup chopped fresh cilantro

TO MAKE THE DRESSING: In a glass measuring cup, whisk together the vinegar, pineapple juice, oil, garlic, cumin, sugar, salt, and pepper.

TO MAKE THE SALAD: In a large bowl, combine the beans, corn, pepper, onion, and cilantro. Whisk the dressing and add to the salad. Toss to coat. Cover and chill for at least 1 hour before serving.

**Makes 10 servings**

*Per serving: 155 calories, 8 g protein, 26 g carbohydrates, 3 g fat, 0.5 g saturated fat, 0 mg cholesterol, 584 mg sodium, 8 g fiber*

# White Bean–Tuna Salad

This salad pulls together quickly and works surprisingly well with less olive oil in the dressing. It makes an excellent lunch. I reduced calories, fat, and cholesterol by:

❖ *Reducing the amount of olive oil*
❖ *Adding garlic for more flavor*

## DRESSING

¼ cup lemon juice

1 tablespoon olive oil

2 garlic cloves, chopped

½ teaspoon salt

⅛ teaspoon ground black pepper

## SALAD

2 cans white cannellini beans (15 ounces each), rinsed and drained

3 cans white tuna packed in water (6 ounces each), drained

½ red onion, chopped

½ cup chopped flat-leaf parsley

¼ cup chopped fresh basil

1 head red or green leaf lettuce, torn into bite-size pieces

TO MAKE THE DRESSING: In a glass measuring cup, whisk together the lemon juice, oil, garlic, salt, and pepper.

TO MAKE THE SALAD: In large bowl, combine the beans, tuna, onion, parsley, and basil. Whisk the dressing and add to the salad. Toss to coat. Line 6 salad plates with the lettuce and top with the salad.

**Makes 6 servings**

*Per serving: 305 calories, 33 g protein, 35 g carbohydrates, 4 g fat, 1 g saturated fat, 26 mg cholesterol, 482 mg sodium, 8 g fiber*

# Lentil Salad

When it comes to legumes, lentils are among the easiest to cook, and they're incredibly healthful. I especially like them in this salad. Calories, fat, and cholesterol were reduced by:

❖ *Reducing the amount of cheese*
❖ *Reducing the amount of oil and replacing it in part with pineapple juice*

## *SALAD*

| | |
|---|---|
| 1 | cup dried lentils, rinsed and sorted |
| 1½ | cups fat-free chicken broth |
| 1 | cucumber, chopped |
| 1 | tomato, chopped |
| ½ | red onion, chopped |
| 2 | tablespoons chopped flat-leaf parsley |

## *DRESSING*

| | |
|---|---|
| 2 | tablespoons pineapple juice |
| 1 | tablespoon red wine vinegar |
| 1 | tablespoon olive oil |
| 2 | teaspoons Dijon mustard |
| 1 | shallot, finely chopped |
| 1 | garlic clove, finely chopped |
| ½ | teaspoon salt |
| ⅛ | teaspoon ground black pepper |
| 3 | ounces goat cheese, crumbled |

TO MAKE THE SALAD: In a medium saucepan, combine the lentils and broth and bring to a boil over high heat. Reduce the heat to medium-low, cover, and cook for 25 minutes, or just until tender. Drain any liquid and set aside to cool completely.

In a large bowl, combine the cooled lentils, cucumber, tomato, onion, and parsley.

TO MAKE THE DRESSING: In a glass measuring cup, whisk together the pineapple juice, vinegar, oil, mustard, shallot, garlic, salt, and pepper. Pour over the lentils and toss to coat. Divide among 6 salad plates and sprinkle with the cheese.

### Makes 6 servings

*Per serving: 205 calories, 14 g protein, 23 g carbohydrates, 7 g fat, 3 g saturated fat, 11 mg cholesterol, 383 mg sodium, 5 g fiber*

# Mango-Gelatin Salad

This makes an absolutely delicious snack. It's also rich in vitamins A and C. Calories, fat, and cholesterol were reduced by:

❖ *Replacing heavy cream with a combination of fat-free yogurt and light whipped topping*

| Nutrition Scorecard | | |
|---|---|---|
| (per serving) | | |
| | before | after |
| Calories | 254 | 194 |
| Fat (g) | 16 | 2 |

| | |
|---|---|
| ¼ | cup mango or peach nectar |
| 1 | package plain gelatin (¼ ounce) |
| 2 | mangoes, peeled and chopped |
| ⅓ | cup sugar |
| 2 | cups fat-free vanilla yogurt (16 ounces) |
| 1 | cup frozen light whipped topping, thawed (2½ ounces) |

Place the nectar in a small saucepan. Sprinkle the gelatin over the nectar and let soften for 5 minutes. Warm over low heat, stirring, until the gelatin is dissolved.

In a food processor or blender, combine the mangoes and sugar. Puree until smooth. Add the gelatin mixture and blend well. Transfer to a large bowl.

Fold in the yogurt and whipped topping. Spoon into 6 custard cups or ramekins, cover with plastic wrap, and refrigerate for at least 2 hours or overnight.

**Makes 6 servings**

Per serving: 194 calories, 5 g protein, 40 g carbohydrates, 2 g fat, 2 g saturated fat, 1 mg cholesterol, 56 mg sodium, 2 g fiber

*Homestyle Hint:* Canned mango nectar and peach nectar are available in the international section of most supermarkets, often near the Latin American foods, and in the juice section.

## Go with Mangoes for Fiber

*One mango has about 4 grams of fiber and provides nearly 100 percent of the recommended amount for vitamin C for adults. If you haven't tried a mango yet, don't wait. They're sweet, juicy, and delicious. Let mangoes ripen at room temperature until they're soft, with a "give" similar to a ripe peach or avocado. And yes, they are a little messy to eat—but they taste so good, who cares?*

# Layered Taco Salad with Sour Cream Dressing

This is one of my daughter's favorite salads. It's crunchy, creamy, and chewy all at the same time. I like it, too, in part because it provides nearly half the daily recommended fiber level for adults. Calories, fat, and cholesterol were reduced by:

*Photo on page 284*

❖ *Using homemade baked tortilla strips instead of tortilla chips*
❖ *Replacing avocado dip with an avocado*
❖ *Using fat-free sour cream instead of regular sour cream*
❖ *Using reduced-fat pepper Jack cheese instead of full-fat cheese*

## TORTILLA STRIPS

4   corn tortillas (6" diameter)
¼   teaspoon salt

## DRESSING

⅓   cup fat-free sour cream (without gelatin), 3 ounces
¼   cup lime juice
¼   cup finely chopped fresh cilantro
4   teaspoons white vinegar
1   tablespoon finely chopped shallot
1   garlic clove, finely chopped
¼   teaspoon salt
⅛   teaspoon paprika

## SALAD

1   head iceberg lettuce, shredded (about 4 cups)
1   can black beans (15 ounces), rinsed and drained
1   tomato, chopped
1   cup shredded reduced-fat pepper Jack cheese (4 ounces)
¼   cup sliced pitted black olives
¼   cup chopped fresh chives
1   avocado, chopped

TO MAKE THE TORTILLA STRIPS: Preheat the oven to 375°F.

Stack the tortillas and cut them in half. Then slice across that cut into ½"-wide strips. Place the strips in a single layer on a large baking sheet. Lightly coat the strips with non-stick spray and sprinkle with the salt. Bake for 10 minutes, or until lightly golden. Remove from the oven and cool.

TO MAKE THE DRESSING: In a glass measuring cup, whisk together the sour cream, lime juice, cilantro, vinegar, shallot, garlic, salt, and paprika.

TO MAKE THE SALAD: Divide the lettuce, beans, tomato, cheese, olives, and chives among 4 plates, layering the ingredients. Spoon the dressing evenly over each serving. Top with the tortilla strips and avocado.

**Makes 4 servings**

Per serving: 345 calories, 18 g protein, 35 g carbohydrates, 16 g fat, 5 g saturated fat, 20 mg cholesterol, 947 mg sodium, 13 g fiber

# Room for Dressings and Mayo

*Don't shy away from salad dressings and mayonnaise altogether. They are good sources of antioxidant vitamin E, which helps lower the risk of heart attack, stroke, cataracts, and some cancers. In fact, dressings and mayo are among the top sources of vitamin E for adults in the United States. When recipes call for these ingredients, use a light hand or low-fat versions. Vitamin E is also found in margarine, fortified cereals, nuts, seeds, and oils.*

# Orange-Pineapple Fluff Gelatin

I grew up on this gelled salad and still find it a refreshing treat. Don't try to substitute fresh pineapple for canned. Oddly enough, this is one case when canned is preferred, since an enzyme in fresh pineapple will prevent the gelatin from setting. I reduced the calories, fat, and cholesterol by:

❖ *Using fat-free cottage cheese*
❖ *Using sugar-free gelatin*
❖ *Using light whipped topping*

| | |
|---|---|
| 1 | can juice-packed crushed pineapple (20 ounces), juices reserved |
| 1 | package sugar-free orange gelatin dessert mix (0.6 ounces) |
| ½ | cup ice cubes |
| 2 | cups fat-free cottage cheese (16 ounces) |
| 1 | container frozen light whipped topping (12 ounces), thawed |
| 1 | can mandarin oranges (11 ounces), drained |

In a medium saucepan, bring 1 cup of the reserved pineapple juice to a boil over medium-high heat. Remove from the heat. Add the gelatin and stir for 2 minutes, or until dissolved. Add the ice cubes and stir until they melt. Refrigerate for 15 minutes, or until partially set.

In a food processor or blender, puree the cottage cheese until smooth. Fold into the gelatin mixture. In separate additions, fold in the whipped topping, pineapple, and oranges. Transfer to a shallow 2-quart dish. Cover and refrigerate for 2 hours, or until firm.

**Makes 8 servings**

*Per serving: 164 calories, 8 g protein, 19 g carbohydrates, 5 g fat, 5 g saturated fat, 5 mg cholesterol, 178 mg sodium, 0 g fiber*

# Cranberry Holiday Gelatin

This salad could double as a dessert, it's so sweet and delicious. You don't have to wait for a holiday to give it a try. Calories, fat, and cholesterol were reduced by:

❖ *Using sugar-free gelatin*
❖ *Reducing the amount of walnuts*
❖ *Using fat-free sour cream instead of regular sour cream*
❖ *Using a combination of light cream cheese and fat-free cream cheese in place of regular*

2 packages sugar-free cranberry or raspberry gelatin dessert mix (0.3 ounces each)

1 cup boiling water

1 can whole-berry cranberry sauce (16 ounces)

1 can juice-packed crushed pineapple (20 ounces), drained

4 ounces light cream cheese, softened

4 ounces fat-free cream cheese, softened

1 cup fat-free sour cream (without gelatin), 8 ounces

2 tablespoons sugar

¼ cup chopped walnuts

In a large bowl, combine the gelatin and water. Stir for 2 minutes, or until dissolved. Stir in the cranberry sauce, breaking up any clumps. Stir in the pineapple. Pour into a shallow 2-quart dish. Cover and refrigerate for 2 hours, or until firm.

In a medium bowl, with an electric mixer set on medium speed, beat the light cream cheese and fat-free cream cheese until smooth. Beat in the sour cream and sugar. Spread over the gelatin salad and top with the walnuts.

## Makes 8 servings

*Per serving: 245 calories, 7 g protein, 44 g carbohydrates, 6 g fat, 2 g saturated fat, 12 mg cholesterol, 166 mg sodium, 1 g fiber*

*Homestyle Hint:* Light cream cheese may be labeled Neufchâtel cheese.

# Fruit Salad
# with Honey–Poppy Seed Dressing

I use melon, pineapple, and strawberries for this salad, but you can use your favorite combinations. I reduced calories, fat, and cholesterol by:

❖ *Using fat-free sour cream instead of regular*
❖ *Using fat-free mayonnaise instead of regular, and less of it*

## Nutrition Scorecard
*(per serving)*

|          | before | after |
|----------|--------|-------|
| Calories | 169    | 96    |
| Fat (g)  | 10     | 1     |

*Photo on page 283*

## DRESSING

½  cup fat-free sour cream (without gelatin), 4 ounces

2  tablespoons fat-free mayonnaise

3  tablespoons chopped crystallized ginger

2  tablespoons honey

2  teaspoons white vinegar

1¼  teaspoons poppy seeds

## SALAD

2  cups cantaloupe balls

2  cups honeydew melon balls

½  fresh pineapple, cut into chunks (2 cups)

2  cups sliced strawberries

Mint leaves (optional)

TO MAKE THE DRESSING: In a glass measuring cup, whisk together the sour cream, mayonnaise, ginger, honey, vinegar, and poppy seeds.

TO MAKE THE SALAD: In a large bowl, combine the cantaloupe, honeydew, pineapple, and strawberries. Whisk the dressing and add to the salad. Toss to coat. Garnish with mint leaves, if using.

**Makes 8 servings**

*Per serving: 96 calories, 2 g protein, 23 g carbohydrates, 1 g fat, 0 g saturated fat, 0 mg cholesterol, 114 mg sodium, 2 g fiber*

# Fixings
and Trimmings

The unassuming side dish is sometimes the tastiest part of a meal. Side dishes can make a significant contribution to nutrition, too, whether by the fiber in Barley Risotto or the rich vitamin A content of Whipped Candied Brandied Yams.

To keep fat and calories in check, I use a variety of simple techniques. In many dishes, simply reducing the amount of oil is all it takes, as in Roasted Asparagus.

🖌 For low-fat crisping, oven-frying instead of deep-frying works wonders. This method makes excellent Cajun Potato Wedges. Just spread the food in a roasting pan, coat with oil (I use cooking oil spray), and oven-fry at 400° to 475°F. The coating of oil and high heat mimics the process of deep-fat frying so you can have great-tasting French fries without the fat.

🖌 Oil spray is the key to healthy sautéing too. A few shots of oil spray are all you need to cook the onions and peppers in Mexicali Corn or the onions and garlic in Shortcut Boston Baked Beans.

🖌 In creamy side dishes, replacing heavy cream with 1% milk saves a bundle of calories, and it tastes surprisingly good. Taste for yourself in the recipe for Homestyle Mashed Potatoes. I also use fat-free evaporated milk in place of cream for some recipes. Evaporated milk works particularly well when you want a rich golden hue.

🖌 When it comes to nuts, the trick is often just using less and toasting them to bring out their full flavor. The small amount of pine nuts in Orzo with Spinach makes all the flavor difference, as do the toasted almonds in one of my favorite dishes from childhood, Rice-a-Noodle.

# Parmesan Zucchini Fans

In this quick dish, zucchini slices are splayed like a hand of cards, which makes an elegant presentation. Broiling the Parmesan cheese brings out its rich flavor. I reduced calories, fat, and cholesterol by:

❖ *Eliminating the butter*
❖ *Slightly reducing the amount of Parmesan cheese*

| Nutrition Scorecard | | |
|---|---|---|
| *(per serving)* | before | after |
| Calories | 239 | 58 |
| Fat (g) | 17 | 3 |

| | |
|---|---|
| 4 | **medium zucchini** |
| ¼ | **teaspoon salt** |
| ⅓ | **cup freshly grated Parmesan cheese (1½ ounces)** |

Cut 5 lengthwise slits through each zucchini to within ½" of the stem end. Arrange the zucchini in one layer in a shallow glass dish. Cover with a glass lid or microwaveable plastic wrap. Microwave for 4 minutes on high power, or until just soft enough so that the slices bend without breaking.

Meanwhile, preheat the broiler. Spread each zucchini out on a baking sheet so that the slices fan out. Sprinkle with the salt. Evenly top with the cheese. Broil for 2 minutes, or until the cheese melts and is lightly browned.

**Makes 4 servings**

*Per serving: 58 calories, 5 g protein, 4 g carbohydrates, 3 g fat, 2 g saturated fat, 7 mg cholesterol, 292 mg sodium, 2 g fiber*

# Mexicali Corn

Fresh, sweet corn makes this simple dish such a treat. It's one of my summer standbys. You can also make it other times of year with frozen or canned corn. Calories, fat, and cholesterol were reduced by:

❖ *Eliminating the butter*

❖ *Using nonstick spray to cook the vegetables*

4   ears corn, shucked

1   onion, chopped

1   red bell pepper, chopped

1   green bell pepper, chopped

⅛   teaspoon salt

⅛   teaspoon ground black pepper

Holding the cobs upright in a bowl, cut the kernels from the cobs with a sharp knife. Discard the cobs.

Lightly coat a large nonstick skillet with nonstick spray and warm over medium-high heat. Add the onion and bell peppers and cook, stirring, for 5 minutes, or until the onion is soft. Add the corn, salt, and black pepper. Reduce the heat to low and cook for 5 minutes longer, or until the corn is heated through.

## Makes 6 servings

Per serving: 65 calories, 2 g protein, 15 g carbohydrates, 1 g fat, 0.5 g saturated fat, 0 mg cholesterol, 99 mg sodium, 4 g fiber

*Homestyle Hint:* If fresh corn isn't available, use frozen corn or drained water-packed canned corn. You will need about 2¼ cups of kernels.

# Whipped Candied Brandied Yams

The combination of orange juice, brandy, and pecans makes this dish irresistible. It's perfect for holidays, but try it anytime. Calories, fat, and cholesterol were reduced by:

❖ *Reducing the amount of brown sugar and brandy*
❖ *Using egg whites in place of whole eggs*
❖ *Eliminating the butter in the yam mixture*

| Nutrition Scorecard | | |
|---|---|---|
| *(per serving)* | | |
| | before | after |
| Calories | 378 | 256 |
| Fat (g) | 12 | 4 |

## YAMS

1 can yams (40 ounces), drained
2 tablespoons brown sugar
2 tablespoons frozen orange juice concentrate, thawed
2 tablespoons brandy or 1 teaspoon rum extract
1 teaspoon cornstarch
1 teaspoon vanilla extract
¼ teaspoon salt
4 egg whites

## TOPPING

½ cup brown sugar
2 tablespoons light butter
¼ teaspoon ground cinnamon
¼ cup chopped pecans

TO MAKE THE YAMS: Preheat the oven to 350°F. In a large bowl, using an electric mixer set on medium speed, beat the yams for 2 minutes, or until well-mashed. Beat in the brown sugar, orange juice concentrate, brandy or rum extract, cornstarch, vanilla extract, and salt. Add the egg whites and beat until smooth. Transfer to a shallow 2-quart baking dish and smooth the surface.

TO MAKE THE TOPPING: In a microwaveable bowl, combine the brown sugar, butter, and cinnamon. Microwave on high power for 30 seconds, or until melted. Stir until blended.

Scatter the pecans over the yams and drizzle with the topping. Bake for 30 to 35 minutes, or until the topping is golden and bubbly.

**Makes 8 servings**

*Per serving: 256 calories, 4 g protein, 50 g carbohydrates, 4 g fat, 0.5 g saturated fat, 4 mg cholesterol, 129 mg sodium, 4 g fiber*

# Sweet Potato–Apple Bake

Parboiling the sweet potatoes makes them easier to slice and reduces the overall baking time. Just one serving of this easy dish provides nearly twice the daily adult need for vitamin A. I reduced calories, fat, and cholesterol by:

| *Nutrition Scorecard* | | |
|---|---|---|
| *(per serving)* | before | after |
| Calories | 244 | 185 |
| Fat (g) | 8 | 1 |

❖ *Replacing full-fat butter with light butter, and using less of it*
❖ *Increasing the amounts of sweet spices to enhance flavor*

4   medium sweet potatoes (about 2 pounds)
3   tart apples
1   tablespoon lemon juice
⅓   cup packed brown sugar
1   tablespoon light butter
½   teaspoon ground cinnamon
⅛   teaspoon ground nutmeg

Preheat the oven to 350°F. Lightly coat a shallow 1½-quart baking dish with nonstick spray.

In a medium saucepan, cover the sweet potatoes with water and bring to a boil over medium-high heat. Cook for 20 minutes, or until slightly tender when pierced with a fork. Drain and let cool. When cool enough to handle, remove and discard the skins. Cut the sweet potatoes crosswise into ½"-thick slices.

Meanwhile, peel and core the apples. Cut crosswise into ½"-thick rings. Sprinkle with the lemon juice to prevent discoloring.

Arrange half of the sweet potato slices in a layer in the prepared baking dish. Top with the apples and then the remaining sweet potatoes.

In a small microwaveable bowl, combine the brown sugar, butter, cinnamon, and nutmeg. Cook in the microwave on high power for 30 seconds, or until melted. Stir until smooth and blended. Drizzle over the sweet potato mixture. Cover with foil and bake for 45 minutes, or until very tender.

### Makes 6 servings

*Per serving: 185 calories, 2 g protein, 43 g carbohydrates, 1 g fat, 0.5 g saturated fat, 3 mg cholesterol, 29 mg sodium, 4 g fiber*

*Homestyle Hint:* I like to use a tart apple, such as Granny Smith, for this dish.

# Roasted Tarragon-Vegetable Medley

Any mixture of vegetables will work here, but this is one of my favorite combinations. Root vegetables such as carrots become delightfully sweet during roasting, as do the peppers. The mushrooms and squash release moisture, and their flavors intensify. For easy cleanup, I like to line the baking sheets with foil. No mess, no fuss! Calories, fat, and cholesterol were reduced by:

❖ *Eliminating the butter and replacing it with chicken broth*
❖ *Using less olive oil*
❖ *Reducing the amount of wine*

| *Nutrition Scorecard* | | |
|---|---|---|
| (per serving) | | |
| | before | after |
| Calories | 177 | 69 |
| Fat (g) | 14 | 2 |

## VEGETABLES

3   carrots, halved lengthwise, then quartered

2   medium crookneck or yellow summer squash, cut diagonally into ½"-thick slices

2   medium zucchini, cut diagonally into ½"-thick slices

2   portobello mushrooms, each cut into sixths

2   red bell peppers, cut into sixths

## GLAZE

2   tablespoons fat-free chicken broth

1   tablespoon dry white wine or fat-free chicken broth

2   teaspoons olive oil

1   tablespoon chopped fresh tarragon or 1 teaspoon dried

4   garlic cloves, finely chopped

TO MAKE THE VEGETABLES: Position one rack in the top third and another in the bottom third of the oven. Preheat the oven to 500°F. Line 2 baking sheets or roasting pans with foil and lightly coat with nonstick spray.

Arrange the carrots, squash, zucchini, mushrooms, and peppers on both baking sheets or pans in single layers. Place the mushrooms with their gills facing up.

TO MAKE THE GLAZE: In a small cup, combine the broth, wine or broth, oil, tarragon, and garlic. Drizzle evenly over the vegetables.

Roast for 20 minutes. Reverse the position of the baking sheets so that the top sheet is on the bottom and vice versa. Roast for 15 minutes longer, or until the vegetables are tender and lightly browned.

**Makes 6 servings**

*Per serving: 69 calories, 3 g protein, 11 g carbohydrates, 2 g fat, 0.5 g saturated fat, 0 mg cholesterol, 30 mg sodium, 5 g fiber*

## Having Trouble Getting Enough Vegetables?

*Double or triple the serving size at dinner. A half-cup of cooked vegetables—about the size of your fist—is considered one serving. Eat 1½ cups with dinner, and you'll have three servings right there.*

# Roasted Asparagus

I'll never forget the first time I roasted asparagus this way for an impromptu dinner gathering. It was so utterly delicious, it never made it to the dinner table! Everyone gobbled it up in the kitchen. Calories, fat, and cholesterol were reduced by:

❖ *Using less olive oil*
❖ *Eliminating butter*

*Nutrition Scorecard*
(per serving)

|          | before | after |
|----------|--------|-------|
| Calories | 148    | 55    |
| Fat (g)  | 11     | 2     |

*Photo on page 131*

| | |
|---|---|
| 1 | bunch thin asparagus (about 1½ pounds) |
| 1½ | teaspoons olive oil |
| 2 | garlic cloves, finely chopped |
| ¼ | teaspoon salt |

Preheat the oven to 500°F. Lightly coat a large baking sheet with nonstick spray.

Bend the asparagus until it snaps and discard the woody ends, if necessary (thin asparagus may not have woody ends). Arrange the stalks in a single layer on the prepared baking sheet.

In small dish, combine the oil and garlic. Drizzle over the asparagus. Sprinkle with the salt.

Roast for 5 minutes. Shake the pan to redistribute the oil. Roast for 3 to 5 minutes longer, or until tender.

### Makes 4 servings

*Per serving: 55 calories, 4 g protein, 8 g carbohydrates, 2 g fat, 0.5 g saturated fat, 0 mg cholesterol, 137 mg sodium, 4 g fiber*

*Homestyle Hint:* **For a touch more flavor, sprinkle the asparagus with 1 tablespoon finely grated lemon peel right when it comes out of the oven. Shake the pan to distribute the peel.**

# Cajun Potato Wedges

My kids love these for snacks. They also go well with burgers. Sometimes I use sweet potatoes instead of baking potatoes. Calories, fat, and cholesterol were reduced by:

❖ *Eliminating the olive oil*
❖ *Using cooking spray for crisping*

|   |   |
|---|---|
| 4 | baking potatoes or sweet potatoes |
| 1 | tablespoon chili powder |
| 2 | teaspoons paprika |
| 1½ | teaspoons ground cumin |
| 1 | teaspoon salt |

Place an oven rack in the lower third of the oven. Preheat the oven to 400°F. Coat a baking sheet with nonstick spray.

Cut the potatoes in half lengthwise. Cut each half lengthwise into quarters. Arrange in a single layer on the prepared baking sheet.

In small bowl, combine the chili powder, paprika, cumin, and salt. Sprinkle over the potatoes and toss to coat the potatoes evenly. Coat the potatoes with nonstick spray and bake for 20 minutes, or until tender.

**Makes 8 servings**

*Per serving: 115 calories, 3 g protein, 26 g carbohydrates, 0.5 g fat, 0 g saturated fat, 0 mg cholesterol, 284 mg sodium, 3 g fiber*

*Health Note*

## Sweet Potatoes: A Nutritional Best Bet

*Sweet potatoes are a terrific source of fiber, with more than 3 grams when baked in their skins. They are also loaded with beta-carotene, providing more than 200 percent of the recommended levels of vitamin A. If you haven't tried a sweet potato lately, don't hesitate. Baked or boiled, they're delicious. Add just a touch of brown sugar or light butter, and you can't go wrong.*

# Homestyle Mashed Potatoes

If my kids had their way, I'd make these every night for
dinner. They're so easy and low in fat that I do make them
often. Calories, fat, and cholesterol were reduced by:

❖ *Replacing cream with 1% milk*
❖ *Replacing full-fat butter with light butter, and using less of it*
❖ *Using red potatoes rather than baking potatoes for a
creamier texture*

*Nutrition Scorecard*

| | *(per serving)* | |
| --- | --- | --- |
| | before | after |
| Calories | 312 | 193 |
| Fat (g) | 15 | 1 |

3 pounds red potatoes
½ cup 1% milk, warmed
1 tablespoon light butter
½ teaspoon salt
⅛ teaspoon ground black pepper

Place the potatoes in a large saucepan and cover with water. Bring to boil over medium-
high heat. Cover and cook for 25 minutes, or until tender. Drain and let cool. When cool
enough to handle, remove and discard the skins. Transfer to a large bowl.

Add the milk, butter, salt, and pepper. With an electric mixer set on medium speed or
with a potato masher, mash the potatoes until smooth. Serve immediately.

**Makes 6 servings**

*Per serving: 193 calories, 4 g protein, 42 g carbohydrates, 1 g fat, 0.5 g saturated fat, 3 mg cholesterol, 210 mg sodium, 3 g fiber*

*Homestyle Hint:* I sometimes leave the skins on the potatoes for this dish. They lend a beautiful red color.

# Roasted Garlic Mashed Potatoes

These are made the same way as the Homestyle Mashed Potatoes (opposite page), but garlic, chicken broth, and olive oil add a richer flavor. Calories, fat, and cholesterol were reduced by:

* ❖ *Using fat-free chicken broth*
* ❖ *Using less olive oil*

*Nutrition Scorecard*
*(per serving)*

|  | before | after |
|---|---|---|
| Calories | 312 | 205 |
| Fat (g) | 15 | 2 |

*Photo on page 184*

| | |
|---|---|
| 3 | pounds red potatoes |
| 1 | whole head garlic |
| 1 | tablespoon fat-free chicken broth |
| ½ | teaspoon olive oil |
| ½ | cup 1% milk, warmed |
| 1 | tablespoon light butter |
| ½ | teaspoon salt |
| ⅛ | teaspoon black pepper |

Preheat the oven to 375°F.

Place the potatoes in a large saucepan and cover with water. Bring to a boil over medium-high heat. Cover and cook for 25 minutes, or until tender. Drain and let cool. When cool enough to handle, remove and discard the skins. Transfer to a large bowl.

While the potatoes are cooking, cut ¼" from the top of the garlic head to expose the cloves. Place the garlic head, root end down, in a small baking dish. Add the broth and drizzle with the oil. Cover with foil and bake for 20 minutes. Remove the foil and bake for 5 to 10 minutes longer, or until the cloves are very soft. Remove from the oven. Using a wooden pick, remove the garlic cloves from their skins and add to the bowl with the potatoes.

Add the milk, butter, salt, and pepper. With an electric mixer set on medium speed or with a potato masher, mash the potatoes until smooth. Serve immediately.

**Makes 6 servings**

*Per serving: 205 calories, 5 g protein, 44 g carbohydrates, 2 g fat, 0.5 g saturated fat, 3 mg cholesterol, 214 mg sodium, 3 g fiber*

# Soufflé Potatoes

Don't let the fancy name intimidate you—this dish is simple to make. But that doesn't mean it's not impressive. Calories, fat, and cholesterol were reduced by:

❖ *Using 1% cottage cheese and fat-free sour cream in place of the full-fat varieties*
❖ *Eliminating butter*
❖ *Eliminating the egg yolks*

> 3 large egg whites
> 3 cups cooked and mashed potatoes
> 1 cup 1% cottage cheese (8 ounces)
> ½ cup fat-free sour cream (4 ounces)
> 3 tablespoons grated onion
> 1 garlic clove, chopped
> ½ teaspoon salt
> ⅛ teaspoon ground black pepper

Preheat the oven to 350°F. Coat a 2-quart baking dish with nonstick spray.

In a large bowl, using an electric mixer on high speed, beat the egg white for 4 minutes, or until stiff peaks form. Set aside.

In another large bowl, combine the potatoes, cottage cheese, sour cream, onion, garlic, salt, and pepper. Beat with the mixer on medium speed for 4 minutes, or until light and fluffy, scraping down the sides of the bowl. Using a rubber spatula or spoon, gently fold the beaten egg whites into the potato mixture.

Gently spoon the mixture into the prepared baking dish. Bake for 1 hour, or until slightly puffed and golden. Serve immediately. (It is natural for the soufflé to fall slightly after a few minutes.)

## Makes 8 servings

*Per serving: 135 calories, 8 g protein, 25 g carbohydrates, 0.5 g fat, 0 g saturated fat, 1 mg cholesterol, 285 mg sodium, 2 g fiber*

*Homestyle Hint:* To make 3 cups mashed potatoes, you'll need about 1½ pounds potatoes (3 medium russets). Peel and coarsely chop the potatoes, place in a saucepan, cover with water, bring to a boil, and boil for 25 minutes, or until tender. Drain and mash well. You can also use unseasoned mashed potatoes.

# Quick Couscous

Couscous is made out of semolina flour—the basis of good old-fashioned pasta. Because couscous is so tiny, it cooks quickly and makes a great side dish for fast meals. I like it with Creamy Chicken Curry (page 116) and Skillet Chicken Paprikash (page 117). Calories, fat, and cholesterol were reduced by:

| *Nutrition Scorecard* | | |
|---|---|---|
| *(per serving)* | | |
| | before | after |
| Calories | 205 | 172 |
| Fat (g) | 4 | 1 |

❖ *Eliminating the oil*
❖ *Incorporating fat-free chicken broth for flavor*

| | |
|---|---|
| 1 | cup water |
| ½ | cup fat-free chicken broth |
| ½ | teaspoon dried oregano |
| 1 | cup dry couscous |

In a medium saucepan over medium-high heat, bring the water, broth, and oregano to a boil. Stir in the couscous. Cover, remove from the heat, and let stand for 5 minutes to absorb the liquid. Fluff with a fork before serving.

**Makes 4 servings**

*Per serving: 172 calories, 6 g protein, 35 g carbohydrates, 1 g fat, 0 g saturated fat, 0 mg cholesterol, 129 mg sodium, 2 g fiber*

# Orzo with Spinach

The pan-toasted pine nuts make this dish a winner. I reduced the calories, fat, and cholesterol by:

❖ *Eliminating the oil for cooking the vegetables*
❖ *Reducing the amount of pine nuts*

*Photo on page 191*

| | |
|---|---|
| 2 | tablespoons fat-free chicken broth |
| 1 | bag washed baby spinach (10 ounces) |
| 4 | teaspoons pine nuts |
| 2 | garlic cloves, chopped |
| 2 | roma tomatoes, chopped |
| 1½ | cups dried orzo |
| ½ | teaspoon salt |
| 2 | tablespoons freshly grated Parmesan cheese |

Combine the broth and spinach in a large skillet. (The pan will be rather full). Cover and cook over medium-high heat for 3 to 5 minutes, or until the spinach is wilted and tender. The volume will reduce by at least half. When the spinach is cool enough to handle, wrap in a paper towel and squeeze to extract as much liquid as possible. Coarsely chop.

Wipe out the skillet and lightly coat with nonstick spray. Add the pine nuts and garlic. Cook, stirring, for 2 minutes, or until the pine nuts are golden. Stir in the tomatoes and spinach. Cook for 1 minute to give the ingredients time to blend. Remove from the heat and set aside.

Cook the orzo according to the package directions. Drain and transfer to the skillet with the spinach mixture and salt. Toss to mix. Sprinkle with the cheese.

**Makes 6 servings**

Per serving: 177 calories, 8 g protein, 40 g carbohydrates, 3 g fat, 1 g saturated fat, 2 mg cholesterol, 263 mg sodium, 3 g fiber

## The Power of Plant Foods

There are more than 4,000 different flavonoids in plants. Flavonoids are a group of phytochemicals that have antioxidant activity that can be several times stronger than vitamins E and C. Researchers found that people who ate diets high in fruits and vegetables (10 servings a day) had high antioxidant blood levels that could not be explained by the recognized antioxidant nutrients alone (such as vitamins E and C). They concluded that the high antioxidant activity came from flavonoids. Another good reason to eat more plant foods.

# Barley Risotto

Toasted pecans and lemon peel make this dish extremely aromatic. I use barley instead of the traditional Arborio rice because it cooks up creamy and has a rich, nutty flavor. Plus, it's high in fiber. Calories, fat, and cholesterol were reduced by:

* ❖ *Eliminating the butter for cooking the onion*
* ❖ *Using fat-free chicken broth*
* ❖ *Reducing the amount of pecans*

| | |
|---|---|
| 1 | onion, chopped |
| 4 | cups fat-free chicken broth |
| 1 | cup quick-cooking barley |
| ⅓ | cup chopped pecans, toasted |
| ¼ | cup chopped flat-leaf parsley |
| 1 | teaspoon finely shredded lemon peel |

Coat a large saucepan with nonstick spray and warm over medium heat. Add the onion and cook, stirring, for 5 minutes, or until tender. Add 3 cups of the broth and the barley. Cover and simmer for 25 minutes, or until most of the liquid is absorbed. Uncover and gradually add the remaining 1 cup broth, about ¼ cup at a time, stirring constantly, and letting each addition be absorbed before adding the next (a total of about 15 minutes).

Stir in the pecans, parsley, and lemon peel. Serve immediately.

### Makes 6 servings

Per serving: 176 calories, 7 g protein, 29 g carbohydrates, 4 g fat, 0.5 g saturated fat, 0 mg cholesterol, 533 mg sodium, 5 g fiber

*Homestyle Hint:* To toast pecans, place them in a dry skillet over medium heat. Cook, shaking the pan often, for 2 minutes, or until lightly browned and fragrant.

## Barley: The Underused Grain

*It's as easy to prepare as rice, and it's a good source of fiber. Just 1 cup of cooked pearl barley (about ¼ cup dry) has 6 grams of cholesterol-lowering fiber. Best of all, barley has a satisfying taste that appeals to both adults and kids.*

# Rice-a-Noodle

I grew up on a commercial boxed version of this side dish. My mom used to make it at least once a week with dinner, and we never grew tired of it. This version is every bit as tasty. I use brown rice rather than white rice for a nutrition boost. I reduced calories, fat, and cholesterol and boosted fiber by:

| Nutrition Scorecard | | |
|---|---|---|
| (per serving) | | |
| | before | after |
| Calories | 270 | 222 |
| Fat (g) | 16 | 7 |

❖ *Replacing butter with light butter and using less of it*
❖ *Using fewer almonds and toasting them for more flavor*
❖ *Replacing white rice with brown rice*

|     |     |
|----:|-----|
| 2 | tablespoons light butter |
| ⅔ | cup vermicelli, crushed |
| 1 | cup long-grain brown rice |
| 2¼ | cups fat-free chicken broth |
| 1 | jar mushroom pieces (4 ounces), drained |
| ⅓ | cup slivered almonds, toasted |

Melt the butter in a large saucepan over medium heat. Add the vermicelli and cook, stirring, for 5 minutes, or until golden.

Stir in the rice, broth, and mushrooms. Bring to a boil over high heat. Reduce the heat to low, cover, and simmer for 45 minutes, or until the liquid is absorbed. Add the almonds and toss to mix.

**Makes 6 servings**

Per serving: 222 calories, 9 g protein, 32 g carbohydrates, 7 g fat, 1 g saturated fat, 5 mg cholesterol, 389 mg sodium, 3 g fiber

*Homestyle Hint*: To toast almonds, place them in a dry skillet over medium heat. Cook, shaking the pan often, for 2 minutes, or until lightly browned and fragrant.

## Go Nuts for a Healthy Heart

*In one study, women who consumed nuts at least five times per week had about a 35 percent lower risk of heart disease compared with women who rarely ate nuts. A handful scattered over a casserole, salad, or rice dish adds flavor and crunch—and good health.*

# Apple-Rice Pilaf

I sprinkle this pilaf with dried apples, but in a pinch, raisins are good, too. Both give the pilaf the sweet lift that makes it delicious. I reduced calories, fat, and cholesterol by:

❖ *Eliminating the oil for cooking the onions*
❖ *Eliminating the butter*
❖ *Using fat-free chicken broth*
❖ *Reducing the amount of almonds and sherry*

| | |
|---|---|
| 1 | onion, chopped |
| 1 | tablespoon sugar |
| ½ | cup brown rice |
| ½ | cup pearl barley |
| 4 | dried apple rings, chopped |
| 2 | cups fat-free chicken broth |
| ¾ | teaspoon salt |
| 1 | tablespoon sherry or apple juice |
| ¼ | cup slivered almonds, toasted |

Coat a large saucepan with nonstick spray and warm over medium-high heat. Add the onion and cook, stirring, for 4 minutes, or until tender. Sprinkle with the sugar and cook for 1 minute. Stir in the rice, barley, apples, broth, salt, and sherry or apple juice. Bring to a boil. Reduce the heat to low, cover, and cook for 40 minutes, or until the liquid is absorbed. Remove from heat, add the almonds, and toss to mix.

**Makes 6 servings**

Per serving: 181 calories, 6 g protein, 32 g carbohydrates, 4 g fat, 0.5 g saturated fat, 0 mg cholesterol, 387 mg sodium, 4 g fiber

*Homestyle Hint:* To toast almonds, place them in a dry skillet over medium heat. Cook, shaking the pan often, for 2 minutes, or until lightly browned and fragrant.

## Brown Rice—Twice the Fiber

*Brown rice is the unprocessed version of white rice with more than two times the fiber. It also takes about twice as long to cook, but the wait is worth it. A cup of cooked brown rice has about 4 grams of fiber and a delicious nutty flavor. If you're rushed, try instant brown rice; it cooks in minutes.*

# Sweet Corn Cakes

Corn cakes often are served as little "tastes" in Mexican restaurants. I like them so much that I usually order an extra side. The first time I tried this recipe at home, I was delighted with the outcome—so much so that they disappeared lickety-split! These are served with a spoon like mashed potatoes, so don't let the name throw you. Calories, fat, and cholesterol were reduced by:

❖ *Using low-fat buttermilk in place of the cream*
❖ *Replacing the butter with a combination of light butter and applesauce*

> 5 **tablespoons light butter, softened**
> ⅓ **cup masa harina**
> ⅓ **cup unsweetened applesauce**
> 2 **cups corn kernels**
> ⅓ **cup sugar**
> 3 **tablespoons cornmeal**
> 2 **tablespoons 2% buttermilk**
> ¼ **teaspoon baking powder**
> ¼ **teaspoon salt**

Preheat the oven to 350°F. Lightly coat an 8" × 8" baking dish with nonstick spray.

In a large bowl, using an electric mixer set on high speed, beat the butter until fluffy. Gradually add the masa harina and applesauce, beating on low speed until incorporated.

In a food processor or blender, coarsely chop the corn. Add to the applesauce mixture along with the sugar, cornmeal, buttermilk, baking powder, and salt. Mix until just blended.

Pour into the prepared baking dish. Bake for 40 minutes, or until firm and lightly golden on top. Let stand for 15 minutes before serving.

## Makes 8 servings

*Per serving: 132 calories, 2 g protein, 23 g carbohydrates, 4 g fat, 0.5 g saturated fat, 10 mg cholesterol, 139 mg sodium, 2 g fiber*

*Homestyle Hint:* Masa harina is corn flour (a finer grain than cornmeal). It's available in the international aisle of most supermarkets, often near the Latin American foods.

# Shortcut Boston Baked Beans

By using canned pinto beans, I shaved hours of soaking and cooking time from this recipe. I like to use the slow-cooker method when I know that I will be taking these to a potluck supper. It makes advance planning easy, I don't have to worry about a thing, and the beans are ready when I am. Calories, fat, and cholesterol were reduced by:

❖ *Eliminating the bacon*
❖ *Using less maple syrup*

> 1 onion, chopped
> 3 garlic cloves, minced
> 1 cup ketchup
> ¼ cup pure maple syrup
> 3 tablespoons brown sugar
> 2 tablespoons molasses
> 2 tablespoons Dijon mustard
> 1 tablespoon cider vinegar or red wine vinegar
> 1 tablespoon soy sauce
> 3 cans pinto beans (15 ounces each), rinsed and drained

Lightly coat a 4-quart saucepan or Dutch oven with nonstick spray and warm over medium-high heat. Add the onion and garlic and cook, stirring, for 5 minutes, or until soft. Stir in the ketchup, maple syrup, brown sugar, molasses, mustard, vinegar, and soy sauce. Bring to a boil. Stir in the beans. Reduce the heat to low, cover, and simmer for 30 minutes, or until the flavors are blended.

**Makes 8 servings**

*Per serving: 232 calories, 10 g protein, 46 g carbohydrates, 2 g fat, 0 g saturated fat, 0 mg cholesterol, 898 mg sodium, 8 g fiber*

*Homestyle Hints:* You can easily make this recipe in a slow cooker. Just combine the ingredients in the slow cooker and cook on the low-heat setting for 4 to 5 hours.

For a hint of smoky flavor, add 2 or 3 drops liquid smoke seasoning along with the soy sauce.

# Crisscross Spiced Apples

My son, Connor, named this dish—at the ripe age of 3! The name comes from a poem about making crisscross apple-sauce. Calories, fat, and cholesterol were reduced by:

❖ *Eliminating the butter*
❖ *Reducing the amount of brown sugar*

| Nutrition Scorecard | | |
|---|---|---|
| *(per serving)* | | |
| | before | after |
| Calories | 212 | 138 |
| Fat (g) | 6 | 1 |

5 apples, peeled and cored
⅓ cup packed brown sugar
1 teaspoon ground cinnamon
¼ teaspoon salt
¼ teaspoon ground nutmeg

Cut the apples in half lengthwise, then slice crosswise to make half-moon shapes. In a medium saucepan over medium heat, stir together the apples, brown sugar, cinnamon, salt, and nutmeg. Cook for 15 minutes, or until the apples are very soft but still somewhat chunky.

**Makes 4 servings**

*Per serving: 138 calories, 0 g protein, 36 g carbohydrates, 1 g fat, 0 g saturated fat, 0 mg cholesterol, 298 mg sodium, 3 g fiber*

*Homestyle Hint:* I like to use a tart apple, such as Granny Smith, for this dish.

## Prostate Problems—Diet Does Make a Difference

*Eating a diet high in fruit appears to lower the risk of developing an enlarged prostate gland, a condition that affects 1 out of 10 men by age 45—and 4 out of 5 men over the age of 80. To help prevent prostate problems, ask the following question whenever sitting down to a meal: How can I add fruit here? Try topping off a bowl of cereal with chopped fruit at breakfast, having a fruit salad with lunch, or crowning frozen yogurt with fresh fruit or frozen berries. It also helps to keep a fruit bowl in plain sight in the kitchen.*

# Best-Loved Desserts

I absolutely love desserts. When I started doing recipe makeovers in the 1980s, I began with desserts. Since then I have learned a lot about what works and what doesn't.

☕ Don't mess with chocolate. There's nothing more disappointing than expecting the taste of chocolate only to end up with a mouthful of carob chips or raisins. To stretch the flavor and texture of chocolate chips, use mini chocolate chips instead of regular. Use cocoa powder in place of solid baking chocolate. To intensify the richness of desserts made with cocoa powder, add strong brewed coffee or instant espresso granules.

☕ Light butter is the answer when a recipe needs the taste of real butter. It has half the fat and calories of regular butter. But be careful how you use it; light butter cannot replace regular butter one-for-one because it contains more moisture. For doughs and batters, reduce the amount of liquid when using light butter instead of regular. For more details, see page 20.

☕ When recipes call for cream cheese, a combination of fat-free cream cheese and light cream cheese works best.

☕ Fruit purees, such as applesauce and baby food prunes, work well in place of oil for cakes and baked goods. Just avoid using too much so that the end product is not gummy.

☕ Fat-free sweetened condensed milk works wonders in place of whole milk or condensed whole milk. I also use 2% buttermilk instead of whole milk for rich texture.

For more makeover tips, see "Recipe Makeover Substitutions" on page 28. The best tip I can give is to *enjoy* dessert. Try not to think of it as forbidden fruit, because if you do, you will never truly enjoy the incredible tastes offered at this part of the meal.

# Aunt Boojie's Chocolate Box Cake

My sister makes the best—and easiest—chocolate cake in the world, although she readily credits me with the fat-cutting techniques. The frosting, which is quite low in fat, is especially rich and satisfying with no skimping on flavor or texture. I happily named this cake in honor of her, partly because she always reserves the center cut of cake just for me—the best part! Calories, fat, and cholesterol were reduced by:

| *Nutrition Scorecard* | | |
|---|---|---|
| (per serving) | | |
| | before | after |
| Calories | 464 | 343 |
| Fat (g) | 26 | 10 |

*Photo on page 288*

* ❖ *Replacing eggs with egg whites*
* ❖ *Using applesauce in place of oil*
* ❖ *Using low-fat buttermilk in place of whole milk for the liquid*
* ❖ *Replacing regular butter with light butter for the frosting, and using less of it*
* ❖ *Using fat-free milk instead of whole milk in the frosting.*

## CAKE

  5  egg whites

1⅓  cups 2% buttermilk

  ⅓  cup unsweetened applesauce

  1  box chocolate cake mix (18¼ ounces)

## FROSTING

  3  cups confectioners' sugar

  ⅔  cup cocoa powder

  6  tablespoons light butter, at room temperature

  ⅓  cup fat-free milk

  1  teaspoon vanilla extract

TO MAKE THE CAKE: Preheat the oven to 350°F. Lightly coat a 13" × 9" baking dish with nonstick spray.

In a large bowl, using an electric mixer set on high speed, beat the egg whites for 1 minute, or until foamy. Beat in the buttermilk and applesauce. Add the cake mix and beat for 2 minutes, or until smooth. Scrape into the prepared pan.

Bake for 30 to 35 minutes, or until a wooden pick inserted in the center comes out clean and the cake is pulling away from the sides of the pan. Cool completely in the pan on a rack.

TO MAKE THE FROSTING: In a small bowl, combine the confectioners' sugar and cocoa, stirring to remove lumps. In a medium bowl, using an electric mixer set on medium speed, beat the butter until fluffy. Gradually beat in the cocoa mixture, milk, and vanilla extract. Beat until very smooth. Spread over the cooled cake, swirling it for a decorative appearance.

### Makes 12 servings

*Per serving: 343 calories, 6 g protein, 62 g carbohydrates, 10 g fat, 2 g saturated fat, 9 mg cholesterol, 447 mg sodium, 3 g fiber*

*Homestyle Hints:* This frosting firms up as it rests. If it becomes too firm to spread, gently warm it in the microwave on medium power for 30 seconds, or until softened.

This cake actually tastes better when made a few hours before serving. As soon as the cake is frosted, cover it with plastic wrap and refrigerate. Let stand at room temperature for about 30 minutes before serving and refrigerate for up to 4 days.

## Restricting Treats Can Backfire

*Well-meaning parents may restrict treats to moderate their children's fat and sugar intake. The problem is that most parents end up with opposite results: It sets up the forbidden food sydrome, where the sheer act of forbidding a particular food makes it more desirable.*

# Upside-Down German Chocolate Snack Cake

This is one of the simplest cakes you'll ever make. The frosting is put on the cake before it's baked—spread on the bottom of the pan. I reduced calories, fat, and cholesterol by:

❖ *Reducing the amount of coconut*
❖ *Using applesauce instead of oil*
❖ *Using fat-free sour cream instead of regular*
❖ *Using low-fat buttermilk for body*
❖ *Using light butter instead of regular butter, and less of it*
❖ *Replacing eggs with egg whites*

## Nutrition Scorecard

(per serving)

| | before | after |
|---|---|---|
| Calories | 330 | 244 |
| Fat (g) | 17 | 9 |

*Photo on page 286*

|   |   |
|---|---|
| 2 | tablespoons light butter |
| ¾ | cup water |
| ⅔ | cup packed brown sugar |
| ¾ | cup flaked sweetened coconut |
| 1½ | cups miniature marshmallows |
| ½ | cup chopped pecans |
| 5 | egg whites |
| 1 | cup 2% buttermilk |
| ½ | cup fat-free sour cream (without gelatin), 4 ounces |
| ⅓ | cup unsweetened applesauce |
| 1 | box German chocolate cake mix (18¼ ounces) |

Preheat the oven to 350°F. Lightly spray a 13" × 9" baking dish with nonstick spray.

In a small saucepan over low heat, melt the butter with the water. Stir in the brown sugar until smooth. Pour evenly into the prepared baking dish. Sprinkle the coconut, marshmallows, and pecans evenly over the melted sugar mixture.

In a large bowl, using an electric mixer set on high speed, beat the egg whites for 30 seconds, or just until frothy. Beat in the buttermilk, sour cream, and applesauce. Add the cake mix and beat on low speed for 30 seconds, or just until moistened. Beat for an additional 2 minutes. Scrape into the pan, smoothing it evenly.

Bake for 40 minutes, or until a wooden pick inserted in the center comes out clean and the cake is pulling away from the sides of the pan.

Cool in the pan on a rack. To serve, cut into squares and invert onto individual plates. Replace any loose topping. Serve warm or cool.

**Makes 16 servings**

Per serving: 244 calories, 4 g protein, 38 g carbohydrates, 9 g fat, 2 g saturated fat, 2 mg cholesterol, 327 mg sodium, 1 g fiber

*Homestyle Hint:* The topping for this cake sticks better when the cake is cooled almost to room temperature.

## Buttermilk for Strong Bones

*One cup of low-fat or fat-free buttermilk has 285 milligrams of calcium, more than 25 percent of the daily amount recommended for most adults. I like to use buttermilk in place of whole milk because it has a richer texture and less fat.*

# Chocolate Spice Zucchini Cake

Aromas of orange zest and cinnamon give this cake wonderful flavor. And thank you, zucchini, for keeping the cake moist! I call it a sneaky ingredient because you don't even see it. Calories, fat, and cholesterol were reduced by:

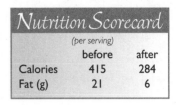

| Nutrition Scorecard | | |
|---|---|---|
| *(per serving)* | | |
| | before | after |
| Calories | 415 | 284 |
| Fat (g) | 21 | 6 |

❖ *Replacing butter with applesauce*
❖ *Using low-fat buttermilk in place of whole milk*
❖ *Using egg whites in place of some of the whole eggs*
❖ *Reducing the amount of walnuts*

## CAKE

2½ cups unbleached or all-purpose flour

1½ cups sugar

½ cup unsweetened cocoa powder

2½ teaspoons baking powder

2 teaspoons finely grated orange peel

1½ teaspoons baking soda

1 teaspoon ground cinnamon

¼ teaspoon salt

2 eggs

2 egg whites

¾ cup 2% buttermilk

½ cup unsweetened applesauce

2 teaspoons vanilla extract

2 cups finely shredded zucchini (about 1 medium)

½ cup chopped walnuts

## GLAZE

¼ cup chocolate chips

1 teaspoon canola oil

TO MAKE THE CAKE: Preheat the oven to 350°F. Generously coat a Bundt pan with nonstick spray.

In a medium bowl, whisk together the flour, sugar, cocoa, baking powder, orange peel, baking soda, cinnamon, and salt. Set aside.

In a large bowl, using an electric mixer set on high speed, beat the eggs and egg whites for 2 minutes, or until frothy and thickened. Add the buttermilk, applesauce, and vanilla extract. Beat just until blended.

Gradually beat in half of the flour mixture. Beat in the remaining flour mixture. Stir in the zucchini and walnuts. Scrape into the prepared pan.

Bake for 45 to 50 minutes, or until a wooden pick inserted in the center comes out clean.

Cool in the pan on a rack for 15 minutes. Loosen the edges of the cake by gently inserting a thin rubber spatula or knife around the sides and center. Invert the cake onto the rack to cool completely.

TO MAKE THE GLAZE: In a small microwaveable cup, combine the chocolate chips and oil. Cook in the microwave on high for 30 seconds and stir. Repeat just until the chocolate can be stirred into a smooth glaze. (The chips will not melt completely in the microwave oven, but they will get shiny and soft enough to stir until smooth.) Drizzle the warm glaze over the cooled cake.

**Makes 12 servings**

*Per serving: 284 calories, 7 g protein, 53 g carbohydrates, 6 g fat, 1 g saturated fat, 36 mg cholesterol, 342 mg sodium, 3 g fiber*

## *Chocolate May Help Protect Your Heart*

Tea is often touted as a good source of catechins, phytochemicals that are powerful antioxidants and may protect against heart disease and boost the immune system. The better news? Chocolate contains even more heart-protecting catechins! In fact, of all the chocolates, dark chocolate is the richest source of this phytochemical.

If you're a milk chocolate lover, the news is still good: An ounce of milk chocolate has more beneficial catechins than a cup of black tea.

# Apple-Carrot Cake

Carrot cake is a favorite in my house, especially when crowned with one of the best cream cheese frostings ever (see the recipe on page 334). Over the years, I've made numerous carrot cakes and tasted even more, and I truly think this is by far the best. Plus, there's a nutritional bonus: One serving provides nearly 40 percent of an adult's daily recommended level of beta-carotene. I reduced calories, fat, and cholesterol and boosted fiber by:

## Nutrition Scorecard
*(per serving, with frosting)*

|          | before | after |
|----------|--------|-------|
| Calories | 544    | 322   |
| Fat (g)  | 35     | 6     |

*Photo on page 285*

❖ *Replacing oil with applesauce*
❖ *Using egg whites in place of some of the whole eggs*
❖ *Using a lightened cream cheese frosting*
❖ *Incorporating whole wheat flour*
❖ *Reducing the amount of walnuts and making them an optional garnish*

| | |
|---|---|
| 1 | cup whole wheat flour |
| 1 | cup unbleached or all-purpose flour |
| 1⅓ | cups sugar |
| 2 | teaspoons baking soda |
| 2 | teaspoons ground cinnamon |
| ½ | teaspoon ground cloves |
| 2 | eggs |
| 2 | egg whites |
| ¾ | cup unsweetened applesauce |
| ½ | cup 2% buttermilk |
| 1 | teaspoon vanilla extract |
| 1½ | cups shredded carrots (about 2 medium) |
| 1 | apple, peeled and shredded |
| 1 | batch Best-Ever Light Cream Cheese Frosting (page 334) |
| ½ | cup chopped walnuts (optional) |

Preheat the oven to 350°F. Lightly coat a 13" × 9" baking dish with nonstick spray.

In a medium bowl, combine the whole wheat flour, unbleached or all-purpose flour, sugar, baking soda, cinnamon, and cloves.

In a large bowl, using an electric mixer set on high speed, beat the eggs and egg whites for 1 minute, or until foamy. Beat in the applesauce, buttermilk, and vanilla extract until blended. Gradually beat in the flour mixture. Stir in the carrots and apple. Scrape into the prepared pan and smooth the surface.

Bake for 35 to 40 minutes, or until a wooden pick inserted in the center comes out clean and the cake begins to pull away from the sides of the pan. Cool completely in the pan on a rack.

When completely cool, spread the cake with the frosting, swirling it for a decorative appearance. Garnish with the walnuts, if using.

**Makes 12 servings**

*Per serving (with frosting): 322 calories, 9 g protein, 59 g carbohydrates, 6 g fat, 2 g saturated fat, 50 mg cholesterol, 488 mg sodium, 3 g fiber*

*Homestyle Hint:* I like to use a tart apple, such as Granny Smith, for this cake.

## Carrots Are Tops

*Carrots are the chief source of beta-carotene in the American diet. Just one medium carrot provides nearly twice the daily requirement for vitamin A (the body turns beta-carotene into vitamin A). If you're not fond of raw carrots, try them in baked goods. They add moisture and a wonderful sweetness.*

# Best-Ever Light
# Cream Cheese Frosting

Every time I make this frosting, my kids beg to lick the beaters (and the bowl and the spatula). Be sure to use the light cream cheese that's packaged in a tub; it's lower in fat than the light cream cheese packaged bar-style. I reduced calories, fat, and cholesterol by:

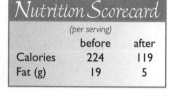

Photo on page 285

❖ *Using a combination of fat-free cream cheese and light cream cheese in place of regular*
❖ *Replacing regular butter with light butter and using less of it*
❖ *Slightly reducing the amount of confectioner's sugar*

| | |
|---|---|
| 1 | tub light cream cheese (8 ounces), softened |
| 8 | ounces fat-free cream cheese, softened |
| 3 | tablespoons light butter, softened |
| 1½ | cups confectioners' sugar, sifted |
| 1½ | teaspoons vanilla extract |

In a medium bowl, using an electric mixer set on medium speed, beat the light cream cheese, fat-free cream cheese, and butter for 2 to 3 minutes, or until smooth and fluffy. Gradually beat in the confectioners' sugar. Stir in the vanilla extract. Use immediately or cover and refrigerate for several hours. Let the frosting return to room temperature and whisk again to lighten it before using.

**Makes about 3½ cups (about twelve ¼-cup servings)**

*Per serving (about ¼ cup): 119 calories, 5 g protein, 14 g carbohydrates, 5 g fat, 2 g saturated fat, 14 mg cholesterol, 242 mg sodium, 0 g fiber*

*Homestyle Hint:* This frosting makes enough to generously frost one 13" × 9" cake or one 9" round 2-layer cake.

Nutrition Scorecard
(per serving)

|  | before | after |
|---|---|---|
| Calories | 224 | 119 |
| Fat (g) | 19 | 5 |

# Tiramisu

I like to bring this to parties because it's such a crowd pleaser. It tastes so good that I no longer order tiramisu in restaurants—I'd rather have my own version at home. And it doesn't require even a minute of cooking—just assembling ahead of time. Be sure to use mascarpone cheese, a naturally sweet Italian cream cheese for which there truly is no substitute. You can find it in Italian delis and large supermarkets. Calories, fat, and cholesterol were reduced by:

*Nutrition Scorecard*
(per serving)

| | before | after |
|---|---|---|
| Calories | 412 | 225 |
| Fat (g) | 34 | 9 |

*Photo on page 292*

❖ *Replacing part of the mascarpone with fat-free cream cheese*
❖ *Using light whipped topping in place of heavy cream*
❖ *Using fat-free sponge cake instead of regular sponge cake*

8 ounces mascarpone cheese
8 ounces fat-free cream cheese, softened
½ cup confectioners' sugar
¾ cup frozen light whipped topping, thawed (6 ounces)
⅔ cup freshly brewed espresso or strong coffee
3 tablespoons coffee liqueur, such as Kahlua, or brewed strong coffee
1 loaf fat-free sponge cake (13 ounces)
½ teaspoon unsweetened cocoa powder

In a large bowl, using an electric mixer on low speed, beat the mascarpone and cream cheese. Beat in the confectioners' sugar until blended. Fold in the whipped topping.

In a measuring cup, stir together the espresso or coffee and coffee liqueur.

Using a bread knife or long serrated knife, cut the cake horizontally into 8 slices. (Don't worry if the slices break. You will still be able to use them.) Arrange half of the cake slices evenly over the bottom of a 10" × 10" pan. Using a spoon, drizzle half of the coffee mixture evenly over the cake. Gently spoon half of the cheese mixture evenly over the cake layer. Repeat layering with the remaining cake slices, coffee mixture, and cheese mixture. Sift the cocoa over the top layer of cheese. Cover and chill for at least 8 hours or overnight.

## Makes 12 servings

Per serving: 225 calories, 6 g protein, 27 g carbohydrates, 9 g fat, 5 g saturated fat, 26 mg cholesterol, 103 mg sodium, 0 g fiber

*Homestyle Hint:* To make *Chocolate Tiramisu*, use a fat-free marble sponge cake instead of the regular sponge cake. (The nutritional figures are almost identical.)

# Sacher Torte

This is quite a beautiful cake. The first time I made it, I left it sitting on the counter. My neighbor stopped by and asked which bakery it was from! But fear not—this cake is not complicated, as it gets a head start from a box mix. The dried apricots studded throughout the cake and the apricot preserve filling make it especially moist and rich. I reduced calories, fat, and cholesterol by:

- ❖ *Replacing whole eggs with egg whites*
- ❖ *Using baby food prunes in place of oil*
- ❖ *Replacing the butter in the glaze with a small amount of oil*
- ❖ *Using slightly fewer almonds*

## CAKE

- 3 ounces dried apricot halves, finely chopped (about ½ cup)
- ½ cup hot water
- 2 teaspoons rum extract
- 6 egg whites
- ¾ cup 2% buttermilk
- 1 jar baby food prunes (2½ ounces)
- 1 teaspoon vanilla extract
- 1 box dark chocolate cake mix (18¼ ounces)

## FILLING

- 1 jar apricot preserves (18 ounces), drained
- 1 teaspoon rum extract

## GLAZE

- 1 cup chocolate chips
- 1 tablespoon canola oil
- ⅓ cup sliced blanched almonds or regular sliced almonds

TO MAKE THE CAKE: Preheat the oven to 350°F. Lightly coat two 8" round cake pans with nonstick spray.

In a small bowl, combine the apricots, water, and rum extract. Set aside to soak for 10 minutes, or until the apricots are very soft.

In a large bowl, using an electric mixer set on high speed, beat the egg whites for 1 minute, or until foamy. Beat in the buttermilk, prunes, and vanilla extract until blended. Add the apricot mixture and the cake mix. Beat on low speed just until moistened. Beat for 2 minutes longer at high speed. Scrape into the prepared pans.

Bake for 35 to 40 minutes, or until wooden picks inserted in the center of the cake layers come out clean. Cool on racks for 15 minutes. Invert onto the racks and cool completely.

TO MAKE THE FILLING: In a small saucepan, melt the preserves and rum extract over low heat. Set aside.

TO MAKE THE GLAZE: In a small microwaveable cup, combine the chocolate chips and oil. Cook in the microwave on high for 30 seconds and stir. Repeat just until the chocolate can be stirred into a smooth glaze. (The chips will not melt completely in the microwave oven, but they will get shiny and soft enough to stir until smooth.)

TO ASSEMBLE THE TORTE: Using a long serrated knife, carefully slice each cake layer in half through the side to make a total of 4 layers. Place 1 layer on a serving plate and spread with one-quarter of the filling. Repeat the layering with the remaining cake and filling. Spread the last of the filling on the top cake layer.

Carefully pour the glaze over the center of the cake, directing the glaze evenly over the top and sides. Allow the glaze to harden for 5 minutes. Press the almonds decoratively into the sides of the cake. Slice with a serrated knife and serve.

**Makes 16 servings**

*Per serving: 314 calories, 5 g protein, 56 g carbohydrates, 10 g fat, 3 g saturated fat, 0 mg cholesterol, 310 mg sodium, 2 g fiber*

## Sweets: A Treat Like No Other

*Sweets like cakes, cookies, quick breads, and doughnuts are the fourth highest source of calories in the American diet. Does this mean that you should give up sweets to reduce calories? No. Just be sure to savor every bite that you eat; that way, you'll be more satisfied, which ultimately results in eating less. This may mean sitting down and enjoying your sweet, rather than driving or walking around while eating it. Ask yourself if you are really savoring what you are eating, versus just eating it because it's there.*

# Hummingbird Cake

This cake is so good that my daughter, who does not like bananas, loves it. It's a joy to watch her gobble it up and know that she is getting all those good nutrients in the bananas and pineapple. The name comes from a classic Southern cake. I reduced calories, fat, and cholesterol by:

Photo on page 293

❖ *Using egg whites in place of some of the whole eggs*
❖ *Using applesauce instead of oil*
❖ *Using fewer pecans*
❖ *Using slightly less sugar in both the cake and the frosting*

## CAKE

- 2 eggs
- 2 egg whites
- ¾ cup unsweetened applesauce
- 1½ teaspoons vanilla extract
- 3 cups unbleached or all-purpose flour
- 1¾ cups sugar
- 1 teaspoon baking soda
- ¼ teaspoon salt
- 2 cups sliced bananas (about 2 medium bananas)
- ½ cup chopped pecans or walnuts
- 1 can crushed juice-packed pineapple (8 ounces)
- ¾ cup sifted confectioners' sugar

Preheat the oven to 325°F. Generously coat a Bundt pan with nonstick spray.

In a large bowl, using an electric mixer set on high speed, beat the eggs and egg whites for 1 minute, or until foamy. Beat in the applesauce and vanilla extract.

In another large bowl, combine the flour, sugar, baking soda, and salt. Add half of the flour mixture to the egg white mixture and beat on medium speed until combined. Add the remaining flour mixture and beat for 1 minute. Stir in the bananas and pecans.

Drain the pineapple, reserving 2 tablespoons of the juice for making the glaze. Stir the pineapple into the batter. Scrape into the prepared pan.

Bake for 60 to 65 minutes, or until a wooden pick inserted near the center comes out clean. Cool in the pan on a rack for 15 minutes. Loosen the edges of the cake by gently inserted a thin rubber spatula or knife around the sides and center. Invert the cake onto the rack and cool completely.

In a small bowl, whisk together the confectioners' sugar and the reserved 2 tablespoons pineapple juice. Drizzle the glaze over the cooled cake.

**Makes 12 servings**

*Per serving: 341 calories, 6 g protein, 71 g carbohydrates, 5 g fat, 0 g saturated fat, 36 mg cholesterol, 171 mg sodium, 2 g fiber*

# For the Love of Walnuts

*These delicious nuts are rich in alpha-linolenic acid, an essential fatty acid that our bodies require from food because we cannot manufacture it internally. Researchers found that men who had higher levels of this essential fatty acid in their blood had a 37 percent decrease in the risk of stroke. To help protect your heart, include walnuts in your diet several times a week.*

# Strawberry Cheesecake

This is my most spectacular-looking cheesecake, especially when those big, juicy strawberries are at the market. With all this flavor, it's hard to believe that more than half of the calories were slashed. I reduced the calories, fat, and cholesterol by:

❖ *Using a combination of fat-free cream cheese and light cream cheese in place of regular*
❖ *Using egg whites in place of whole eggs*
❖ *Using fewer graham cracker crumbs and less brown sugar in the crust*
❖ *Using less sugar in the filling*
❖ *Using fat-free sour cream instead of regular in the topping*

## CRUST

⅓ cup graham cracker crumbs
2 tablespoons brown sugar

## FILLING

2 packages light cream cheese (8 ounces each), at room temperature
2 packages fat-free cream cheese (8 ounces each), at room temperature
1⅔ cups sugar
3 tablespoons unbleached or all-purpose flour
3 tablespoons lemon juice
2½ teaspoons vanilla extract
8 egg whites, lightly beaten

## TOPPING

2 cups fat-free sour cream (without gelatin), 16 ounces
3 tablespoons sugar
½ teaspoon vanilla extract
4 cups whole strawberries, hulled
⅔ cup seedless strawberry or raspberry jam

TO MAKE THE CRUST: Preheat the oven to 350°F. Generously coat a 10" springform pan with nonstick spray.

In a small bowl, combine the graham cracker crumbs and brown sugar. Scatter evenly over the bottom of the prepared pan.

TO MAKE THE FILLING: In a large bowl, using an electric mixer set on medium-high speed, beat together the light cream cheese and fat-free cream cheese until smooth. Adding one ingredient at a time, beat in the sugar, flour, lemon juice, and vanilla extract. Beat in the eggs until just blended, stopping occasionally to scrape down the sides of the bowl. Scrape the batter into the crust.

Bake for 55 minutes, or until puffed and lightly golden. Cool on a rack for 10 minutes. Do not turn off the oven.

TO MAKE THE TOPPING: In a medium bowl, stir together the sour cream, sugar, and vanilla extract. Spoon the topping over the cheesecake, spreading to the edge of the pan. Bake for 5 to 7 minutes, or until the topping is just set. Remove from the oven. Run a knife between the crust and pan to loosen. Cool on a rack. When cooled to room temperature, cover with plastic wrap and chill for 8 hours or overnight.

Release the sides from the pan. Arrange the strawberries, points up, on top of the cheesecake, covering it completely.

Place the jam in a small bowl and microwave on high power for 1 to 2 minutes, or until melted. Brush the melted jam over the berries, allowing some to drip between.

**Makes 12 servings**

*Per serving: 392 calories, 15 g protein, 62 g carbohydrates, 9 g fat, 6 g saturated fat, 32 mg cholesterol, 429 mg sodium, 1 g fiber*

*Homestyle Hints:* The easiest way to melt jam is to microwave it on high power for 1 minute, or until just warm enough to drizzle.

Be sure to use a mixture of light and fat-free cream cheeses in this cheesecake. Attempts to cut more fat and calories by using only fat-free cream cheese will result in a cake that does not have a pleasing texture or flavor. This is the voice of experience!

# One More Benefit of Vitamin C

*Research shows that vitamin C may play a role in preventing lead, a toxic metal, from accumulating in the body. To get more vitamin C, look to foods like strawberries, bell peppers, oranges, broccoli, kiwifruit, mango, pink and red grapefruit, pineapple, and cantaloupe.*

# Raspberry Jewel Pie

As soon as raspberries are in season, my kids plead for me to make this. It's especially easy to make because I use a ready-made low-fat graham cracker crust. Fat-free ricotta cheese offers a nutritional boost—one serving of the cake provides 20 percent of the recommended calcium needs for adults. Not bad for a dessert. Calories, fat, and cholesterol were reduced by:

❖ *Using a low-fat graham cracker crust*
❖ *Using a combination of light cream cheese and fat-free ricotta for the filling*

## PIE

1  package plain gelatin (¼ ounce)
¼  cup fat-free milk
1  tub light cream cheese (8 ounces)
1  cup fat-free ricotta cheese (8 ounces)
⅓  cup sugar
1  teaspoon vanilla extract
1  ready-made low-fat graham cracker crust

## TOPPING

⅓  cup sugar
1  tablespoon cornstarch
¾  cup peach nectar
10  ounces fresh raspberries (about 2 cups), rinsed and patted dry

TO MAKE THE PIE: In a small saucepan, sprinkle the gelatin over the milk and set aside for 1 minute, or until softened. Cook, stirring, over medium-low heat for 3 to 5 minutes. Do not boil. Set aside.

In a medium bowl, using an electric mixer set on low speed, beat together the cream cheese, ricotta, sugar, and vanilla extract until smooth. Gradually beat in the milk mixture. Pour into the crust. Cover with plastic wrap and refrigerate.

TO MAKE THE TOPPING: In another small saucepan, combine the sugar and cornstarch, stirring to remove any lumps. Gradually stir in the nectar. Cook, stirring, over medium-high heat, for 2 minutes, or until bubbly. Remove from the heat and set aside for 10 minutes, or until cooled.

Arrange the raspberries, points up, over the top of the pie. Drizzle the peach glaze evenly around the raspberries. Cover with plastic wrap and chill for at least 2 hours, or until set.

**Makes 8 servings**

*Per serving: 291 calories, 11 g protein, 45 g carbohydrates, 8 g fat, 4 g saturated fat, 18 mg cholesterol, 258 mg sodium, 3 g fiber*

*Homestyle Hint:* Canned peach nectar is available in many supermarkets in the international aisle, often near the Latin American foods, and in the juice section.

## The Life and Times of Sugar

In the early 1900s, most of the sugar that was produced went directly into our homes, which meant that control was in the hands of the person who bought it. Today, the opposite is true. More than 75 percent of the sugars produced today go to the food and beverage industries. Less than 25 percent is brought home.

# Peanut Butter Pie

This is one of my husband's favorite pies. Who can blame him? It's rich, creamy, and combines chocolate and peanut butter. Calories, fat, and cholesterol were reduced by:

❖ *Using chocolate cookie crumbs for the crust*
❖ *Using a combination of light cream cheese and fat-free cream cheese instead of full-fat*
❖ *Using fat-free sweetened condensed milk instead of whole milk*
❖ *Reducing the amount of peanut butter*

*Nutrition Scorecard*
(per serving)

|  | before | after |
|---|---|---|
| Calories | 665 | 336 |
| Fat (g) | 47 | 13 |

*Photo on page 294*

| | |
|---|---|
| 8 | chocolate wafer cookies, crushed |
| ½ | cup creamy peanut butter |
| 4 | ounces light cream cheese |
| 4 | ounces fat-free cream cheese |
| 1 | can fat-free sweetened condensed milk (14 ounces) |
| 2 | tablespoons lemon juice |
| 1 | cup frozen light whipped topping, thawed (8 ounces) |
| 2 | teaspoons chocolate syrup |

Lightly coat a 9" pie plate with nonstick spray. Scatter the cookie crumbs evenly over the bottom. Set aside.

In a large bowl, using an electric mixer set on medium speed, beat together the peanut butter, light cream cheese, and fat-free cream cheese until smooth. Gradually beat in the milk and lemon juice. Fold in the whipped topping. Spoon into the pie plate, spreading evenly over the crumbs. Drizzle with the chocolate syrup. Using the tip of a knife, decoratively swirl the chocolate syrup. Cover with plastic wrap and chill for at least 4 hours, or until set.

## Makes 8 servings

*Per serving: 336 calories, 13 g protein, 43 g carbohydrates, 13 g fat, 5 g saturated fat, 14 mg cholesterol, 227 mg sodium, 1 g fiber*

# Blueberry Crisp

Cinnamon and lemon really bring out the natural flavor of blueberries. For an extra treat, I like to serve this with low-fat vanilla ice cream. Calories and fat were reduced by:

❖ *Using less sugar and adding sweet spices to compensate*
❖ *Using light butter instead of regular butter, and less of it*
❖ *Reducing the amount of nuts*

## Nutrition Scorecard

(per serving)

|  | before | after |
|---|---|---|
| Calories | 451 | 251 |
| Fat (g) | 22 | 5 |

## COMPOTE

8   cups fresh blueberries, rinsed and sorted (about 2½ pints)

½   cup sugar

2   teaspoons cornstarch

½   teaspoon ground cinnamon

½   teaspoon ground nutmeg

1   tablespoon lemon juice

## TOPPING

1   cup packed brown sugar

⅔   cup rolled oats

½   cup unbleached or all-purpose flour

3   tablespoons walnuts

1   teaspoon ground cinnamon

¼   teaspoon salt

6   tablespoons chilled light butter, shredded

TO MAKE THE COMPOTE: In a large saucepan, combine 2½ cups of the blueberries and the sugar. Cook, stirring, over low heat for 5 to 8 minutes, or until the berries soften.

In small cup, combine the cornstarch, cinnamon, and nutmeg. Stir in the lemon juice until smooth. Add to the cooked blueberries. Raise the heat to medium and cook, stirring, for 1 minute. Stir in the remaining 5½ cups blueberries. Transfer to a 13" × 9" baking dish.

TO MAKE THE TOPPING: Preheat the oven to 350°F. In a food processor or blender, combine the brown sugar, oats, flour, walnuts, cinnamon, and salt. Pulse once or twice, just until mixed. Add the butter and pulse until crumbly. Sprinkle over the berries.

Bake for 45 minutes, or until the topping is golden. Cool slightly before serving.

## Makes 10 servings

*Per serving: 251 calories, 3 g protein, 50 g carbohydrates, 5 g fat, 0 g saturated fat, 9 mg cholesterol, 165 mg sodium, 4 g fiber*

# Lemon Heaven Meringue Squares

I find that it's essential to use egg yolks in this recipe for their beautiful golden color and delicate thickening. But I do use fewer of them. Remember to zest the lemons before you squeeze out the juice. Calories, fat, and cholesterol were reduced by:

*Photo on page 291*

❖ *Replacing some of the egg yolks with cornstarch*
❖ *Using light butter instead of regular for the crust*

## CRUST

1⅓ cups graham cracker crumbs

2 tablespoons sugar

⅓ cup light butter, melted

## FILLING

1¼ cups sugar

½ cup cornstarch

1⅔ cups water

2 egg yolks

4 lemons

## MERINGUE

4 egg whites

½ teaspoon cream of tartar

½ cup sugar

TO MAKE THE CRUST: Preheat the oven to 350°F. Lightly coat a 13" × 9" baking dish with nonstick spray.

In a large bowl, combine the graham cracker crumbs and sugar. Using a fork, work in the butter. With your hands, lightly press the crumb mixture onto the bottom of the baking dish.

TO MAKE THE FILLING: In a medium saucepan, combine the sugar and cornstarch. Stir until no lumps remain. Gradually stir in the water until smooth. Cook, stirring, over medium-high heat, for 3 minutes, or until boiling. Remove from the heat.

Place the egg yolks in a small bowl and whisk in about ½ cup of the hot sugar syrup, 1 tablespoon at a time. Return to the pan. Cook, stirring, over medium heat, for 1 to 2 minutes, or until thick and bubbly. Remove from the heat. Grate the outer peel (but not the inner white part) of 2 of the lemons to make 2 tablespoons lemon peel. Add to the filling. Roll all 4 lemons on a countertop, cut them in half, and squeeze to make ½ cup lemon juice. Stir into the filling. Pour the filling over the prepared crust.

TO MAKE THE MERINGUE: In a large bowl, using an electric mixer set on high speed, beat the egg whites until foamy. Add the cream of tartar and beat until soft peaks form. Gradually beat in the sugar and continue beating until stiff, shiny peaks form.

Spread the meringue over the warm filling to the edges. Bake for 25 to 30 minutes, or until the meringue is golden brown. Cool on a rack for 1 hour. Cover with plastic wrap and chill for at least 1 hour before serving. Cut into squares.

**Makes 12 squares**

Per square: 199 calories, 3 g protein, 38 g carbohydrates, 5 g fat, 1 g saturated fat, 42 mg cholesterol, 134 mg sodium, 1 g fiber

*Homestyle Hint:* Rolling lemons (or any citrus fruit) on a countertop before squeezing them will yield more juice.

## How Much Sugar Is Too Much?

*The USDA's Food Guide Pyramid recommends these upper limits of sugar: 6 teaspoons if you eat 1,600 calories a day; 12 teaspoons if you eat 2,200 calories a day; or 18 teaspoons if you eat 2,800 calories a day.*

# Pumpkin Streusel Custard

I like to eat this treat as a snack as well as a dessert. Just one serving provides more than half of your beta-carotene needs for the day. I reduced calories, fat, and cholesterol and boosted fiber by:

❖ *Using egg whites in place of some of the whole eggs*
❖ *Replacing whole milk with fat-free evaporated milk*
❖ *Using frozen light whipped topping rather than dairy whipped topping*
❖ *Using fewer pecans*
❖ *Replacing all-purpose flour with wheat germ*

### CUSTARD

| | |
|---|---|
| 2 | eggs |
| 2 | egg whites |
| 1 | can plain pumpkin puree (15 ounces) |
| 1 | can fat-free evaporated milk (12 ounces) |
| ¾ | cup packed brown sugar |
| 1½ | teaspoons pumpkin pie spice |
| 1 | teaspoon vanilla extract |
| ¼ | teaspoon finely shredded orange peel |
| 1½ | cups frozen light whipped topping, thawed (12 ounces) |

### STREUSEL

| | |
|---|---|
| ⅓ | cup pecans |
| ¼ | cup packed brown sugar |
| 3 | tablespoons wheat germ |
| ½ | teaspoon ground cinnamon |
| ¼ | teaspoon ground nutmeg |
| 2 | tablespoons chilled light butter, shredded |

TO MAKE THE CUSTARD: Preheat the oven to 350°F. Lightly coat twelve 6-ounce custard cups with nonstick spray.

In a medium bowl, beat the eggs and egg whites with a whisk. Stir in the pumpkin puree, milk, brown sugar, pumpkin pie spice, vanilla extract, and orange peel. Mix until completely blended. Fold in the whipped topping.

Pour into the prepared custard cups. Place the cups in a shallow baking dish and pour 1" of water into the baking dish around the cups. Bake for 20 minutes, or until the sides of the custard start to set but the centers are still loose.

TO MAKE THE STREUSEL: Meanwhile, in a food processor or blender, combine the pecans, brown sugar, wheat germ, cinnamon, nutmeg, and butter. Pulse until the mixture resembles coarse crumbs. Sprinkle over the custard. Bake for 10 to 15 minutes, or until a knife inserted near the center comes out clean. Cool on racks. When cool, cover with plastic wrap and chill for at least 3 hours before serving.

**Makes 12 servings**

Per serving: 157 calories, 5 g protein, 22 g carbohydrates, 5 g fat, 1 g saturated fat, 39 mg cholesterol, 71 mg sodium, 2 g fiber

*Homestyle Hint:* If you don't have custard cups, pour the custard into a shallow 2-quart shallow baking dish. Place the dish in a larger baking dish and pour 1" of water into the larger dish. Bake at 350°F for 40 minutes and proceed with the recipe.

# Record Sugar Consumption

*Americans are eating record amounts of sugar—averaging 154 pounds of sweeteners per year. The number one source of sugar in the American diet is carbonated soft drinks. If that's the case with you, try drinking naturally flavored sugar-free teas, such as passion fruit or mint. Or get in the habit of drinking water. It's surprisingly delicious with a wedge of lemon or lime or a splash of grenadine.*

# Lemon Dream Cheesecake Bars

These lemony cheesecake-like bars are irresistible, and they're a cinch to make. Calories and fat were reduced by:

- ❖ *Using light butter in place of regular, and much less of it*
- ❖ *Replacing a whole egg with an egg white for the crust*
- ❖ *Using a smaller amount of cake mix*
- ❖ *Replacing whole milk with fat-free sweetened condensed milk*
- ❖ *Using light tub-style cream cheese rather than regular*

| *Nutrition Scorecard* | | |
|---|---|---|
| (per bar) | | |
| | before | after |
| Calories | 155 | 95 |
| Fat (g) | 8 | 3 |

### CRUST

| | |
|---|---|
| 1 | box single-layer yellow cake mix (9 ounces) |
| ½ | cup walnuts |
| ¼ | cup chilled light butter, shredded |
| 1 | egg white |

### FILLING

| | |
|---|---|
| 1 | tub light cream cheese (8 ounces) |
| 1 | can fat-free sweetened condensed milk (14 ounces) |
| 3 | tablespoons lemon juice |
| 1 | large egg |
| 4 | teaspoons finely shredded lemon peel |

TO MAKE THE CRUST: Preheat the oven to 350°F. Lightly coat a 13" × 9" baking dish with nonstick spray. In a food processor or blender, combine the cake mix, walnuts, butter, and egg white and pulse until crumbly. Press into the prepared baking dish and bake for 10 minutes, or until set. Remove from the oven and cool on a rack for 5 minutes. Do not turn off the oven.

TO MAKE THE FILLING: In a large bowl, using an electric mixer set on medium-high speed, beat the cream cheese until fluffy. Gradually beat in the milk, lemon juice, egg, and lemon peel. Pour into the partially baked crust, smoothing the surface of the filling. Bake for 25 minutes, or until a wooden pick inserted in the center comes out clean. Cool completely on a rack. Cut into bars.

**Makes 36 bars**

*Per bar: 95 calories, 2 g protein, 13 g carbohydrates, 3 g fat, 1 g saturated fat, 11 mg cholesterol, 99 mg sodium, 0 g fiber*

*Homestyle Hint:* If you can't find a 9-ounce box of single-layer cake mix, use half a package of double-layer cake mix (the 18-ounce box), which equals 2 cups plus 2 tablespoons mix.

# Mom's Rich Double-Chocolate Pudding

Here's a quick way to satisfy a "chocolate tooth"—if you can wait for the pudding to cool down before gobbling it up. Try it with whipped cream or whipped topping. I reduced calories, fat, and cholesterol by:

❖ *Using 1% milk instead of whole milk*
❖ *Reducing the amount of solid chocolate*
❖ *Eliminating the butter*

### Nutrition Scorecard
*(per serving)*

|  | before | after |
|---|---|---|
| Calories | 464 | 251 |
| Fat (g) | 23 | 5 |

*Photo on page 289*

⅔  cup sugar

¼  cup unsweetened cocoa powder

3  tablespoons cornstarch

2  cups 1% milk

1  ounce bittersweet chocolate or 3 tablespoons chocolate chips

1  teaspoon vanilla extract

In a medium saucepan, whisk together the sugar, cocoa, and cornstarch until no lumps remain. Gradually stir in the milk over medium heat, just until bubbly and thickened. Remove from the heat. Stir in the bittersweet chocolate or chocolate chips and vanilla extract and cook for 1 minute, or until the chocolate melts. Pour into 4 custard cups or ramekins. Cover with plastic wrap and chill for at least 3 hours before serving.

**Makes 4 servings**

Per serving: 251 calories, 6 g protein, 51 g carbohydrates, 5 g fat, 3 g saturated fat, 5 mg cholesterol, 130 mg sodium, 2 g fiber

*Homestyle Hint:* To make *Mint-Flavored Chocolate Pudding*, use 3 tablespoons mint-flavored chocolate chips in place of the bittersweet chocolate.

## Get Milk

*During the World War II era, Americans drank more than 4 times as much milk as soda. Today, we gulp nearly 2½ times more soft drinks than milk. No wonder most Americans are not getting enough calcium in their diets. This is one trend we can reverse.*

# Chocolate-Dipped Cookies

These cookies are utterly delicious and absolutely irresistible. They're also a tasty way to introduce whole wheat flour into your family's diet. I reduced calories, fat, and cholesterol and boosted fiber by:

❖ *Using a combination of light butter and canola oil instead of regular butter*
❖ *Incorporating whole wheat flour*

*Nutrition Scorecard*

| (per cookie) | before | after |
|---|---|---|
| Calories | 114 | 53 |
| Fat (g) | 7 | 2 |

*Photo on page 290*

### COOKIES

½  cup sugar

2  tablespoons light butter, softened

2  tablespoons canola oil

1  egg

1  teaspoon vanilla extract

1  cup unbleached or all-purpose flour

½  cup whole wheat flour

½  teaspoon baking powder

¼  teaspoon ground cinnamon

⅛  teaspoon salt

### GLAZE

½  cup chocolate chips

1  teaspoon canola oil

TO MAKE THE COOKIES: Preheat the oven to 350°F. Lightly coat 2 baking sheets with nonstick spray.

In a large bowl, using an electric mixer set on medium-high speed, beat together the sugar, butter, and oil until light and fluffy. Add the egg and vanilla extract and beat until smooth.

In a small bowl, stir together the unbleached or all-purpose flour, whole wheat flour, baking powder, cinnamon, and salt. Add to the egg mixture. Beat on low speed for 30 seconds, or just until combined.

Divide the dough in half and press each half into a disk. Place each disk on a sheet of waxed paper and cover with another sheet of waxed paper. Using a rolling pin, roll out the dough between the waxed paper to a thickness of about ⅛".

Remove the top sheets of waxed paper. Using a 3" cookie or biscuit cutter, cut out the cookies. Reroll the scraps and cut out more cookies. Place the cookies on the prepared baking sheets. Bake for 8 to 10 minutes, or until golden around the edges. Transfer the cookies to racks to cool completely.

TO MAKE THE GLAZE: In a small microwaveable cup, combine the chocolate chips and oil. Cook in the microwave on high for 30 seconds and stir. Repeat just until the chocolate can be stirred into a smooth glaze. (The chips will not melt completely in the microwave oven, but they will get shiny and soft enough to stir until smooth.)

Place a large sheet of waxed paper on a work surface. Dip half of each cooled cookie into the melted chocolate. Lift the cookie, allowing any excess chocolate to drip back into the cup. Place the dipped cookies on the waxed paper and allow to harden.

**Makes 36 cookies**

*Per cookie: 53 calories, 1 g protein, 8 g carbohydrates, 2 g fat, 0 g saturated fat, 7 mg cholesterol, 21 mg sodium, 1 g fiber*

*Homestyle Hint:* To make *Jam-Filled Cookies*, omit the chocolate glaze. Stir ½ cup finely chopped walnuts into the dough. Instead of rolling out and cutting the cookies, roll the dough into 1" balls with your hands. Press your thumb into the center of each ball to make a well. Bake at 350°F for 8 to 10 minutes, or until golden around the edges. Fill each well with ½ teaspoon of your favorite jam (I like raspberry jam and apricot jam). The nutritional figures are almost identical to those for *Chocolate-Dipped Cookies*.

## *Where Do Carbs Come From?*

Many Americans think that pasta is our number one source of carbohydrates. Think again. Here are the top 10 carbohydrate food sources in the American diet.

1. Yeast breads
2. Soft drinks
3. Cakes, cookies, quick breads, doughnuts
4. Sugar, syrups, jam
5. Potatoes (white)
6. Ready-to-eat cereal
7. Milk
8. Pasta
9. Rice and other cooked grains
10. Flour and other baking ingredients

# Barbara's Layered Banana Pudding

When my friend Barbara and I first met, she had a simple request: Could I lighten her signature dessert recipe? I sure did. And with winning results! I cut calories, fat, and cholesterol by:

❖ *Using light vanilla wafers instead of regular vanilla wafers*
❖ *Using light whipped topping rather than whipped cream*
❖ *Using fat-free milk instead of water for a nutrition boost*
❖ *Eliminating sweetened condensed milk and increasing the amount of fat-free milk*

3  cups fat-free milk

2  packages instant banana pudding mix (3.4 ounces each)

1  cup frozen light whipped topping, thawed (8 ounces)

1  box light vanilla wafers (12 ounces), 8 to 10 cookies reserved

4  bananas, peeled and sliced

In a large bowl, using an electric mixer set on medium speed or a whisk, beat the milk and pudding mix for 3 to 5 minutes, or until well-blended. Fold in the whipped topping.

Spoon one-third of the pudding mixture over the bottom of a 13" × 9" glass baking dish. Arrange a layer of cookies (about half of the box) over the pudding and then arrange a layer of half of the banana slices. Repeat to make a second layer of pudding, cookies, and bananas. Top with the remaining pudding. Crush the reserved 8 to 10 cookies and sprinkle over the top. Cover with plastic wrap and chill for at least 3 hours before serving.

**Makes 20 servings**

*Per serving: 160 calories, 3 g protein, 31 g carbohydrates, 3 g fat, 2 g saturated fat, 0 mg cholesterol, 162 mg sodium, 1 g fiber*

## Go Bananas

*One medium banana provides one-third of your daily needs for vitamin $B_6$, an important vitamin for growth and fighting infections. Try bananas on top of cereal, mixed with other fruits, or whipped into smoothies.*

# Resources

## Chapter 1: Nutrition Update

American Dietetic Association. "Position of the American Dietetic Association: Phytochemicals and Functional Foods." *Journal of the American Dietetic Association* 95 (4):493-496 (April 1995).

Anderson, J. W. "Meta-Analysis of the Effects of Soy Protein Intake on Serum Lipids." *New England Journal of Medicine* 333:276-282 (August 3, 1995).

Ascherio, A., et al. "Trans Fatty Acids and Coronary Heart Disease." *New England Journal of Medicine* 340:1994-1998 (June 24, 1999).

Connor, W. E. "Alpha-Linolenic Acid in Health and Disease." *American Journal of Clinical Nutrition* 69:827-828 (1999).

Craig, W. J. "Phytochemicals: Guardians of Our Health." *Journal of the American Dietetic Association* 97 (10 supplement 2):s199-s204 (October 1997).

Deckelbaum, R. J., et al. "Summary of a Scientific Conference on Preventive Nutrition: Pediatrics to Geriatrics." *Circulation* 100 (4):450-456 (July 27, 1999).

Frazao, E. (ed). "America's Eating Habits: Changes and Consequences." Food and Rural Economics Division, Economic Research Service, U.S. Department of Agriculture, Bulletin No. 750, pp. 23, 24 (1999).

Horton, et al. "Fat and Carbohydrate Overfeeding in Humans: Different Effects on Energy Storage." *American Journal of Clinical Nutrition* 62:19-29 (1995).

Hu, F. B., et al. "Dietary Intake of Alpha-Linolenic Acid and Risk of Fatal Ischemic Heart Disease among Women." *American Journal of Clinical Nutrition* (69):890-897 (May 1999).

Jacobs, D. R., et al. "Is Whole Grain Intake Associated with Reduced Total and Cause-Specific Death Rates in Older Women? The Iowa Women's Health Study." *American Journal of Public Health* 89 (3):322-329 (March 1999).

Lichtenstein, A. H., and Van Horn, L. "Very Low Fat Diets." *Circulation* 98:935-939 (September 1, 1998).

National Institutes of Health. "Facts about the DASH Diet." NIH publication no.98-4082 (September 1998).

Obarzanek, E., and J. T. Moore. "The Dietary Approaches to Stop Hypertension (DASH) Trial." *Journal of the American Dietetic Association* (8 supplement):s9-s104 (August 1999).

Siguel, E. N., and R. H. Lerman. "Role of Essential Fatty Acids: Danger in the U.S. Department of Agriculture Dietary Recommendations ('Pyramid') and in Low-Fat Diet." *American Journal of Clinical Nutrition* 60:973 (1994).

Tucker, et al. "Potassium, Magnesium and Fruit and Vegetable Intakes Are Associated with Greater Bone Mineral Density in Elderly Men and Women." *American Journal Clinical Nutrition* 69 (4):727-736 (April 1999).

USDA Center for Nutrition Policy and Promotion. "Is Total Fat Consumption Really Decreasing?" *Nutrition Insight* 5 (April 1998).

Wolk, A., et al. "Long-Term Intake of Dietary Fiber and Decreased Risk of Coronary Disease Among Women." *Journal of the American Medical Association.* 281 (21): 1998-2004 (June 2, 1999).

## Chapter 2: Recipe Makeover Secrets

"Most Popular Reduced-Fat Products." National Consumer Survey, Calorie Control Council.

## Chapter 3: Homestyle Bakery

Craig, W. J. "Phytochemicals: Guardians of Our Health." *Journal of the American Dietetic Association* 97 (10 supplement 2):s199-s204 (October 1997).

Korol, D. L. and P. E. Gold. "Glucose, Memory and Aging." *American Journal of Clinical Nutrition* 67 (supplement):764s-771s (1998).

Rainey, C. H. "Daily Boron Intake from the American Diet." *Journal of the American Dietetic Association* 99:335-340 (March 1999).

Subar, A. F., et al. "Dietary Sources of Nutrients Among U.S. Adults, 1989 to 1991." *Journal of the American Dietetic Association* 98 (5):541 (May 1998).

## Chapter 4: Brunch Specials

Brown, L., et al. "Cholesterol-Lowering Effects of Dietary Fiber: A Meta-Analysis." *American Journal of Clinical Nutrition* 69 (1):30-42 (January 1999).

Kerstetter J. E., et al. "Dietary Protein Affects Intestinal Calcium Absorption." *American Journal of Clinical Nutrition* 68 (4) :859-865 (1998).

Murphy, J. M., et al. "The Relationship of School Breakfast to Psychosocial and Academic Functioning." *Archives of Pediatrics and Adolescent Medicine* 152:899-907 (September 1998).

## Chapter 5: Nibbles for One or a Crowd

Craig, W. J. "Phytochemicals: Guardians of Our Health." *Journal of the American Dietetic Association* 97 (supplement 2):s199-s204 (October 1997).

Frazao, E. (ed). "America's Eating Habits: Changes and Consequences." Food and Rural Economics Division, Economic Research Service, U.S. Department of Agriculture, Bulletin No. 750, p. 217 (1999).

Westerterp-Plantenga, M. S. and C. R. T. Verwegen. "The Appetizing Effect of an Aperitif in Overweight and Normal Weight Humans." *American Journal of Clinical Nutrition* 69 (2):205-212 (February 1999).

## Chapter 6: 15-Minute Meals

Clemens, L. H., et al. "The Effect of Eating Out on Quality of Diet in Premenopausal Women." *Journal of the American Dietetic Association* 99 (4):442-444 (April 1999).

Fernandez, E., et al. "Fish Consumption and Cancer Risk." *American Journal of Clinical Nutrition* 70 (1):85-90 (1999).

Harnack, L. H., et al. "Guess Who's Cooking? The Role of Men in Meal Planning, Shopping, and Preparation in U.S. Families." *Journal of the American Dietetic Association* 98 (9): 995-1000 (September 1998).

Jones, A. J., E. Hill, and E. Bohm. *Healthy Dining in Los Angeles* (3rd ed.), Accents on Health: San Diego (1998).

Neumark-Sztainer, D., et al. "Factors Influencing Food Choices of Adolescents: Findings from Focus-Group Discussions with Adolescents." *Journal of the American Dietetic Association* 99 (8): 929-937 (August 1999).

## Chapter 7: Relax while It Cooks

American Dietetic Association. "Lycopene: An Antioxidant for Good Health." ADA Fact Sheet. American Dietetic Association Foundation (1999).

Kleiner, S. "Water: An Essential but Overlooked Nutrient." *Journal of the American Dietetic Association* 99:200-206 (February 1999).

Saketkhoo, K., et al. "Effects of Drinking Hot Water, Cold Water, and Chicken Soup on Nasal Mucus Velocity and Nasal Airflow Resistance." *Chest* Oct 74 (4):408-410 (October 1978).

## Chapter 8: Homestyle Beef and Pork

Frazao, E. (ed). "America's Eating Habits: Changes and Consequences." Food and Rural Economics Division, Economic Research Service, U.S. Department of Agriculture, Bulletin No. 750, p.137 (1999).

Houston, D. K., et al. "Age-Related Hearing Loss, Vitamin $B_{12}$, and Folate in Elderly Women." *American Journal of Clinical Nutrition* 69 (3):564-571 (March 1999).

Lloyd, T., et al. "Fruit Consumption, Fitness, and Cardiovascular Health in Female Adolescents: The Penn State Young Women's Health Study." *American Journal of Clinical Nutrition* 67:624-30 (1998).

Misciagna, G., et al. "Diet, Physical Activity, and Gallstones—A Population-Based, Case-Control Study in Southern Italy." *American Journal of Clinical Nutrition* 69:120-126 (January 1999).

*Nutrition Research Newsletter* "Is Lean Red Meat Really That Bad?" page 16 (August 1999).

Subar, A. F., et al. "Dietary Sources of Nutrients Among U.S. Adults, 1989 to 1991." *Journal of the American Dietetic Association* 98 (5):539 (May 1998).

## Chapter 9: Finger-Lickin' Chicken and Turkey

Frazao, E. (ed). "America's Eating Habits: Changes and Consequences." Food and Rural Economics Division, Economic Research Service, U.S. Department of Agriculture, Bulletin No. 750, p.173 (1999).

## Chapter 10: Family-Pleasing Meatless Meals

Smit, E., et al. "Estimate of Animal and Plant Protein Intake in U.S. Adults: Results from the Third National Health and Nutrition Examination Survey, 1988-1991." *Journal of the American Dietetic Association* 99:813-820 (July 1999).

## Chapter 11: Pastabilities

Subar, A. F., et al. "Dietary Sources of Nutrients Among U.S. Adults, 1989 to 1991." *Journal of the American Dietetic Association* 98 (5):539 (May 1998).

## Chapter 12: Salads Big and Small

Frazao, E. (ed). "America's Eating Habits: Changes and Consequences." Food and Rural Economics Division, Economic Research Service, U.S. Department of Agriculture, Bulletin No. 750, p.173 (1999).

Subar, A. F., et al. "Dietary Sources of Nutrients Among U.S. Adults, 1989 to 1991." *Journal of the American Dietetic Association* 98 (5):542 (May 1998).

## Chapter 13: Fixings and Trimmings

Cao, G., et al. "Increases in Human Plasma Antioxidant Capacity after Consumption of Controlled Diets High in Fruit and Vegetables." *American Journal of Clinical Nutrition* 68 (5):1081-1087 (November 1998).

Hu, F. B., et al. "Frequent Nut Consumption and Risk of Coronary Heart Disease in Women: Prospective Cohort Study." *British Medical Journal* 317:1341-1345 (November 1998).

## Chapter 14: Best-Loved Desserts

Arts I. J. C., et al. "Chocolate as a Source of Tea Flavonoids." *Lancet* 354 (9177) (August 7, 1999).

Fisher, J. O., and L. L. Birch. "Restricting Access to Palatable Foods Affects Children's Behavioral Response, Food Selection, and Intake." *American Journal of Clinical Nutrition* 69 (6):1264-1272 (June 1999).

Frazao, E. (ed). "America's Eating Habits: Changes and Consequences." Food and Rural Economics Division, Economic Research Service, U.S. Department of Agriculture, Bulletin No. 750, pp. 142, 152 (1999).

Simon, J. A., et al. "Serum Fatty Acids and the Risk of Stroke." *Stroke* 26 (5):778-782 (May 1995).

Simon, J. A., and E. S. Hudes. "Relationship of Ascorbic Acid to Blood Lead Levels." *Journal of the American Medical Association* 281(24):2289-2293 (June 1999).

Subar, A. F., et al. "Dietary Sources of Nutrients Among U.S. Adults, 1989 to 1991." *Journal of the American Dietetic Association* 98 (5):539, 543 (May 1998).

## Nutritional Information Source

Nutrient data analyzed with Food Processor V 2.2 software, ESHA Research: Salem, OR (1995).

# Index

Underscored page references indicate Health Notes or boxed text. **Boldface** page references indicate photographs.

Cholesterol, in eggs, <u>53</u>, <u>89</u>
Chowders
    Parmesan-Corn Chowder, 159
    Potato-Bacon Clam Chowder,
        **129**, 158
Clams
    Potato-Bacon Clam Chowder,
        **129**, 158
Cocoa powder, 26, <u>31</u>. *See also*
    Chocolate
Coffee cake
    Sour Cream–Streusel Coffee
        Cake, **61**, 84–85
Coleslaw. *See* Slaws
Condiments, <u>24</u>
Cookies
    Chocolate-Dipped Cookies,
        **290**, 352–53
    Jam-Filled Cookies, 353
Corn
    Chicken-Tortilla Soup, **124**, 144
    Enchilada Strata, 234
    Festive Black Bean Salad, 296
    Fresh Corn Tamales, 247
    Jalapeño Cornbread, 52–53
    Mexicali Corn, 307
    Mixed Bean Tamale Pie,
        236–37
    Parmesan-Corn Chowder, 159
    Shepherd's Pie, 178–79
    Sweet Corn Cakes, 322
    Tex-Mex Skillet, **122**, 136
Cornmeal
    Chili with Cornbread
        Dumplings, **127**,
        160–61
    Cornmeal-Fried Fish, 137
    Fresh Corn Tamales, 247
    Jalapeño Cornbread, 52–53
    Mixed Bean Tamale Pie,
        236–37
    Polenta Lasagna, **192**, 232–33
    as thickening agent, 25
Cornstarch, in sauces, 24–25, <u>31</u>
Cottage cheese
    Baked Zucchini with Dill Seed,
        241
    Beef Stroganoff Bake, 167
    Creamy Pesto Pasta, 256

Deviled Eggs, 89
    Orange-Pineapple Fluff
        Gelatin, 302
    Parmesan Spinach–Stuffed
        Potatoes, 248
    Pierogi Lasagna, 265
    Soufflé Potatoes, 316
Couscous
    Garden Couscous Salad, **187**,
        276
    Quick Couscous, 317
Cranberries
    Cranberry Bread, 44, **56**
    Cranberry Holiday Gelatin,
        **281**, 303
Cream, substitutions for, 22, 25,
    <u>31</u>
Cream cheese
    Best-Ever Light Cream Cheese
        Frosting, **285**, 334
    Chicken–Cream Cheese
        Bundles, **187**, 222–23
    Chocolate Tiramisu, 335
    Cranberry Holiday Gelatin,
        **281**, 303
    Lemon Dream Cheesecake
        Bars, 350
    Peanut Butter Pie, **294**, 344
    Raspberry Jewel Pie, 342–43
    in recipe makeovers, 21, 25,
        <u>28–29</u>
    Southwest Pinwheels, 91
    Strawberry Cheesecake, **287**,
        340–41
    Stuffed French Toast, **60**,
        72–73
    Tiramisu, **292**, 335
    Tuxedo Brownie Muffins,
        40–41, **57**
Crisps
    Blueberry Crisp, 345
Cucumbers
    Barley Salad, 295
    Lentil Salad, 298
Curry
    Creamy Chicken Curry, 116
Custards
    Pumpkin Streusel Custard,
        348–49

# D

Dairy products. *See also specific*
    *dairy products*
    in Food Guide Pyramid, 6
    low-fat alternatives for, 25–26,
        <u>28–29</u>
DASH (Dietary Approaches to
    Stop Hypertension),
    13–14, <u>14</u>, <u>85</u>
Dates
    Hearty Hot Cereal, 86
    Orange-Date Bran Muffins, 38
Desserts. *See also* Cakes and
    Frostings
    Barbara's Layered Banana
        Pudding, 354
    Blueberry Crisp, 345
    Chocolate-Dipped Cookies,
        **290**, 352–53
    Chocolate Tiramisu, 335
    Jam-Filled Cookies, 353
    Lemon Dream Cheesecake
        Bars, 350
    Lemon Heaven Meringue
        Squares, **291**, 346–47
    Mint-Flavored Chocolate
        Pudding, 351
    Mom's Rich Double-Chocolate
        Pudding, **289**, 351
    Peanut Butter Pie, **294**, 344
    Pumpkin Streusel Custard,
        348–49
    Raspberry Jewel Pie, 342–43
    Tiramisu, **292**, 335
Dill
    Baked Zucchini with Dill Seed,
        241
Dips
    Hot Spinach-Artichoke Dip,
        **67**, 94
    Texas Caviar, 90
Dumplings
    Chili with Cornbread
        Dumplings, **127**,
        160–61
    Pizza Dumpling Bake, 180–81,
        **183**

# E

Eggplant
    Baked Eggplant and Provolone, 231
    Linguine with Eggplant-Basil Sauce, 259
Eggs
    Artichoke Frittata, **62**, 79
    Artichoke Squares, 103
    Baked Cheddar Grits, 81
    Baked Zucchini with Dill Seed, 241
    cholesterol in, <u>53</u>, <u>89</u>
    Crustless Garden Quiche, 240
    Deviled Eggs, 89
    egg substitutes, 27
    fat-saving tips for, 27
    in Food Guide Pyramid, 5
    Mini Broccoli Quiche, 104
    nutritional profile of, <u>89</u>
    Overnight Brunch Bake, 75
    powdered whites of, 21–22
    Southwest Soufflé Roll-Up, **64**, 76–77
    Stuffed French Toast, **60**, 72–73
    Tex-Mex Frittata, 80
Enchiladas
    Cheesy Green Enchiladas, 238
Evaporated milk, fat-free, 22, 25, <u>28</u>

# F

Fast foods, <u>98</u>
Fat-free foods, in recipe makeovers, 18–19, 21–22, <u>28–31</u>
Fats
    in Food Guide Pyramid, 7
    harmful types of, 11
    health benefits from, 7
    healthy types of, 8–11
    in recipes, reducing, 23–27, <u>29–31</u>

in restaurant foods, <u>98</u>, <u>113</u>, <u>117</u>
Feta cheese
    fat-saving tips for, <u>28</u>
    Feta Pita Wedges, 93
    Feta-Spinach Rice Bake, 243
Fettuccine
    Fettuccine with Spicy Spinach and Tomatoes, 255
Fiber
    for children, <u>51</u>
    dietary sources of, <u>3</u>, <u>73</u>, <u>299</u>, <u>313</u>, <u>319</u>, <u>321</u>
    health benefits from, <u>86</u>
Fish. *See also* Shellfish
    Broiled Sole with Parmesan-Olive Topping, 138
    Cornmeal-Fried Fish, 137
    Creamed Tuna on Toast, 142
    in Food Guide Pyramid, 5
    health benefits from, <u>138</u>
    Tuna-Noodle Skillet Supper, **196**, 262
    White Bean–Tuna Salad, 297
Flavonoids, <u>15</u>, 16, <u>318</u>
Flavor-boosting tricks, <u>24</u>
Flour, cake, 54
Folate, 5, <u>173</u>, <u>267</u>
Food Guide Pyramid, 2–8
Frankfurters
    Corn Dog Bites, **66**, 99
French toast
    Stuffed French Toast, **60**, 72–73
Frittatas
    Artichoke Frittata, **62**, 79
    Tex-Mex Frittata, 80
Frostings
    Best-Ever Light Cream Cheese Frosting, **285**, 334
Fruit. *See also specific fruits*
    citrus, to boost flavors, <u>24</u>
    in Food Guide Pyramid, 4–5
    health benefits from, 5, <u>15</u>, 16, <u>203</u>, <u>318</u>, <u>324</u>
    puree, in baked goods, 23, <u>29–30</u>
Frying, in oven, 23
Fusilli

Creamy Pesto Pasta, 256
Garlicky Fusilli with Broccoli and Dried Tomatoes, 258, **280**

# G

Garlic
    Fettuccine with Spicy Spinach and Tomatoes, 255
    Garlicky Fusilli with Broccoli and Dried Tomatoes, 258, **280**
    immunity-boosting effects of, 16
    Roasted Garlic Mashed Potatoes, **184**, 315
    Roasted Garlic–Potato Soup, 156–57
    Spicy Garlic Shrimp, **119**, 139
Gelatin salads
    Cranberry Holiday Gelatin, **281**, 303
    Mango-Gelatin Salad, 299
    Orange-Pineapple Fluff Gelatin, 302
Ginger
    Gingerbread Pancakes, **63**, 74
    Gingered Carrot Soup, 153
    peeling and grating, 153
Goat cheese
    fat-saving tips for, <u>29</u>
    Festive Cheese Log, **68**, 92
    Fettuccine with Spicy Spinach and Tomatoes, 255
    Lentil Salad, 298
Grains. *See also specific grains*
    adding to diet, 32
    in Food Guide Pyramid, 2–3
    good sources of, 3, <u>3</u>, <u>73</u>
Greens, <u>278</u>. *See also* Cabbage; Lettuce; Spinach
Grilling foods, to boost flavors, <u>24</u>
Grits
    Baked Cheddar Grits, 81

# Conversion Chart

These equivalents have been slightly rounded to make measuring easier.

### VOLUME MEASUREMENTS

| U.S. | Imperial | Metric |
|---|---|---|
| ¼ tsp | – | 1 ml |
| ½ tsp | – | 2 ml |
| 1 tsp | – | 5 ml |
| 1 Tbsp | – | 15 ml |
| 2 Tbsp (1 oz) | 1 fl oz | 30 ml |
| ¼ cup (2 oz) | 2 fl oz | 60 ml |
| ⅓ cup (3 oz) | 3 fl oz | 80 ml |
| ½ cup (4 oz) | 4 fl oz | 120 ml |
| ⅔ cup (5 oz) | 5 fl oz | 160 ml |
| ¾ cup (6 oz) | 6 fl oz | 180 ml |
| 1 cup (8 oz) | 8 fl oz | 240 ml |

### WEIGHT MEASUREMENTS

| U.S. | Metric |
|---|---|
| 1 oz | 30 g |
| 2 oz | 60 g |
| 4 oz (¼ lb) | 115 g |
| 5 oz (⅓ lb) | 145 g |
| 6 oz | 170 g |
| 7 oz | 200 g |
| 8 oz (½ lb) | 230 g |
| 10 oz | 285 g |
| 12 oz (¾ lb) | 340 g |
| 14 oz | 400 g |
| 16 oz (1 lb) | 455 g |
| 2.2 lb | 1 kg |

### LENGTH MEASUREMENTS

| U.S. | Metric |
|---|---|
| ¼" | 0.6 cm |
| ½" | 1.25 cm |
| 1" | 2.5 cm |
| 2" | 5 cm |
| 4" | 11 cm |
| 6" | 15 cm |
| 8" | 20 cm |
| 10" | 25 cm |
| 12" (1') | 30 cm |

### PAN SIZES

| U.S. | Metric |
|---|---|
| 8" cake pan | 20 × 4 cm sandwich or cake tin |
| 9" cake pan | 23 × 3.5 cm sandwich or cake tin |
| 11" × 7" baking pan | 28 × 18 cm baking tin |
| 13" × 9" baking pan | 32.5 × 23 cm baking tin |
| 15" × 10" baking pan | 38 × 25.5 cm baking tin (Swiss roll tin) |
| 1½ qt baking dish | 1.5 liter baking dish |
| 2 qt baking dish | 2 liter baking dish |
| 2 qt rectangular baking dish | 30 × 19 cm baking dish |
| 9" pie plate | 22 × 4 or 23 × 4 cm pie plate |
| 7" or 8" springform pan | 18 or 20 cm springform or loose-bottom cake tin |
| 9" × 5" loaf pan | 23 × 13 cm or 2 lb narrow loaf tin or pâté tin |

### TEMPERATURES

| Fahrenheit | Centigrade | Gas |
|---|---|---|
| 140° | 60° | – |
| 160° | 70° | – |
| 180° | 80° | – |
| 225° | 110° | – |
| 250° | 120° | ½ |
| 300° | 150° | 2 |
| 325° | 160° | 3 |
| 350° | 180° | 4 |
| 375° | 190° | 5 |
| 400° | 200° | 6 |
| 450° | 230° | 8 |
| 500° | 260° | – |